A MAGICAL EDUCATION

A MAGICAL EDUCATION
Talks on Magic and Occultism

John Michael Greer

AEON

First published in 2019 by
Aeon Books Ltd
12 New College Parade
Finchley Road
London NW3 5EP

British Library Cataloguing in Publication Data

A C.I.P. for this book is available from the British Library

ISBN-13: 978-1-91280-702-4

Typeset by Medlar Publishing Solutions Pvt Ltd, India

www.aeonbooks.co.uk

CONTENTS

ABOUT THE AUTHOR

One of the most widely respected voices in contemporary occult studies, **John Michael Greer** is the award-winning author of more than fifty books, including *The New Encyclopedia of the Occult, The Druidry Handbook, The Celtic Golden Dawn,* and *Circles of Power: An Introduction to Hermetic Magic.* An initiate in Freemasonry, the Hermetic Order of the Golden Dawn, and the Order of Bards, Ovates and Druids, Greer served as the Grand Archdruid of the Ancient Order of Druids in America (AODA) for twelve years. He lives in Cumberland, Maryland, an old mill town in the Appalachian mountains of western Maryland, with his wife Sara.

John Michael Greer is also the author of four books on peak oil and the future of industrial society, *The Long Descent, The Ecotechnic Future, The Wealth of Nature* and *Not The Future We Ordered,* and also blogs weekly on politics, magic, and the future of industrial society at www. ecosophia.net.

FOREWORD

The talks included in this book were all written and presented during the decade that ran from 2001 to 2010, when I was a regular presenter at Pagan and occult conferences in various corners of North America. All of them were presented several times to a variety of audiences and adapted for each presentation to address issues that happened at that time to be of particular interest to their listeners, or to me. There were others—all told, I must have given upwards of thirty different talks to such conferences during those years—but these are the ones that I was most often requested to give, and the ones that people since that time have most often asked me to make available in printed form.

I've resisted the temptation to turn these talks into essays: to reorganize them to fit some less fluid narrative outline, equip them with the standard scholarly impedimenta of footnotes and bibliographies, and so on. The point of talks like these is to inspire curiosity and reflection, not to set out an ironclad case for this or that point of view; readers of this volume, like members of these talks' original audiences, will have to chase down the books and other sources I've cited by themselves—though in the age of Google this is hardly a difficult task. The one exception is "Healing Through The Elements"; audiences for that talk were given a handout that included a short bibliography, and the handout is reprinted here right after the talk.

There are many different ways to approach the mystery teachings. Those I've sketched out in these talks are only a few of them. If any of the perspectives these talks offer are of use to those who are seeking the ways of the Mysteries, this volume will have served its purpose.

—John Michael Greer

CHAPTER ONE

A magical education

I'd like to thank all of you for being here. We have a lot of stuff to cover, and probably everybody in this room will be offended by at least one thing I say during the next hour and a half. That can't be helped. I've studied and practiced magic for thirty years now and taught it for nearly twenty; I've seen a lot of very capably done magic during that time but a lot more that was, well, pretty feeble. I've drawn a few conclusions from my experiences, but of course, your mileage may vary. Take what follows for whatever it's worth.

In a world that's still giddy over J. K. Rowling's Harry Potter novels, talk about a magical education carries a certain amount of baggage but it also has an important lesson to teach. Rowling's tales of young witches and wizards at school have reminded a lot of people in the magical scene that magic is something that has to be learned. This is a point that some mages these days have tried to avoid facing since it's a lot easier to decide that you already know it all, or that your inborn magical talents are all you need. Sounds great, but as any craftsperson can tell you, raw talent isn't worth all that much unless it's developed through training and practice, and the people who think they know everything are generally those who know the least. It's a mark of people who actually know something about magic—or any other craft—that they're aware of just how little they actually know. For that reason, I don't think it's out of line to talk here about how to get a magical education.

I want to stress the last word. Today's magical community has plenty of technically competent mages. I'm also going to talk about how to become one of those, in case you don't happen to be one already. But we have a shortage of educated mages—mages who can not only do magic, but who understand what they're doing and can not only teach it to others by rote but explain it to them so *they* can understand what they're doing. We do have some. Given the obstacles in the way of getting a real magical education these days, it speaks very well of the passion and commitment with which so many of today's mages pursue their art. But we don't have as many as we ought to, and some of the barriers that interfere most with the growth and development of the magical community come from that fact.

If our society were less terrified of magic, there would be schools of magic in every large city, and people who wanted to become mages could register for classes and come out the other end as competent and well-educated practitioners of the magical arts. There are some projects heading in that direction right now, and some people are hard at work trying to make that vision a reality. For the time being, though, most of us who want to become competent and well-educated practitioners of the magical arts are going to have to do the job ourselves. Even if you're studying with a teacher, or belong to a coven or a magical lodge, or have the chance to participate in one of the schools of magic I've just mentioned, you still have to do a good deal of the job yourselves. Education is lighting a lamp, not filling a bucket, and every teacher knows all too well that the best teaching in the world won't do a thing for a student who isn't willing to take responsibility for his or her education.

I mentioned a moment ago that there are obstacles in the way of getting a real magical education these days, and I want to discuss two of those right now. Those of you who know your way around the Cabalistic Tree of Life may recall that the path through the Veil of the Sanctuary leads past two fierce guardians: Death and the Devil, or in more prosaic language, the potentials for disastrous imbalances of force and form that beset the would-be initiate on his or her way to mastery of magic. Well, there are two guardians flanking the path to a useful magical education in modern culture, too. They're not quite the same as the ones on the Tree of Life, but they're every bit as fierce, and I'm sure everyone in this room knows people who have fallen victim to one or both.

The first of the guardians is the many-headed monster of fantasy fiction and media magic. That's a tough one to face because most people who get involved in magic in the first place do it because something in the image of magic in our culture's entertainment media struck a chord somewhere deep. I speak from personal experience here. At age ten, I knew exactly what I wanted to be when I grew up. I wanted to be Gandalf. Try telling that to your school guidance counselor! When I stumbled across my first-ever book of Golden Dawn ritual magic a few years later, I flung myself into it with all the rapture an overenthusiastic teenager can manage, which is saying something. It took me years of study and magical practice, not to mention additional maturity, to really notice the fact that magic in novels and movies is not the same thing as the magic that actually works here and now, in the only world we actually inhabit.

I know this is an unpopular thing to say, but magic isn't whatever you want it to be. Some things work, and some things don't. Traditions of magic around the world have settled on remarkably similar collections of technique—I've had the chance to talk shop with a Shinto priest, and we both discovered that Shinto esotericism and Druid Revival ritual magic have a lot more in common than either of us expected. That's because certain things, certain processes and techniques and odd corners of human neurology, allow you to bend the universe of human experience to your will more effectively than others.

This has uncomfortable implications for those of us—and remember, I'm talking about myself here too—who grow up on fantasy fiction or movies about magic, and decide we want to be mages just like Gandalf, or Harry Potter, or whoever. That's exactly what we can never be. Novelists or screenplay writers, remember, don't come up with the magic in their imaginary worlds to teach us how to do magic in this one. They create their magical systems and spells as plot engines for the sake of the story. The problem, of course, is that magical systems created for fictional effect usually have exactly that—fictional effects—when you try to put them to use in the world we actually live in.

Here's an example. Quite a few years back, I spent some time frequenting alt.magick on Usenet, and I remember one guy who made a plaintive post. He'd wanted to keep his roommate out of his dorm room for a couple of hours, and since he'd been reading Katherine Kurtz' Deryni novels, he'd cast the Wards Major, a powerful protective spell that Kurtz' Deryni magicians use all the time to good effect. Damn if the roommate didn't walk right in despite his spell. He posted to alt.magick wanting to know what he'd done wrong. I think someone suggested that he obviously didn't have enough Deryni blood to make it work. Cold but accurate enough.

In the same way, there are a lot of people who try to do Klingon magic, or Darkover magic, or we-can't-tell-you-what-it-is-because-Mercedes-Lackey-will-sue-us magic, and run into the same problem. Here in the world we live in, there's a real shortage just now of matrix crystals, tickets to the Klingon homeworld, and cute telepathic horsies with big blue eyes. Now some would suggest that there's also a real shortage of reality testing, but I think they're missing the point. People turn to fantasy literature and the like because the world that's presented to them by the schools and the media is as imaginary as Middle Earth, and pretty damn dismal into the bargain. One of the things that makes it dismal is that it flatly denies the reality of magic, a reality that's woven into our blood and bones and nervous systems. So when fantasy novels and movies offer a glimpse of the living reality of magic, it's no wonder a lot of people embrace it as passionately as they do.

But that passion has to be integrated into a clear sense of what works and what doesn't in real-world magic. I can raise my hands to the sky and shout *Naur an edraith ammen! Naur dan i ngaurhoth!* until my face turns blue, and I won't be able to launch firebolts from my fingertips the way Gandalf did. But I can study a proven system of word magic, learn how to shape sound with my voice so that it sends changes cascading through my nervous system and the minds and bodies of the people around me, and get some pretty remarkable effects. You can also do as some Chaos magicians have done and borrow symbolism from fantasy fiction—but you'll notice that those Chaos magicians combine the fantasy symbolism with distinctly nonfantasy technique, which they got from solidly proven magical traditions. So the many-headed monster of fantasy can become a source of inspiration and enthusiasm in magical training, and if it's handled carefully, it can also become a source of evocative symbolism. The problems come when it's treated as a source of accurate technical knowledge.

But too many people flee from that guardian only to fall into the jaws of the other. Plenty of would-be mages become disgusted by the fantasy, the make-believe, the dress-up games, and roleplaying that too often disguises itself as magical practice in the occult community these days, and they decide to look for real magic, proven magic, magic from some historical period where such nonsense didn't exist yet. Fair enough; but too many of them fall into the opposite trap, and come to think that the only way to do real magic is to limit themselves strictly to some tradition or system handed down from the distant past. They become the prey of the other fierce guardian of the path, the hobgoblin of authenticity.

Now historical authenticity is a very good thing if you're a historian. If you want to know how mages practiced magic in the Renaissance, or in the Middle Ages, or in ancient Greece or Mesopotamia, questions of authenticity should be near the very top of your checklist. This is particularly true because there's a huge amount of fantasy fiction disguised as history in the magical community, an endless torrent of grandmother stories and claims of ancient lineage used to bolster magical systems that date from the mid-twentieth century when they weren't invented last week over beer at the local pizza parlor's all you can eat night. But when you want to know what sort of magic you should practice here and now, authenticity is irrelevant.

That's also an unpopular thing to say these days because a lot of people are very deeply invested in being authentic this or traditional that. There's a real ego boost in being able to claim that you're a *real* Hermeticist or Druid or traditional Wiccan or whatever, while anyone who doesn't fit your definition of authenticity is a fake. Some people become so addicted to the ego high that you'll find them barging onto one Yahoo group after another, where they can parade their superior knowledge and tell everyone else how wrong they are. But even those who don't fall victim to this sort of galloping idiocy lose something crucial by an unthinking worship of authenticity. If historical authenticity is all that matters, then creativity is bad; innovation is bad. And a tradition that abandons creativity and innovation is dead. You may be able to keep the mummified corpse on display like Lenin in his tomb, but eventually, the makeup is going to wear off and people will realize that what you've got isn't a living tradition; it's a corpse.

The irony here is that an obsession with authenticity is perhaps the single most inauthentic thing you can do in magic. We know one thing for sure about magicians in the past—anywhere in the past: they used what worked. The oldest and most authentic tradition in all of magic is the tradition of stealing anything that's not nailed down and bringing along a crowbar for use on the things that are. Choose any magical tradition from the past, look into its roots, and you'll find a fantastic gallimaufry of sources. There are no culturally pure magical traditions. That's a simple fact of the history of magic. Imposing purity tests on magical traditions may feed people's egos, not to mention fostering ethnic and cultural divisions of the sort the world could very well do without these days, but it's not going to make you a better magician.

The hobgoblin of authenticity is very much an American hobgoblin, and it crops up in a lot of different corners of American culture these days. In the martial arts scene, for example, I've met people who have studied some authentic traditional style, and boast that they do every detail of every form exactly the way it's been handed down to them. Mention that to any of the elderly Chinese guys who participated in the martial arts scene in Beijing or Shanghai before 1949 and they may just laugh themselves into hiccups.

In those days, if you did everything exactly the way your teacher did, it meant that you were a lousy student—you didn't have the initiative or the imagination to adapt the form to your own body, or to come up with anything new to add to the teachings of your style and your kwoon. And yet people boast of that nowadays. In the same way, you'll meet people who tell you with pride that they perform such and such a ritual in exactly the same way the founder of their tradition did back in the 1950s or whenever. What that means is that neither that person, nor their teacher, nor anyone in their lineage has learned a single new thing about how to perform that ritual since the 1950s—and I find it hard to see anything in that worth boasting about.

Does this mean that history is irrelevant, or that we have nothing to learn from the past? Of course not. What it means is that the lessons of the past have to be tested against the touchstone of the experiences and needs of today. As mages, we turn to the past to learn what kinds of magic worked back then. We turn to living traditions in the present to learn what kinds of magic work right now. But we can't ever abandon the need to create, to innovate, and to learn something new, because that's where we'll find the kinds of magic that will work in the future.

Ah, you're thinking, but doesn't that contradict the crabby comments I made about fantasy fiction magic a few minutes ago? Don't the people who take their magic from old Michael Moorcock novels have exactly the sort of creative, innovative approach to magic I'm proposing now? Well, no. The problem with fantasy fiction magic isn't that it doesn't come from some provably authentic ancient source. The problem with fantasy fiction magic is that most of the time it doesn't work—or to be more precise, the effects you can get are a lot more limited than the effects you can get from magic that's designed to have nonfictional results. Fantasy magic isn't meant to work, and in fact, the whole genre of fantasy fiction assumes that magic belongs to faraway worlds, to Oz and Middle Earth and Valdemar—not to the here and now. Ironically, the cult of authenticity makes exactly that same assumption by thinking that real magic has to come from some distant time, some faraway place, some exotic culture—anywhere but here and now. Real magic starts from the opposite idea. Paul Foster Case said it best: all the power that ever was or will be is right here. Right now. And that's why real magic works, right here and right now.

Of course, here we get into circles within circles, since there's always the question of what magic is meant to do. In one sense, the posers in the magical community—the folks whose magical practice is limited to dressing in black, wearing twenty-three pounds of assorted silver jewelry, and leaving books by Aleister Crowley on the coffee table to impress dates—are the most effective mages among us. They know what they want to accomplish, and they accomplish it. It's just that magic can be used for many things other than acting out a social role. In the same way, if your ambition in magic is to identify yourself with the lead character from your favorite fantasy novel, then fantasy magic may be exactly what you want. If your goal is to get that good warm glow of self-righteousness that comes from knowing that you're right and everyone else in the world is wrong, then the cult of authenticity may be exactly what you're looking for.

But magic can do a lot more than that. One of the problems we have in the magical community these days, due to the lack of well-educated mages I referred to earlier, is that too many people have a very cramped and restricted idea of what magic can accomplish. That's not surprising; nearly all of us have grown up in a culture that flatly rejects the idea that magic can do anything at all and measures "doing anything at all" using technology as a yardstick. Magic isn't technology, and it doesn't do the things that technology does. It does different things, and it does them extremely well. Magical work, thoroughly learned and competently performed, can totally transform yourself and your world. It can take problems most people don't think they can ever get past, limits that most people think are just part of being human, wads them up and jump-shot them into the nearest trash can. The problem is that nearly everything in our society pushes us in the other direction.

We live in a society where rich men get richer by convincing everyone else to give up their own abilities, their own talents, their own potential in order to buy some shoddy technological gimmick that pretends to do the same thing. Instead of learning how to bake bread, buy a bread machine; instead of learning how to remember, buy a palm pilot; instead of learning how to think, buy a television and let the media think for you! It's as though they convinced everyone to cut off their own legs, so they could buy the latest high-tech prosthetics, which don't work as well as real legs but are much more fashionable. The usual claim made by the prosthetics merchants is that using machines to do what you can do better saves time, which is true, but only if you don't count the time you put in earning the money to buy the thing, maintain it, power it, and deal with the mess it inevitably creates.

Not all the prosthetics on sale in our prosthetic society are machines. There are also prosthetic identities; instead of figuring out who you really are, buy an identity off the rack! But of course, that's something we've talked about already. One of the reasons many would-be magicians get gobbled by the many-headed monster of fantasy magic is that they're trying to take on a pre-fab identity that appeals to them, the identity of a character in some fantasy epic who seems to have everything they lack, and the magic is part of the kit. One of the reasons many other would-be magicians become authenticity orcs is that they're trying to fit themselves into an identity that appeals to them, and they think that if they're more authentic than anyone else, they get to stop being who they actually are. In either case, magic turns into a humorless sort of roleplaying. Again, if that's what you want from magic, go for it.

But magic can be much more than that, infinitely much more than that. Every person in this room has the capacity for genius, for magnificence, in some field of human action. Every person in this room—every one of you—has potentials that would flabbergast you if you caught the merest glimpse of just what you can be. Machines do what they're built to do, and when people reduce themselves to the level of machines, they do what they're told to do. You can do more than that; you can be more than that. Researchers into what the jargon mechanics call "exceptional human capacities" have found time and again that in the right circumstances, the most ordinary people can accomplish unbelievable things. The purpose of magical training is to be able to do that whenever you choose, to make any circumstances the right circumstances for the lightning to strike.

So it's crucial not to aim your magic too low. That's part of becoming a competent and well-educated mage. But if you want to become a competent and well-educated mage, how do you avoid the two fierce guardians? It's a complicated process. I usually recommend that people find some established system of magic that appeals to them and practice it steadily for a couple of years. If you're doing that in a teacher/ student relationship, whether as a teacher or as a student, you need to pay attention to both of the guardians. If you're the teacher, you need to think hard about what parts of the material you're passing on are essential, and what parts can be modified or replaced by something else better suited to your student's capacities and interests. If you're the student, you need to think hard about whether your dislike for any given part of the material you're given is worth following, or whether you'll gain more by confronting the thing you don't like and learning the lessons it has to teach. If you're learning on your own from books and internet resources, the way most mages in training do these days, you have to fill both roles. That's a tricky balancing act, though it can certainly be done.

At this point, though, we can move past the two fierce guardians, and we can start talking about the nuts and bolts of a magical education—the secrets of learning magic, in a certain sense. There's a common bad habit of thinking that the way to learn magic is to get hold of secret teachings nobody else has. I call this the Yoda Fallacy: "Master Yoda or the nearest available equivalent you find, and the secrets of the Force get him to teach you, and a Jedi Knight that makes you." Right? Wrong. That might possibly have had a scrap of truth to it back when magical teachings were hard to come by, but these days the magical secrets of the ages are sitting on bookshelves in every occult bookstore in the country. You can get all the secrets of the Force you want and that by itself won't make you a mage. For the would-be mage, the most important "secrets" of magic aren't secret at all, and they're not even particularly exotic.

What are these secrets, then? They're exactly the same factors that bring success in any other human activity—a point that's led more than one mage to argue that all human activities, no exceptions, are forms of magic.

Imagine for a moment that instead of wanting to be a mage, you've decided to become a guitar player. You're not going to get there by wishing, or by decorating your place with posters of your favorite lead guitarist, or by reading lots of novels about rock bands, or by buying guitars and leaving them all over your apartment for visitors to admire, or by attending a concert and listening to someone else perform eight times a year. You need three things in order to get from the desire to the reality. First, you need to decide what kind of guitar music you want to play, and learn as much as you possibly can about it, while picking up a good general knowledge of music theory and some background in other styles and instruments. Second, you need to get a guitar and practice playing it for half an hour or an hour a day, seven days a week, fifty-two weeks a year. Third, you need to learn from your practice, and to compare what you can do with what you want to do, not so you can puff up your ego or wallow in how bad you think you're failing, but so you can see what you need to work on next and measure how your learning process is coming along.

These same three factors—knowledge, practice, and the ability to learn—are the keys to magic. That's the secret. If you study magic, practice magic, and learn from your experiences, you'll become a capable and well-educated mage. It really is as simple as that.

But of course "simple" is not necessarily the same thing as "easy." In particular, there's a deep paradox in magical training, because the tool you're working with and the material you're working on is the same thing: yourself. To study magic is to develop the magical imagination by giving it the images and ideas it needs to work on. To practice magic is to develop the magical will by challenging it to push past the common bad habits of the everyday self. To learn from your experiences is to develop the magical memory by teaching yourself to face experience as it is, and not as you want it to be or fear it might be. The problem is that imagination, will, and memory are also the tools you need to accomplish these things. It's as though the key you need to open the door is locked inside the door, or as though the first step in building a house was to make tools that you need those same tools to make.

It's not quite as bad as that since everybody has some capacity to imagine, will, and remember, and those give you something to start from. Most of the techniques of magical training, from the most basic to the most baroque, are simply ways of getting past this difficulty by boosting the ordinary supply of imagination, will, and memory. But the core of study, regular practice, and learning from your experiences— those are the foundation level on which all other magical methods build. We'll take them one at a time.

The first one's study. To become a competent and well-educated mage, you need to learn about magic. You need to learn a *lot* about magic. Of course, you need to start by learning the rituals and teachings of whatever system of magic you happen to fancy. You need to learn them by heart, by the way. Reading a ritual out of a book or off a sheet of paper is fine to begin with, but to make the ritual really catch fire you need to be able to concentrate on it totally, and that's not going to happen while you're trying to read the next line through the incense smoke. In the same way, you don't really understand a piece of magical theory or philosophy until you can explain it in your own words, without looking at the book you got it from.

But you can't stop there, not if you want to become the sort of well-educated mages we've been talking about. Too many people who know their own system of magic very well don't know any other system at all, and this has a variety of problems. It gets in the way of talking shop with other mages at gatherings like this one; it can also lead you to make a fool of yourself by assuming that your tradition's approach is common to every other magical tradition when odds are it isn't. Thus, it's a good idea to read about other magical traditions, and once you've got your feet under you in your own, it's a good idea to practice another magical tradition now and again. Johann Wolfgang von Goethe used to say that someone who only knew one language didn't really know any language at all. In the same way, if you only know how to practice magic using one system, there are things about practicing magic you don't know, and you'll never learn.

I like to encourage students to practice magic that isn't just from a different tradition but from a different cultural and linguistic background than the main tradition they practice. You learn most by challenging your boundaries. If you like to practice a refined, intellectual, stuffy magic like the Golden Dawn tradition, the system I originally trained in, do something entirely different: break out the mojo bags, the High John the Conqueror Root and the goofer dust, and take up hoodoo. I promise you you'll get a completely new perspective on your magical practices—I certainly did. These days you can get access to magic from just about anywhere in the world right here in America, so don't set your sights too narrowly.

A good general knowledge of world magic is especially worth having because the effects of magical practice don't necessarily pay any attention to the boundaries of culture and tradition. Here's an example.

I know a guy who spent twenty-odd years practicing ceremonial magic. One day he was meditating and started feeling these funny sensations in the base of his spine: heat, upward pressure, that sort of thing. They got more and more intense as he kept practicing and started moving up his spine. Now if he'd only paid attention to the specific tradition he practiced, he would have been completely baffled, and he might have been in very deep trouble. Fortunately he'd read enough Hindu occult literature that he knew the signs of awakening kundalini, and was able to get the sushumna, the central channel of his spine, relaxed and open enough that the kundalini energy went the right direction, instead of shorting out into one of the side channels and frying his nervous system. That's a nice fringe benefit, and there's also the far from minor benefit that his magical work has gone into overdrive since that process started.

So, a knowledge of world magic is worth having. It's at least as important to get a sense of the history of magic. You're not going to get this by reading the obligatory chapter about the Burning Times in the front of every other book on Pagan magic written in the last fifty years; you need real history written by real historians. The history of magic is extremely complex and it's remarkably continuous. Most people in the Neopagan community these days, for example, aren't aware that there have been public Neopagan groups in Britain and America since the eighteenth century. You hear constantly that we're in the middle of a brand-new magical revival, but there were at least as many occultists per capita in the US in the 1920s as there are now, and there may have been more.

The magical history of America, in particular, is practically a black hole in the modern magical scene. How many people in this room know that there were fully functioning, chartered temples of the Hermetic Order of the Golden Dawn in Los Angeles and San Francisco a hundred years ago? Those were just two of more than a hundred magical lodges, Pagan circles, and other occult groups in California at that time. They weren't secret, either—they advertised in the daily newspapers, for heaven's sake. The whitewashed all-Christian image of the American past projected by fundamentalists, and uncritically accepted by too many people in the magical community today, is utter horseradish. From Rosicrucian communes in colonial Pennsylvania to all of us here today, America has always been awash with magic, crawling with wizards and witches and sorcerers. If more of today's magicians knew that, we could reclaim more of our real history, rather than inventing bogus fam-trad lineages, or pretending we belong to someone else's culture or insisting that the Burning Times didn't end until 1965 and handing the fundamentalists the right to define our history for us.

The fringe benefits of this sort of historical awareness aren't small. On the off chance that any of you hanker after a career writing occult nonfiction, I'm about to tell you my deep dark secret for coming up with material that nobody else in the magical community has ever heard of. Ready? Read books that were written more than a hundred years ago. Almost nobody in the American occult community these days does that. Better yet, read books that were written more than a hundred years ago, in a language other than English. There's a joke in Europe these days; you know that a person who speaks three languages is called trilingual, and a person who speaks two languages is called bilingual; what do you call a person who only speaks one language? American.

There's any number of difficulties that come out of the stark terror most Americans feel at the thought of learning a foreign language, but the one that's most relevant here is parochialism. We end up thinking that the magical traditions we happen to have right here and now are the be-all and end-all of magic when they're a tiny sample of the much larger and livelier magical heritage of the world. Learn just about any language you care to, and you can easily double the amount of magical information at your disposal. Choose your language well and it goes up by an order of magnitude or more. Most people in the American magical scene have no notion just how much untranslated magical lore you can get by picking up a decent reading knowledge of Latin, or French, or German, and we're not even going to talk about the astonishing stuff you can get into with a reading knowledge of classical Chinese. There's a whole world of magic out there waiting for you; go get it.

I should say that all this assumes you can read at least one language to start with, and, of course, these days that's not an assumption we can necessarily make. America's been sliding down the curve of economic and political decline for some decades now, and one result of that is that a school system that used to be one of the best in the world is now worse than those in some Third World countries. Illiteracy is very common in this country and marginal literacy is much more so. As that gets more common still, one of the things the Pagan and magical community might consider doing for its members is organizing volunteer literacy programs. In the meantime, if you have any experience teaching reading, ask around in your local magical scene and see if there's anyone who would welcome your help. If you have problems reading or can't read at all, don't feel bad about that—it's very common. Ask around and see if there are any adult literacy programs in your area and get some help.

So you're studying your own magical system, and you're learning something about one or two others, and picking up a general knowledge of world magic, and learning French so you can get access to some of those amazing nineteenth-century French magical textbooks written by people who out-Gothed today's Goth scene a hundred and twenty years in advance. Does that complete your education as a well-rounded mage? Not a chance. Dion Fortune, who was an excellent practical mage as well as a first-rate magical theoretician, and launched a magical order that's still active today, wrote that a good well-rounded education for a magical initiate should include a solid general knowledge of all the natural sciences, plus history, mathematics, logic and philosophy, psychology, and comparative religion. A modest goal! Of course, the amount of information to be had in any of these fields has soared exponentially since she wrote, and there are also quite a number of other sciences that didn't even exist in her time but have plenty to teach the aspiring magician. Cybernetics, systems theory, semiotics, ecology—the list could go on for days.

But there's zero point in setting goals that only the most fanatic magical students will ever be able to reach. More realistically, there are three general fields of study outside magic and a foreign language that deserve a central place in a magical education. The first is mythology and folklore. Why? Because it's the raw material of magical symbolism and ritual. Every magical system, however abstract and philosophical it becomes, has its roots in the rich soil of myth and folk belief. If you know your way around myth and folklore, thinking like a mage is a lot easier, and thinking like a mage is one of the major steps you need to take to become one.

A lot of people in Pagan magical traditions study mythology, but most of them limit their studies to the myths and legends of whatever culture really turns their crank. That's a good starting point, but Goethe's comment about languages also applies to mythologies; if you only know one, you don't really know any. Choose at least one other to study, from the other end of the world, and learn as much about it as you know about the myths of your favorite culture. That way you have some perspective; you start to notice what the common themes are, and what's specific to each individual culture. While you're at it, take in some of the writers who try to synthesize all the world's myths into a single pattern. A lot of people find Joseph Campbell really good for this, though I have to admit I can't stand him; Giorgio de Santillana and Hertha von Dechend's astonishing book *Hamlet's Mill* is more my speed. Don't take them as gospel, or for that matter cast them into the outer darkness with wailing and gnashing of teeth; read them, think about them, draw your own conclusions about where they have good points and where they fall short.

This might be a good point, by the way, to mention that you aren't reading all these books to find out what the truth is and then cling to it like grim death. Jiddu Krishnamurti used to say that truth is a pathless land; you won't get there by following anyone else's map. You're reading these books and studying these subjects to learn how to think and to give yourself relevant things to think about. Most people in our society these days don't think. Remember what I said about prosthetics? The media is the prosthetic mind. Listen to conversations these days and most of what you hear is quotes from the media. I remember a political argument I overheard a few years back in which every single word was a sound bite from TV ads for one candidate or the other. Thus, it's a good idea to read books you disagree with, and make yourself try to get inside the author's point of view, understand why what he or she is saying makes sense from that particular perspective; just as it's a good idea to read books you agree with and pick apart every single flaw in them you can possibly find. Having the right opinions is worth nothing in magic. Being able to think your own thoughts, and not just parrot someone else's, is worth everything.

Back to the reading list. The second thing I'd recommend that every aspiring magician study is at least one natural science. Which one? Any one you like. Depending on the kind of magic you do, one may be more useful than another. If you like doing magic with herbs, botany is going to be quite a bit of help. If you ever plan on taking up laboratory alchemy, a good background in practical chemistry is essential. Astrology and astronomy used to be the same thing until four hundred years ago, and the best astrologers know their planetary astronomy inside and out. And the list goes on. It's crucial to actually get your hands grubby, to practice the science you study and learn the technical language, rather than reading the stuff that gets written for laypeople. If you study botany, in other words, you need to spend time keying out plants and examining them under a low-power microscope; if you take up chemistry, you need to pull on the lab coat and the safety goggles and head into the laboratory; if you study astronomy, plan on spending long nights with one eye up against the eyepiece of a telescope. Learning science without practicing it is like learning magic without practicing it.

Why should mages study science? In a few minutes, I'm going to say some very rude things about the ideology that informs most sciences these days, but practical scientific work is another matter. Here and now, there's no better way to learn the difference between what you know, what you think you know, and what you really don't have a clue about. The scientific method has its limits, but it's a great cure for the sort of pompous nonsense and wishful thinking that play far too large a role in today's magical community. Beyond that, there are practical advantages—if you've spent time in a chemistry lab, for instance, and then you take up alchemy, you're a lot less likely to poison yourself or blow yourself to kingdom come—and there are deeper issues.

Modern science evolved out of magic. As Lynn White pointed out in a crucial article three decades ago, it lost track of some core insights in the course of its evolution, and those losses have a lot to do with the ecological crisis that's flooding over the sand castles of industrial society just now. If today's mages can begin the process of bringing science back into contact with its occult roots, and with the magical vision of the universe as a living unity instead of a collection of objects banging into one another in the void, we can lay the foundations for a way of thought that can save the best achievements of today's science but keep from wrecking the biosphere on which all our lives depend.

The third thing I'd propose as essential study for mages is a basic grasp of philosophy. Magic used to be considered the highest form of applied philosophy; there's a reason why Cornelius Agrippa's great book, the most notorious sorcerer's manual of the Renaissance, went by the title *Three Books of Occult Philosophy*. Again, to become a mage you need to be able to think like a mage; that implies that you need to be able to think; and the way to learn how to think is to think about what you're thinking, to turn your attention to your own thoughts and see if they actually make sense. If you can't critique your own thoughts and opinions, you don't have thoughts; your thoughts have you. Philosophy is how you learn to think about thoughts, look at the basic assumptions that underlie them and explore different ways of making sense of the world. It's essential to the mage in training.

An astonishing number of the squabbles that have kept the magical community from accomplishing much of what it could have accomplished in the last thirty years could have been avoided with even a little undergraduate philosophy. A few years back the meaning of the word "witch" was a hot button that drove endless bickering; in some circles, the meaning of the word "druid" is becoming the same sort of rhetorical football today. Nearly everyone involved talked as though the word had some fixed, essential meaning that you could get from its etymology. It doesn't take much philosophy of language to show that words are tools, not truths; that the meaning of a word is determined by usage, not etymology. The word "black" originally meant "white"; it's an exact cognate of the French word *blanc*. Attention to that might have spared the community a good deal of bickering and saved time and effort for something more useful.

But philosophy has other uses for the mage. I've suggested above that modern science can be fitted back into the worldview of magic. Quite a few writers on magic in the last hundred and fifty years or so have tried the opposite trick and struggled to find some way to stuff magic into the worldview of modern science. The recent attempts to find room for magic in quantum mechanics are just the latest in a long string of such efforts. The appeal is understandable, but all the same, it's a sucker's game, because scientific ideology was designed to exclude magic and everything like it.

I mentioned reading real history by real historians a little while back. Frances Yates and Margaret Jacobs are two of the latter who belong close to the top of the list. Both talk about the way that the ideology of modern science evolved out of magical philosophy, and Jacobs talks about the conscious political motivations that drove the creators of modern science in the seventeenth century to redefine the world in a way that made magic impossible. That's material for a different talk, but the point that's relevant here is that the worldview taught by the cheerleaders of modern science isn't simple common sense or reality. It's an ideology with its own ulterior motives, and it actually doesn't have that much to do with the realities of laboratory work and fieldwork—another reason to study at least one science, as I suggested a little earlier.

The ideology of modern science is also built on some exceptionally shaky philosophical ground—on assumptions about the nature of reality, truth, and meaning that won't stand up to fifteen minutes of serious examination. Modern philosophers as different as Arthur Schopenhauer and Alfred North Whitehead have put together serious, coherent philosophies that leave plenty of room for magic. Older philosophies assume the reality of magic as a matter of course. The modern Pagan scholar Don Frew has put a lot of time into discussing the role of Neoplatonism as the core mystical philosophy underlying modern Pagan spirituality. It's also the core magical philosophy underlying most of the traditions of Western magic, and some background in Neoplatonist philosophy is a great way to get a handle on older magical traditions—not to mention a great way to get a sense of the possibilities of magic, and get past the cramped and restricted view of magic's potentials I critiqued earlier.

Another branch of philosophy that deserves some attention in a course of magical study is ethics. I know this is an unpopular subject to bring up, because far too many of us grew up in families and churches where ethics gets confused with morality, and morality gets confused with some jerk in a minister's outfit yelling at people on Sunday for the sins he himself commits the other six days of the week. That's not what I'm talking about. There are three big questions that cover nearly everything in philosophy, and the three main branches of philosophy—ontology, epistemology, and ethics—exist to deal with them. What exists? That's ontology. What can I know? That's epistemology. What should I do? That's ethics. Since magic is mostly about doing things, it's inevitably about ethics, and some background in the philosophy of ethics will get you past the sort of hypocritical Sunday school moralizing that passes for ethical thought all through our culture—including large parts of the Pagan and magical subculture—and start grappling with ethical issues themselves, considering the consequences of their actions, and thinking their own thoughts about what words like "good" and "bad" actually mean.

Mythology, philosophy, and at least one natural science, plus magical lore, the history and traditions of magic from around the world, and a foreign language: there's your basic course of study. A lot of work, but within the reach of most people—like magic itself. Those of you who are attending college, or will be going to college, or can arrange to go back to college even for the occasional evening class, have a huge advantage here, by the way. Every one of the subjects I've mentioned except for practical magic itself can be picked up at any college or university. It may not be Hogwarts, but for now, it's the next best thing. If you're in a degree program, choose your electives carefully and by graduation day you'll have a solid magical education and can swap the mortar-board for a tall pointy hat with moons and stars on it.

So much for study. Study is essential so that you know what to do, why to do it, and how it fits into the big picture, but it's not going to teach you *how* to do magic. For that you need practice. Remember the would-be guitar player I mentioned earlier? If all he does is read books on music theory and guitar technique, he's going to be very well informed, but he still won't know how to play the guitar. To do that, he's got to pick up the guitar every single day, for a half hour or an hour or more, and practice.

Now, this is one of the things people who want to learn magic tend to shy away from. Partly it's a function of the modern social context of magical practice. A lot of people who want to study and practice magic these days come out of countercultures that rebel against our society's rigid timetables and routines, and the thought of buckling down to half an hour of magical practice a day, seven days a week, fifty-two weeks a year, sounds way too much like the sort of class schedule or work schedule most of us would like to see Cthulhu rise from the deeps and drag away in his tentacles forever. So would-be mages often try to avoid regular practice. They try to be spontaneous, to do magic when the spirit moves them. It's a great idea, in theory. The only problem is that I've yet to meet a really competent magician who trained that way.

Learning magic is work. It's hard work. It takes time, effort, passion, and patience. The people who master it are the people who put in the work, day in and day out, for years. Again, our guitar player is a good comparison. You know the kind of guitarist who practices for two hours a day every day, and you know the kind that plays when he feels like it, which usually adds up to once a week or so when his friends come over to jam. You know and I know which kind actually end up knowing how to play the guitar well enough to make it in a band worth listening to. Magic is exactly the same way.

It's also something that takes years to master. No matter who you are or how much talent you think you have, you're not going to go from novice to adept in a few weeks or a single year. Ultimately, magic takes a lifetime to learn, but then you've got a lifetime to learn it. One of my teachers, when he decided you might have what it took to learn more than the kindergarten level of what he had to teach, would sit you down and tell you in very serious tones that it would take you at least ten years to get anywhere with the stuff he was teaching. That scared a lot of people off. When he told me that, I thought about it, and told him that I was still going to be studying and practicing in ten years, so why not? It turned out that that was the answer he was looking for. Becoming a first-rate mage will take you many years, but if you're still going to be doing magic many years from now, you might as well get started.

What I recommend for beginning students is that they choose a single basic practice from the magical tradition of their choice, and work up to doing it once a day, every day. Many magical traditions have specific practices designed for this sort of work. If you're a Golden Dawn mage, it's the Lesser Ritual of the Pentagram and the Middle Pillar exercise. If you're a Thelemite, the Star Ruby, or perhaps the Mass of the Phoenix. The older Druid orders each have their basic practice: in OBOD it's the Light-Body exercise, in AODA it's the Sphere of Protection, and so on. If you're a Wiccan, you can cast a circle and call the quarters. In most traditions, the basic practice teaches you how to open and close magical space, and how to contact and work with magical energies. When you do it daily, you get good at it. That means that when you need to use your magical skills to accomplish something, you can. You can create magical space, clear it of unwanted energies, call in the energies you want, work with them, and then disperse leftover energies and close down the space between the worlds, quickly, cleanly, competently, and with no fumbling or wasted effort. All that for fifteen minutes a day.

To begin with, though, if you don't have much background in magical practice, once a day may be too much. Magic is intense, and it puts strains on the body and mind. No matter who you are, or how much talent you think you have, you may not be up to the strain of daily practice to start with. For starters, do your practice once a week. When you've done that for a little while, go to twice or three times a week. Fill in the spaces as you feel ready for them. Pay attention to how you feel after magical work. If you're feeling spacy, dizzy, disconnected from the ordinary world, cut back on the pace a bit, make sure you're getting enough B vitamins, and get a massage; that will help you reconnect to your body.

A word of warning for any of you who choose a vegetarian diet, by the way. Many people find that a meat-free diet doesn't work well with ritual magic. Eating meat helps bring your awareness back into contact with your physical body, which after all is made of meat. It doesn't happen with everyone, but fairly often people who try to learn magic while eating a vegetarian diet have trouble with their nerves. If you're learning magic and avoiding meat, and you find that you're becoming hypersensitive, jittery, and easily stressed out, you may have to choose between your diet and your magic. Just remember that there are other spiritual paths, and there are also other healthy diets.

Of course, you'll want to add other magical workings to the schedule of basic practices. There's a lot of value in the systematic practice of basic magical exercises, and some traditions have beginners work on those, and nothing but those, until they've made some serious progress. I understand the point of that, but I'm not at all sure it's necessary. There's much to be gained by actually performing magical workings intended to cause a change in the world around you, and seeing what happens. When they fail, you get a very good glimpse of the distance between where you are and where you want to be, which is an excellent cure for the sort of beginner's grandiosity we too often see in the magical community, where people with six months' practice beneath their belt become convinced that they're Ipsissimi and can do anything. When your workings succeed, on the other hand, you start to learn just what you can do. Of course, you're likely to make some mistakes, but that's how you learn. As a magical novice you don't yet have the ability to make mistakes you won't recover from, and if you burn your fingers a few times, you'll know better by the time you get within range of serious trouble.

You may also want to add other types of training. Most mages I know practice at least one system of divination. Golden Dawn initiates of the old school were expected to prove their competence in three—Tarot, geomancy, and horary astrology—and while the Golden Dawn did tend to go over the top a little bit, or more than a little bit, getting a working mastery of at least one method of divination is a good thing. Divination is to magic what the eye is to the hand. They work together very well, and nearly all magical traditions have at least one system of divination that's closely allied to their magical working methods.

There are also plenty of what I've called auxiliary arts in the magical tradition, though most people in the occult community these days don't know much about them. What are auxiliary arts? Well, think of Kwai-Chang Caine, the hero of the old TV series Kung Fu. He was primarily a Buddhist monk; that means his primary training was in meditation and ritual, though of course, that wasn't what you saw most of through the blurry flashback scenes of Master Po and the Shaolin Temple.

His ability to cure diseases, heal wounds, and kick the stuffing out of a dozen cowboy-hatted heavies without working up a sweat—those were sidelines, things Buddhist monks in the Shaolin tradition did when they weren't busy with the core work of meditation and ritual.

Those are auxiliary arts. The occult traditions of the West used to have dozens of them, and there are still quite a few hanging around in old books if you know where to look. There was at least one Hermetic magical martial art—a system of swordsmanship based on sacred geometry and magical proportion, drawn from Agrippa's *Three Books of Occult Philosophy* no less, which was a going concern during the seventeenth century but dropped out of use thereafter. There are nineteenth-century Western systems of exercise and internal energy work that you'd need a microscope to tell from Qigong. There's the Art of Memory, which is a system of training that allows you to chuck your palm pilot and get an instant recording and recall out of your own brain. There are healing systems, dozens of them. There are traditions of art, music, and so on. Do you need to get into these to be a capable and well-educated mage? No, but if you have an interest in one or more of these, you might as well—and there again, that means practice.

So you're doing all these practices, and if you remember the third secret of magical training I mentioned earlier, you know you need to learn from them, use them to figure out what works for you and what parts of your magical skills need more work. There are plenty of ways to do this, starting with sheer brute repetition, but most Western magical traditions have a special tool to help you learn from your experiences. It's called the magical journal.

What's a magical journal? A blank book that you fill with details of your own magical practices. *February 19th, 2005, 6:30 AM, morning meditation, thirty minutes. Theme was thus and such. Mental focus was shaky at first, but I managed to get it under control after a few minutes. I understood X, Y, and Z; still not sure what W means, have to work on that. 10:50 PM, Pentagram ritual and Middle Pillar exercise. Somewhat improved, but the visualizations of the archangels still need work. Energy was moderate. 11:44 PM, daily review. Got about halfway back before I fell asleep. February 20th,* and so on.

Now some magical lodges and traditions require you to keep a magical journal as part of their training program. We do that in the AODA, for example. It's one way to encourage people to do the coursework, and if you require students to pass an examination before they go on to the next degree, as we do in AODA, you can have them go back into their journal and pull out stuff for the exam. But too often this is seen as the be-all and end-all of keeping a magical journal, and the real value of the exercise gets lost.

The real value of the exercise is that when you keep a magical journal, you can check your memory against something a little more stable, and that's crucial in magical training. Most people don't realize just how much memory bends and sways with each little breeze of awareness. There's a thing called state-dependent memory; when you're in a given mental state, you have a very easy time remembering things you took in when you were in the same state in the past, and a much harder time remembering things you took in when you were in a different state. I knew people in college who found that out the hard way. They'd guzzle coffee all night studying for a test, then go take the test the next afternoon with no coffee at all, and they couldn't remember a thing: too much blood in their caffeine stream, or something like that.

Emotion is the same way. When you're angry, you click into state-dependent memory, so you remember all sorts of things that made you angry in the past. When you're depressed, you click into state-dependent memory and remember all sorts of miserable, depressing things. You can learn to break out of it, there are skills and techniques for accessing memory from different states, but those have to be learned and they're not easy at first.

And finally, magical states of consciousness are the same way. You can have amazing magical experiences, and three weeks later you'll have lost most of the details. That's annoying, and it can also be a practical problem because one of the things that happens in magical states of consciousness is that you get symbolism, teachings, techniques that you can put to use in your magical practice. That's where the really innovative and powerful stuff comes into your magical work, by the way—realizations that come out of your own practice and your own experience. Your magical journal is where you copy down those realizations while they're still fresh, before the details have slipped away, and you copy down everything, not just the stuff that seemed important at the time, because a week or a month or a year from now the detail that didn't seem important at the time may turn out to be the key to whole new realms of magic. That's happened to me more than once, and it's happened to most of the mages I know.

There's another fringe benefit to the magical journal if you think you might want to write books about magic someday. I already mentioned one of my deep dark secrets for writing magical nonfiction;

here's another. During the late 1980s, I spent something like five years using meditation, scrying, and ritual to work my way through the whole structure of the Cabalistic Tree of Life. It was a lot of work, and I forget how many blank books I filled up keeping up my magical journal during those years. When I was finished, I had a good basic understanding of the Tree of Life—and I stress the word "basic"; gaining a mastery of the whole tree is a lifetime's work—but I also had about ninety percent of the material for my first two books.

So there you have it. Study, of magic, including the magical traditions of other places and times; of mythology and folklore; a natural science; philosophy; and a foreign language. Practice, including a daily magical working, but also including practical workings of various kinds, divination, and any auxiliary arts that might interest you. Keeping a magical journal. A lot of work? Yes, but no more than you'd expect to put into becoming a good musician, or a martial artist, or a schoolteacher, or a dentist, or anything else. Magic is work; it has to be learned, studied, practiced, for years—like anything else worth doing. The payoffs, for those willing to do the work, are literally beyond imagining. Are you willing to take up that challenge? That, my friends, depends on you.

CHAPTER TWO

Magical ecology

The words "magical" and "ecology" don't often share space in the same paragraph, much less cuddle up as closely as they're doing in this talk, and some of you may have been scratching your heads and wondering just how I'm going to manage to connect them. Now of course I write books on both topics; and it wouldn't surprise me one bit if half of you are readers of my books on magic who hope that I'll just kind of skim over the ecology stuff, and the other half of you are readers of my books on ecology who hope that I'll just skim over the magic stuff.

But this is where things get interesting. There's a reason why I write books on both magic and ecology, and I hate to disappoint you, but it's not because I live a double life, like some kind of very minor league superhero: mild-mannered organic gardener and peak oil researcher John Michael Greer suddenly ducks into a phone booth, comes out in a spandex outfit with a cape, and fathoom! It's John Michael Greer, occultist and Archdruid! No. I promise you, I don't look good in spandex. And I don't live a double life; I have quite enough trouble keeping track of one.

No, I write on both subjects, and incorporate both of them into my life, because when properly understood they're not two different subjects;

they're one. They're also nothing like as exotic as they probably seem to many of you. I practice magic; so does everyone else in this room; the only difference is that I'm conscious of doing so, and some of you may not be. I also live in an ecological relationship with Nature; so does everyone else in this room, the only difference, once again, is that I'm conscious of doing so and some of you may not be. And the magic, and the ecological relationship, I suggest, are ultimately not two different things. We'll discuss that identity a good deal more in a bit.

We can't get into that right away because that awkward word "magic" carries with it one thumping truckload of misunderstandings. To begin with, a majority of people in today's industrial societies will tell you up front that magic doesn't exist. And they're right; what they think the word "magic" means doesn't exist. I can promise you, for example, that no matter who your parents were and what school you go to and how many times you mumble words in bad Latin, you're not going to be able to make a broomstick go whizzing through the air the way the actors do in Harry Potter movies. You're not going to make lightning bolts jump out of your fingertips or conjure up a stampeding herd of unicorns, or do any of the other things that keep the computer geeks at Industrial Light and Magic well fed on takeout pizza.

That kind of magic does not exist. No amount of wishful thinking will make it exist. That's probably just as well; the world is enough of a mess without throwing in aerial broomsticks and irate unicorns on demand. The only problem is that a lot of people think that that sort of thing is what the word "magic" means, and in fact, they'll argue themselves blue in the face insisting that that's what magic means—that magic by definition involves claiming to do impossible things. It doesn't help that this insistence got swallowed whole by the entertainment industry back when printed books were a hot new technology, and ever since then, every form of entertainment has been full of absurdities dressed up like magic.

Imagine, for comparison, that magic rather than science won the reality wars at the end of the Renaissance. Go to your local university in this alternate world and you'll find departments of astrology, alchemy, and what have you; all very dry and dull, though of course some of it has useful applications in everyday life. Go to the movies, though, and you're sure to find an exciting fantasy flick about science. You must have seen the Barry Trotter movies—you know, about the kid who finds out his parents were scientists, and he gets to go to this mysterious Institute where people wear white lab coats all the time, and they mutter an algebraic formula, jump onto a test tube, and fly to the Moon. That's what science is, right? And so you'd have groups like the Committee for Magical Investigation of Claims of the Scientific, who go around denouncing anyone who claims to have observed a material cause and effect relationship at work.

In that alternate world, you'd probably end up with a subculture of people who call themselves scientists; some of them would actually be practicing science, and some of them would be trying to act out Barry Trotter fantasies and fly to the Moon astride a test tube, and some of them—perhaps the majority—would be working with a jumbled mess of ideas from both sources, so that even if they were using actual scientific methods and tools, they might very well approach them with the idea that if they get it just right, they can straddle a test tube and fly to the Moon. And finally, I can predict with absolute certainty that you would get entrepreneurs who would make a very large amount of money pandering to the fantasy and trying to convince the gullible that they can teach them how to make science work for them.

I can predict this with absolute certainty because, in this world, where the reality wars of the Renaissance went the other way, we've got a bumper crop of entrepreneurs making boatloads of money convincing people that they can do the equivalent of flying a test tube to the Moon. How many of you remember that very popular New Age book of a couple of years back, *The Secret* by Rhonda Byrne? It was also a video, and an audio tape, and I have no idea what all else; it was one of the most stunningly effective bits of mass marketing the New Age scene has witnessed any time in the last thirty years or so; you know, all the sages of antiquity laboring down through the ages to pass down the ultimate secret of the universe to *you!*

Except it wasn't the ultimate secret of the universe. It wouldn't have been a secret to anybody, except that next to no one in the occult or New Age scenes these days reads books older than they are, and the last time this same point was made in a big way in mass market books was back in the 1950s. The time before that was the 1920s; before that, the 1880s—I could keep going on, but I trust you get the point.

What *The Secret* had to offer underneath all the glitz and heavy PR, in point of fact, was one of the basic exercises that the old occult lodges used to give rank beginners to work with, so they'd have a taste of some of the possibilities, and some of the limitations, of what they'd be working with later on. It so happens that if you convince yourself that you're destined to achieve something, that the whole momentum of the universe is backing your efforts to achieve it, your chances of achieving it can go up sharply, because you jam up a good many of the self-defeating habits so many of us use to keep ourselves from getting the things we think we want. So the old lodges would teach their neophytes some variation on *The Secret*'s Law of Attraction—basically, the idea is that if you put your head in the right space and believe strongly enough, anything you want will magically show up in your life.

So the old lodges used to teach newbies this, and they'd tell them, go give it a spin. After a few weeks the neophytes would be nicely baffled, because some of the things they tried to get using the Law of Attraction would, in fact, show up in their lives, including some things that seemed completely improbable to them; and a lot more of the things that they tried to get wouldn't appear whatever they did, including some things that seemed like pushovers. So then, the neophytes would go back to their tutors, wanting to know what happened and why they couldn't get that 1928 Rolls Royce to suddenly materialize in the carport they didn't have yet. Then the tutors would say basically, "Okay, good. Now that we have your attention, you can start learning how this stuff actually works."

Unfortunately, neither Rhonda Byrne nor her marketing team wrote a sequel to *The Secret* titled *Now That We Have Your Attention*. Instead, a flurry of New Age entrepreneurs followed up the publication of *The Secret* with all kinds of seminars on "How to make the Law of Attraction work for you." A few months later they started running seminars on "Why the Law of Attraction isn't working for you," and then—well, by then most of the eager beavers had gone scampering off to seminars on how to make godzillions of dollars flipping real estate, with equally good results. Not all of them; the news a little while back carried an ugly story about one of the New Age entrepreneurs whose high-intensity retreat for getting the Law of Attraction to work—at nine thousand dollars plus a pop, mind you—ended up costing two of his clients their lives.

There are any number of lessons to be learned from this fiasco. One of them is a bona fide law of magic: if you try to use magic to get stuff you haven't earned, you *will* get soaked. Yes, that's a law of magic, or rather it's one application of a very important law of magic I'll discuss later.

Another lesson is the great mystical teaching passed on long ago by the great mystical adept Benjamin Franklin: a fool and his money are soon what? And of course, there are plenty of other lessons for anyone in this room who's considering a career making fast bucks off the gullible—which is one growth industry that somehow never seems to be hampered by recessions.

But there's another lesson here, and the best way to point it out is to reference a very similar story in a very different field. A few years ago, a startup company called GreenFuel announced that it had the answer to the awkward little problem that the petroleum reserves that power our civilization are starting to run short. There are these species of algae—basically, pond scum—that produce a modest amount of oil in their tissues. So the wonks at GreenFuel worked out this technology that would grow huge amounts of oily pond scum in big waterfilled plastic tubes in the southwestern deserts of the US, extract the oil, and sell it as biodiesel.

You can imagine how eagerly people on the green end of things embraced this prospect, not least because GreenFuel's public-relations people were not exactly modest in their claims. They insisted, in fact, that plastic tubes full of pond scum could not only replace a huge percentage of the gluttonous American appetite for oil, but they could also absorb so much CO_2 from power plants in the process that their pond scum would save the world from global warming. Oh, and the processed pond scum sans oil was going to be sold en masse to the animal feed industry as a cheap ecologically sound feedstock. It all sounded great, but then so did the Law of Attraction.

The trouble was that nobody had done the numbers. The people at GreenFuel made some very optimistic estimates and forgot to check them against the laws of Nature, and the eager beavers who poured investment dollars into GreenFuel—well, the only numbers in the GreenFuel press releases they paid attention to were the wildly inflated estimates of return on investment. Finally, a botanist named Krassen Dimitrov noticed that there was something very odd about GreenFuel's figures and ran the numbers. It turned out that the expenses involved in running those plastic tubes full of pond scum were so high that GreenFuel's algal biodiesel would make money once diesel fuel costs, oh, a mere $800 a gallon. And, by the way, their figures for the conversion of energy from sunlight to oil somehow assumed that the second law of thermodynamics didn't apply to them. Oops.

There was a bit of a fracas over Dimitrov's report in the alternative energy scene, spiced with angry counterclaims from GreenFuel, and then GreenFuel suddenly went bankrupt and closed its doors. It turned out that the venture capitalists who were funding them read Dimitrov, ran the numbers themselves, and slinked away in shame, taking their money with them. Mind you, this hasn't prevented a dozen other algal biodiesel firms from insisting, on the basis of equally dubious numbers, that their very similar pond scum technologies will save the world.

What links the GreenFuel debacle and the Law of Attraction isn't simply the fact that a lot of people make decisions without checking the fine print. At the root of both fiascos was the same very popular piece of bad logic. The Law of Attraction assumes that the only reason you don't get everything you want is that you don't know how to go about getting it. The algal biodiesel industry is making the same assumption in a narrower field. That may not be obvious to some of you, and it's important enough that I want to take a few minutes to explore it.

The basic notion driving algal biodiesel, and a baker's dozen or so of similar projects, is that since the world's petroleum resources are being depleted very quickly—much more quickly than new reserves are being found, by the way—we need to find some other abundant, concentrated fuel source to keep industrial civilization going. That's the difficulty, though, because there is no other fuel source as abundant and concentrated as petroleum or the other fossil fuels. It's not just that we haven't found one yet; one doesn't exist, and it's not too hard to show that.

The oil we're now using at the astonishing rate of eighty-four million barrels a day didn't just show up because we all decided to conjure it into being by affirmations, you know. To get a barrel of oil, you've got to start with sunlight falling on shallow prehistoric seas for millions of years, driving the everyday miracle of photosynthesis that turns solar radiation into the chemical energy that keeps all living things going. You let the remains of living things in those shallow seas sink to the bottom in just the right conditions and get buried with mud, and then with more mud, until the mud begins to harden into rock; you then apply another hundred million years or so of heat and pressure from the Earth itself. All of this energy—the sunlight, the heat, the pressure—goes into making a barrel of crude oil one of the most energy-rich naturally occurring substances in the known universe.

If you want to make a barrel of oil from raw materials today, without a mess of dead plesiosaurs and a hundred million years of processing time, you need to put in something like the same amount of energy that goes into naturally occurring petroleum. That's the trap that swallows up most alternative energy schemes; it takes energy—lots of energy—to collect energy, to concentrate it, to convert it from one form to another, or really to do much of anything with it, and you can't get that energy by muttering some words in bad Latin. With fossil fuels, Nature put that energy into the mix long before our species showed up. With other fuels, we have to do that, and it's when we have to pay the energy costs ourselves that alternative fuels suddenly stop being paying propositions.

Nobody wants to hear this. We've got a global industrial civilization that keeps itself chugging along by burning through the world's fossil fuel reserves at an almost unimaginable rate—alongside those eighty-four million barrels of oil, the world's daily take of energy resources includes twelve and a half million short tons of coal and eight billion cubic meters of natural gas. We live on a finite planet that contains an even more finite amount of these fuels, and we're pumping and digging them faster than we're finding new reserves. That's a recipe for real trouble; and yet because we believe in something not too far from the Law of Attraction when it comes to energy, the only response most people are willing to consider is to accelerate the search for a replacement for fossil fuels, even though it only takes a little bit of basic physics to realize that one doesn't exist.

Now when I say that online or in a talk like this one, there's almost always somebody who stands up and insists that that's not true, haven't I heard of algal biodiesel, or Bussard fusion reactors, or zero-point energy, or—well, the list goes on for quite a time. Yes, I've heard of them. I've looked into them. At the end of the day, the same rule applies: there ain't no such thing as a free lunch. The only reason we think we don't have to obey that rule is that our civilization has spent the last three hundred years raiding the Earth's stashes of stored carbon and burning it to power a technological joyride. We think we've gotten away with it; we'll see what our descendants, who will have to deal with the mess we're leaving behind, think of that logic.

But there's another interesting parallel between the Law of Attraction and GreenFuel's pond scum Ponzi scheme that I want to bring up here. A lot of people who read and tried to use *The Secret* thought that they were doing something magical. A lot of people who bought into GreenFuel's hype thought that they were doing something ecological. Both were wrong, and for the same reason, because GreenFuel and

The Secret ignore the same central principle that's common to both magic and ecology: the reality of limits.

That's an extraordinarily unpopular principle, you know. Not long ago, I was invited to speak at a conference on Nature and spirituality at a retreat center over on the west coast. There was a pretty wide range of attendees, from many different spiritual traditions, and each of the speakers were supposed to present some insights their tradition offered about the relationship between spirit and Nature. So I decided—I was about to say, "to grab the bull by the horns," but it was a vegetarian retreat center, so we'll say I decided to grab the broccoli by the stem and talk about the reality, importance, and goodness of limits. It was a warm summer day, but the effective temperature in that lecture room dropped by about thirty degrees before I finished speaking half a dozen sentences. They heard me out, and I think a few of them actually grappled with what I was saying, but when the next speaker got up you could feel the sense of relief. Across that whole spectrum of spiritual traditions, what I'd suggested was blasphemy.

Yet it's also the key to magical power. Real magic, I mean. There is such a thing. It's not supernatural; personally, I don't think there is anything supernatural, anything outside the laws and balances of Nature, though it's tolerably likely that Nature has wrinkles and connections that get missed by the sort of extreme reductionalist rationalism that's fashionable these days. What you can accomplish with magic is limited by the laws of Nature, so you'll have to do without the aerial broomsticks and the stampeding unicorns. What you can do is influence the flow of events so that the things you want to happen are more likely to happen.

How does it work? Nobody knows. It's not as though people who practice magic can get grant money to research what they're doing. From my own experience and that of other people who practice this stuff, it has a lot to do with will and imagination; with changing your own attitudes and expectations; with the nonrational parts of the mind and nervous system. We all do it, all the time—we've all seen the way attitudes and expectations become self-fulfilling prophecies, for example. The difference between magicians and the rest of humanity is that magicians try to figure out how to do it consciously; to shape the world of their experience deliberately.

That's magic. Now, I don't need bad Latin to hear you thinking: Oh, but what about the wands and robes and funny hats? What about the billowing incense, the candles on the altar, the sonorous incantations, and all that entertaining stuff? Those are training wheels. Those are the things you use, when you're in training, to learn how to work with the nonrational parts of your self, and hook up with certain complicated patterns of causation that nobody understands very well, but magicians—real magicians—use all the time. At a certain point, you can skip the hardware, though a lot of us still use it; it's fun, and besides, you get in the habit. But the key to magic isn't in the hardware. The key to magic is in the self, and the hardware is just a set of symbolic tools you use to sort out the ways that the nonrational parts of yourself shape the universe of your experience.

It works. If you learn how it's done, and practice it regularly, you'll find pretty quickly that you can get results that take a lot of special pleading to explain away. Of course, there's a substantial body of effort dedicated to just that sort of special pleading; no matter how remarkable the results, it's always possible to insist that it was just a coincidence. Of course, it was just coincidence; magic is the art and science of causing coincidence in accordance with will. Put another way, it's the art of tweaking the balance so that things are just that little bit more likely to turn out the way you want. No unicorns; no broomsticks; just will and imagination, and some kinds of causality we don't understand yet, adding that little extra push where needed. That's real magic.

Does it always work? Of course not. Neither does anything else. Buildings fall down, airplanes drop out of the sky, promising new algal biodiesel companies go bankrupt, you name it; every field of human endeavor has its flops; and magic is tricky; it takes practice and a lot of hard work to make it function. Still, there's a reason why every human society on Earth, as far back as records go, has practiced magic. It's not foolproof, but very often, if you know what you're doing and aim for what's possible, you can tilt the odds significantly in your favor.

What's most interesting to me in this context is what magicians around the world say about how their odd and tricky craft gets its results. They'll tell you that there are connections linking everything in the world with everything else; that it's possible to tap into that web of connections in a subtle way, not just by the blunt instrument of ordinary, rationally understood cause and effect; that if you know about the subtle ways and use them, you can get surprising results even when the things you do have no visible connection to the results you get.

For the sake of comparison, sit down with an ecologist sometime, and ask how the processes of Nature work. The ecologist will tell you that there are connections linking everything in the world with everything else; that that web of connections works in ways that don't always make sense in terms of the blunt instrument of ordinary, rationally understood cause and effect; and that actions taken in a living ecosystem can have surprising results, even when the things you do have no visible connection to the results you get.

You may notice a little similarity there. I've come to think that it's not accidental: the world of subtle connections understood by magicians, and the world of subtle connections understood by ecologists, are actually the same world. Magic, real magic, is the traditional craft of tweaking the ecological connections that link everything together. This is why so much magic among what we like to call primitive peoples has to do with maintaining the right relationships between human beings and the animals they hunt and the plants they gather; and why so much magic among people who practice agriculture focuses on what we'd now call soil fertility and the ecological balance among crops, soil, and weather that makes the harvest come in.

You can find this in ancient traditions all over the world. One of the things that used to make archeologists scratch their heads, for example, was the location of ancient Greek temples of Demeter. Every Greek temple had an area of sacred ground around it that you couldn't farm, and you couldn't graze animals on—if your livestock wandered into the temple precincts, according to ancient Greek law, the god or goddess took ownership of the animal and it was immediately offered up as a sacrifice. Not exactly an incentive to let your cow stray on the god's side of the fence, you must admit.

Now Demeter, the grain goddess, had a lot of her shrines in places that made no sense in practical terms—miles away from the nearest town, in a lot of cases. Sometimes there wasn't even a temple, just a grove of trees that belonged to her, and you did *not* harm them. In most ancient Greek cities, cutting a tree in one of those groves got you the death penalty. The archeologists had a heck of a time figuring out why these groves were where they were, and why they had this complex of taboos around them that the ancient Greeks took so seriously.

Then some ecologist pointed out that most of the groves of Demeter had something in common: erosion control. They were in places where a big patch of natural vegetation would catch rainwater and slow it down, so the topsoil didn't get washed away by floods. Demeter was the goddess of grain and arable soil; the groves were sacred to her because they protected the arable soil and made it possible to grow grain successfully on the rugged Greek peninsula. Good religious magic, and also very sound ecological logic.

You'll find the same thing to this day in Japan. Inari is the rice god of Shinto, the old polytheist faith of Japan, and he's got shrines all over the place in rural Japan. A Shinto shrine is traditionally surrounded by trees and gardens and green stuff, like a Greek temple, and some of them have entire mountains back behind them that are off-limits to all but religious uses. That's especially common with old rural shrines to Inari, and wouldn't you know it, the sacred groves of the rice god are once again in places that keep erosion under control and provide steady water supplies to the rice paddies.

Inari likes foxes, by the way. Foxes are his messengers, and you'll have a hard time finding anybody in rural Japan who will do anything to inconvenience a fox; it's very, very bad luck. Does this have something to do with the fact that foxes are the number one predator of the rodents that are a major problem for rice farmers? You do the math.

There's a lot of this stuff in the old magical and religious lore. That is to say, there's a lot of stuff that makes obvious ecological sense. The thing that interests me, though, is that there's a great deal more that isn't as obvious but may just make a subtler kind of ecological sense. In traditional American folk magic, for example, if you need to cleanse yourself from negative forces, you take a bath containing certain ingredients, including plant extracts. You save the water from the bath, or at least some of it, and then you go out and throw the water onto the trunk of the biggest and healthiest tree you can find.

Now, of course, the folklorists have come up with all kinds of theories about how this symbolizes this, that and the other thing. Still, it occurs to me that something else may be going on here. Trees communicate with one another; botanists know that now. They release complicated chemical pheromones into the air and the soil, and other plants pick up on those; if a tree gets an insect infestation, for example, its pheromones warn every other tree within a certain range to start boosting the anti-insect compounds in their sap and cells that are their equivalent of an immune system. There's some reason to think that animals also tap into this conversation, and add their own chemical voices to it.

So when you take a bucket of water full of your own skin oils and pheromones, along with a mess of botanical products with their own chemical messages, and toss it onto a tree, what are you saying to the tree? And what is the water, and the tree, saying to every other life form within range? We don't know—but maybe we need to start thinking about the possibility that things like this have more to do with magic than anybody has suspected.

Now there's a pretty fair gap between the Law of Attraction and talking to trees with a bucket of bathwater, and it's not at all unlike the gap between pond scum in plastic tubes and the kind of changes we're actually going to have to make in our lives as the age of cheap abundant energy comes to an end. *The Secret* and GreenFuel both made sweeping promises they couldn't fulfill because they only got half the lesson that magic and ecology teach. They got the half that says that there are all kinds of possibilities in the universe around us; they missed the half that says that there are also all kinds of limits in the universe around us. So they failed.

Now of course you can fail just as badly by paying attention to the limits and never pursuing the possibilities, and a lot of people do that, but that just proves that the opposite of a bad idea isn't necessarily a good idea; most of the time, it's just another bad idea, and in the process of swinging from one extreme to the other, you slid right past a good idea in the middle. That's a law of magic, by the way; it's also one of the great secrets of initiation; some of you may know it as the Royal Secret; and its name is equilibrium. If you insist that equilibrium doesn't matter, and the universe exists to give you whatever you happen to want, then equilibrium is going to kick your butt. It's when you recognize equilibrium, and learn to move with it and ride it, that you become able to achieve great things—not everything you want, quite possibly not even the thing you most want, but things that from an ordinary perspective seem hopelessly out of reach.

The same rule of equilibrium applies to the predicament of industrial civilization, by the way. For the last three hundred years we've been doing our level best to ignore the law of equilibrium; we've burnt nearly half the Earth's supply of stored carbon, and wasted most of it, and of course the half that we burnt was the stuff that was easy and cheap to extract, leaving the difficult and expensive stuff for later. We've known collectively since the 1970s that we were backing ourselves into a corner, and then we went ahead and did it anyway. So by this point a lot of options have been foreclosed; a lot of choices that could have given us a soft landing on the way down are no longer within reach. But there are still things that can be accomplished; there are still options that could make the future a lot less rough than it could be, and if we stop kidding ourselves—stop insisting that the universe is under some kind of obligation to give us the lifestyles we happen to want, just because we happen to want them—we can still make the best of the opportunities that are still open.

Now, of course, this implies that the future isn't limited to the only two options that contemporary popular culture is willing to consider. You know, business as usual forever, leading to some sort of Star Trek future metastasizing across the galaxy, or a really cool cataclysm that wipes seven billion extras off the planet, so some Hollywood stars can act out the role of plucky survivors. You'd be amazed how many people literally can't imagine a future other than those. I call that the Fuller Fallacy, after Buckminster Fuller, who wrote a book titled *Utopia or Oblivion* arguing that those were the only two possibilities we had, and of course he was dead wrong. There's a lot of very complicated cultural history behind that weird two-way tunnel vision, which I don't have time to go into just now. Let's just take it as given that once again, the meaningful option is the one between the two extremes.

That means we're in for a very rough ride over the next few centuries. It's not the end of the world; it is very likely the end of industrial civilization, and the end of a lot of things many of us take for granted; and the same sort of troubles and crises and local catastrophes that make up so much of history before our time will very likely make up about the same amount of history in the future. Civilizations fall—it's one of the most predictable things about them—and most of the time, they fall because they overshoot the resource base that supports them. That's what we're doing, too, and our civilization is already showing most of the standard historical signs of imminent decline.

Now it so happens that in the past, when civilizations have gone into decline, magic has tended to become even more popular than it usually is. There's a reason for that. When a civilization's political system is frozen in gridlock, and its economic system is riddled with incompetence and corruption, and its religious traditions have either fossilized into meaningless dogma or been chucked out as so much superstition, and its resource base is running short enough that it has trouble getting much of anything done in the usual ways—do any of these sound familiar?—then a way to accomplish things that does an end run around the usual ways, that makes use of subtle connections to get unexpected results, has an obvious appeal. I don't think it's accidental that so many people were so eager to find some magical way to accomplish things with their lives that they were willing to swallow *The Secret* hook, line, and sinker.

Equally, though, it wasn't an accident that so many people were so eager to find some more ecologically sane way to power our society that they got taken in by GreenFuel. If I'm right and ecology and magic are two different ways of talking about the same reality, the web of subtle connections that weave together all living things in the biosphere, these are two sides of the same leaf. Since the dawn of the industrial age, we've been using brute force methods to get things done; if we've got a problem with some insect, say, we dump chemical poisons anywhere the insect might be found, and end up struggling with a truckload of unintended and unwanted consequences. It never occurs to most of us that there's a better way—that we can figure out what subtle disorder in the ecosystem is allowing that insect to get out of balance, and that we can do things to the ecosystem, subtle things, to bring the balance back.

I've come to believe that that's going to be one of the most important developments of the decades and centuries ahead of us—the evolution of what I call the ecotechnic crafts, the ways of doing things that work constructively with the subtle balances of Nature so that everybody benefits. We've got just the very first rough sketches of the ecotechnic crafts and industries of the future, in the appropriate technology movement, the organic farming movement, some of the less delusional forms of green energy, and a lot of ancient craft traditions that evolved back when we didn't have the cheap abundant energy to use brute force methods, so we had to be smart instead. We have to be smart again; I've come to think that those who spearhead that return to basic ecological intelligence—who pioneer the ways of living that will allow us to lead humanly becoming lives in some kind of harmony with the broader patterns of the biosphere—are the cutting edge of the future, the people whose work will still be remembered when those old stories about flights to the Moon have become fairy tales nobody believes anymore.

And magic? In one sense, that's a given; there has never been a human society anywhere, as far as we know, that didn't have at least an occult subculture that enthusiastically practiced magic. So we can be sure that whatever the future holds, it will hold some kind of magic; people will keep on trying to figure out the subtle web of connections that link all things together, and they'll keep on trying to tweak it for their own benefit.

In another sense, it's anybody's guess, for the twilight years of a civilization are a time when the whole legacy of the past is up for grabs. What appeals to one or another of the emerging successor cultures gets preserved, and what doesn't, gets to rot in the ruins. Magic is as much a part of that process as anything else. We live at a time when the magical legacy of the past is right here at our fingertips; teachings and practices that were the jealously guarded secrets of inner circles of initiates as little as a few centuries ago are sitting on the shelves at your local bookstore. How much of that will still be around when the industrial age is over? Good question. To some extent that depends on us; to a larger extent, it depends on which of those legacies turn out to be useful in the very difficult years ahead of us, and so become part of the toolkit that our successors use to make sense of their world and take action in it.

But there's also a third sense that has to be considered when the future of magic comes up for discussion, and that's the odd parallelism between magic and ecology that I've tried to point out in tonight's talk. If I'm right, and magic works by way of ecological relationships, or at least functions in a way that parallels ecological principles, the old magical disciplines may just have a special gift for us at this turning of history's wheel.

What we in the industrial world need, more than anything else right now, is to learn how to think ecologically, to relate our actions to the needs and limits of a wider world, to move away from the clumsy brute force methods of making things happen toward subtler means that work with rather than against the natural flow of events. Magic can teach that; ecology can teach that; and it's just possible that a deliberate fusion of the two—a magical ecology, or an ecological magic, or some larger thing not yet even imagined that embraces both—could become a very potent tool of transformation to reshape our relationship to the planet that sustains our lives.

I don't have such a magical ecology in my pocket. Nobody does, not yet, and it will most likely take generations for one to evolve out of the raw materials we've got to hand now. Still, there's good reason to start the process of bringing it to birth right now. So I'm going to suggest to those of you who came here to hear about magic that maybe you should consider learning a little about ecology, and put that knowledge into practice; and those of you who came here to hear about ecology might want to learn a little about magic, and put that into practice, too.

There are many other traditions, and many other practices, that could well become part of such a fusion of magic and ecology. Equally, there's no reason to think that there will only be one such fusion—nor any reason to think that there should only be one. One of the basic laws of ecology is that diversity is a good thing. But I'd like all of you, whatever brought you to this evening's talk, whatever beliefs and commitments guide you, and whatever future you expect, to put a few moments of thought at least into how your life relates to the bigger picture of the biosphere, at this moment of history, and to ask yourself if there are things you can and should be doing differently. If anything is going to help make the future a better place, it's not going to be pond scum or New Age hokum or any other attempt to deny the reality of the limits that define the universe of our experience; it's going to be the choices that each of us make at each moment, as parts of the great web of connections that weaves the world together.

CHAPTER THREE

The secret history of Neopaganism

Talking about the history of Neopaganism these days is rather like waving a red cloth in front of a bull deity. Some of the bitterest political struggles in recent Pagan memory have been fought at least partly over issues of history. But it's interesting to note that nearly always in a modern Pagan context, the word "history" has referred to origins. The origins of our traditions, of course, form one of the more interesting issues in Pagan history and is one in which I've argued for certain viewpoints in the past. But to say that the history of modem Paganism is entirely about where it originally comes from is a little like saying that someone's biography should deal entirely with the details of her conception and birth. While those do have a certain amount of prurient interest, the rest is more than just afterthoughts. That's particularly true in the case of modem Paganism because the history of today's Neopaganism goes back a good deal further than many modern Pagans realize.

So, I'd like to begin this exploration with a scene that ought to sound familiar to many of us here. The setting? A London park toward the end of September. A small group of people, some in white robes, some in ordinary clothes, have just cast a ceremonial circle and are about to perform a Druid ritual to celebrate Alban Elfed, the autumn equinox, under the gaze of a medium sized mob of baffled onlookers. The guy who leads the group claims to have received ancient Druidic traditions handed down in secret since pre-Christian times; he's a poet with a drug problem and a day job to make ends meet. The other members are artists and urban intellectuals, most of them far to the left in politics and culture, into new and alternative ideas of all sorts.

You could have found a similar crowd not far from there last September, or in the 1970s, or for that matter in the 1920s, doing pretty much the same thing. But this particular autumn equinox ceremony at Primrose Hill in London was in 1792. The fam-trad Druid and opium addict was Edward Williams, better known these days by his craft name Iolo Morganwg.

Iolo and his Druid Grove weren't the only Pagans running around London in those days, by any means. Another was the astonishing Thomas Taylor, whom newspapers of the time called "the Pagan High Priest of England." I'm not sure Taylor would have agreed with the "High Priest" part, he was a fairly modest man, but he had no problem at all with "Pagan." He was a brilliant scholar of Greek and Latin literature; in fact, during his lifetime he translated every surviving scrap of Greek and Roman Pagan religious and philosophical writing into English and got them into circulation in alternative religious circles all over the English-speaking world. And it wasn't just a job for him. He publicly referred to Christianity as a "barbarous superstition" which he hoped would be replaced someday soon by the true religion of humanity: Paganism.

Mind you, what he meant by Paganism wasn't exactly what most of us mean when we use the word. Taylor was a Greek Pagan Neoplatonist; he was powerfully influenced by people such as Iamblichus of Chalcis and Proclus Diadochus, the last great theoreticians of classical Greek spirituality, who used Neoplatonist metaphysics to provide a theology for the traditional practices of Greek Pagan religion. When Taylor spoke of Paganism, in other words, he was talking about sacrificing cattle to Zeus—in a very philosophical and erudite way, of course, though I doubt that mattered much to the cattle. As far as I know nobody has been able to document that Taylor actually sacrificed an ox to anybody, but he had altars to the gods of Olympus, poured them libations of wine—all the other things a devout person would have done as a matter of course in Greece, say, two thousand years earlier.

He wasn't alone. From the late eighteenth century to the early part of the twentieth, there was quite a sizable Greek Pagan scene all through British society, with some very important artists, writers, and cultural figures in it up to their eyeballs. Many of you probably grew up reading Kenneth Grahame's children's classic *The Wind in the Willows*; you may not have known that Grahame also published a collection of essays titled *Pagan Papers* in which he called himself a follower of the Old Religion. That wasn't Gardner's Old Religion; Gerald Gardner was still taking care of rubber plantations in Sumatra when Grahame's book came out. It was Thomas Taylor's Old Religion, which is why the Greek god Pan puts in a cameo appearance in one of the best-loved books in British children's literature.

Of course in those days a good education meant learning enough Latin and Greek to read the classics in the original. Quite a few educated Englishmen and women were struck pretty hard by the contrasts between the classical Paganism they read about and the religion of their own place and time. Whatever you happen to think about Greek Pagan religion, it's unquestionably more fun than sitting through a two-hour sermon every Sunday. It's particularly appealing if you happened to be gay, and were looking for a spirituality that made room for that, as, of course, Victorian Christianity didn't. So, in particular, there were a lot of gay Victorian gentlemen whose religion involved going out into the back garden and pouring libations of wine over an altar while chanting "Io Pan, Io Pan Pan."

Now the Greek Pagan subculture extended well beyond that, of course, and, in a bit, I'll return to the astonishing afterlife of classical Greek Paganism. But first I'd like to go to a third vignette. (I'm a Druid, and, of course, Druids like to do things in threes.) The time is just a bit earlier—1798, to be precise—and the place is a small town in the Hudson River Valley of New York State. A meeting is about to start. It's a meeting of the first documented American Pagan organization, the Society of Ancient Druids.

The Society actually started out its existence as a Masonic lodge, but there was one little problem with that connection. The members of that particular lodge, like many other Masons before and since, entered the Craft because they wanted access to deep spiritual mysteries, which in practice meant just about anything other than the sort of narrow Protestant piety that was standard issue in America just before and during the Revolution. The problem is that Masonry is basically a men's social club with a set of medieval initiation rituals that even most Masons don't understand. Its reputation as a secret school of arcane mysteries, or for that matter the sort of world-dominating conspiracy Matt Groening parodied to death in the one episode of *The Simpsons* most Masons know by heart, was invented by its enemies, and then adopted by some of its more overenthusiastic supporters. Don't get me wrong; I'm a Freemason myself and very fond of the Craft, but it's not all it's been cracked up to be. We don't control the British Crown, we don't keep the metric system down; we don't, we don't.

And this is what the future members of the Society of Druids found out when they'd all been entered, passed, and raised to the sublime degree of Master Mason. The very real virtues of Masonry were not what they were looking for. They wanted arcane spiritual mysteries, and not Christian ones, either, thank you very much. So the whole lot of them voted to disconnect their lodge from the Masonic fraternity, and they turned it into a Society of Ancient Druids.

Why Druids? For that matter, why Druids in London in 1792? Especially, why Druids when the only information anybody had about Druids in those days consisted of around ten pages of scrappy quotations in old Latin and Greek sources, half of them contradicting the other half, most of them second- or third-hand quotations of someone else's work, and none of them actually written by Druids, or by people with direct detailed knowledge of Druids?

It's a complicated question; why does anything from hula hoops to nose piercing become fashionable when it does? The fact of the matter was that Druids were fashionable, in much the same circles that Druids are fashionable today. A lot of people in Britain and America in 1798 thought that Celts were cool; now admittedly this didn't include the British government, which was hard at work trying to wipe them out in Ireland and Scotland just then, but that's another story. In the first stages of the Industrial Revolution, also, there were quite a few people who had an inkling of just how suicidally stupid the Western world's war on the Earth was going to become, and a lot of them borrowed the image of the Druid worshiping in sylvan groves as a way of talking about the spiritual importance of Nature. Thus one of the first books in English on planting trees, a 1734 handbook of oak culture, was titled *The Modern Druid*.

Then there was the Irish writer John Toland, who could easily fill up a talk like this all by himself. Toland lived before the internet. This was probably a good thing, because the guy was a walking, talking, one-man flamewar. He was a very controversial figure. Lacking an AOL account and access to Usenet, he made do with the printing press instead, issuing books and pamphlets that landed him in every conceivable kind of hot water. This is the guy who invented the word "pantheism" for his own religious beliefs, and who—in 1696—published a book suggesting that someone ought to go through the Bible and the doctrines of Christianity, take everything that violated the rules of common sense and everyday logic and chuck them out. Did I mention that he was a controversial figure?

It's been claimed, though as far as I know nobody's been able to document it yet, that Toland headed one of the earliest English Druid organizations. Certainly, he was interested in Druids. He thought they were ancient pantheists—they were wise, of course, they agreed with him, right? Other people in the early days of the Druid movement insisted that Druids had been a sort of advance party of liberal Anglicans. This offended Toland—everything offended Toland—and so Toland's one book on the Druids was an extended satire on the Anglican Church, presenting Druid proto-Anglicans or proto-Anglican Druids as fakers who were doing the religion schtick in order to get out of working for a living. But even there, his Druids were pantheists, and so people in Europe and America who liked pantheism decided that since they were pantheists, they might as well be Druids too.

So, in fact, the members of the Society of Ancient Druids were flaming pantheists. That is, they believed that the universe was God, that matter and spirit were the same thing, that Nature was the proper object of human worship, and that the rules and prohibitions of conventional Christian religion were a load of malarkey. They weren't alone, either, even in the American colonies. In fact, no less a figure than Thomas Jefferson took Toland at his word and produced an edition of the Christian gospels from which everything, as he put it, that would not be admitted as evidence in a court of law had been cut out. That includes little things like the Virgin Birth and the Resurrection, in case you're wondering. So much, by the way, for our Christian founding fathers.

Now, these three vignettes make a point that should be looked at before we go on to talk about the origins and results of all this eighteenth-century Paganism. The point is that almost nothing in today's Pagan movement is as new as most of today's Pagans tend to think. The modern Pagan scene didn't suddenly leap out of the New Forest in the late 1940s like Athena from the head of Zeus. Most of the things that define the modern Pagan subculture also defined urban middle-class Pagan subcultures in Britain and America two hundred years ago. As we'll see, they also defined other Pagan subcultures a good deal further back.

All this flatly contradicts a way of looking at the past of Paganism that has been very influential, particularly here in America, in the last few decades. The model in question was created by the late Isaac Bonewits and introduced to the Pagan community in his writings from the 1970s onwards. Most likely everyone here knows it. It divides the Pagan past into three sections. First come the Paleo-Pagans, the people who followed Pagan religions back in the days before Christianity. Without too much risk of satire we could simply call them "real Pagans." Next come the Meso-Pagans, about which Bonewits had almost nothing good to say. They were people who tried to revive something they thought was Paganism in the eighteenth and nineteenth centuries, but according to Bonewits they were stuffy, basically Christian, and had their history all wrong. Finally, we come to the Neo-Pagans, who revive Paleo-Pagan traditions and turn their backs on those awful Meso-Pagans and all their works.

It's an interesting model and very revealing in its way; it's just that what it reveals doesn't actually have that much to do with the history of Pagan spirituality before the 1970s. One of the things it reveals most clearly, for instance, is Mr. Bonewits' own position in the political squabbles that rocked the 1970s Druid scene. I doubt it's an accident that while he was developing and circulating this model, he was also extracting himself from the Reformed Druids of North America. To judge from his writings of the time, he thought the RDNA was stuffy, basically Christian, and had their history all wrong, just like his Meso-Pagans. He then went on to launch Ar nDraiocht Fein, a Druid organization which he intended to be exactly the sort of Neopaganism his model proposes.

This sort of historical hindsight, projecting today's politics onto the past, is of course very common, and not just in Pagan circles. But it's not the only thing behind Bonewits' Paleo-Meso-Neo-Pagan model. The same sort of three-step waltz to the music of Time has been standard in progressive circles all through the Western world since the twelfth century when a Christian theologian named Joachim of Flores invented the concept. Joachim's three ages of Law, Grace, and Love formed a bad to so-so to good sequence, but most of his followers thought it made better rhetoric to suggest that the middle period was the really bad one. In these later Joachimist schemes you're always right at the end of the second period, about to move into the third, and so it gave a nice satisfying dualistic contrast between good and evil. Of course, this same pattern was adopted wholesale into Marxism by way of Hegel, giving us the ever-receding revolution of the proletariat, and you also get exactly the same model in Aleister Crowley's doctrine of the three Aeons of Isis, Osiris, and Horus.

A third factor—you knew there was going to be a third factor, didn't you?—is a very clever bit of strategy that modern Pagans have been using on the academic establishment for around three hundred years now. Bonewits' view of the Meso-Pagans was modeled very closely on the views of archeologists and historians such as Stuart Piggott, whose 1968 book *The Druids* was in large part a broadside aimed at the English Druid movement of Piggott's own time. Piggott talked about "bodies of self-styled Druids who today represent the fag-end of the myth" and called them "pathetic." Very moderate, unemotional language, as you see. Bonewits basically took this and said, "Well, yes, of course, but that's those old-fashioned Meso-Pagan Druids over there. We're different, and none of your argument applies to us."

It's a great piece of rhetorical jujitsu, and the best thing about it is that you can do it over and over and over again. Every time the academic establishment winds up and throws another punch, you step to one side, redefine Paganism in a way that slips right past their critique, and add their book to your First Degree recommended reading list. Then a few years later you do the same thing, and Ronald Hutton goes onto the reading list right next to Stuart Piggott. You're a moving target, always one step ahead of them.

The downside to this very elegant strategy is that it fosters a curious sort of historical blindness in the Pagan community. If you're constantly disavowing the last decade's Pagan traditions, not to mention those of fifty and a hundred years ago, it's difficult to learn from them—or even to recognize that there are things you might want to learn from them. And there's quite a bit you might want to learn from them.

A different strategy might be worth borrowing here from the world of advertising. You've all noticed, I'm sure, that every year or so your favorite brand of whatever suddenly shows up with packaging announcing that it's new, improved, better than ever! Of course, it still tastes the same, and you roll your eyes and put it in the shopping cart. But some companies have realized that you can get the same market boost with packaging that says, "Old-fashioned, just like Grandma used to microwave," or what have you. That way you don't even have to make-believe that you messed with the formula.

Maybe it's time for some of that in the Pagan community. We've seen plenty of the new and improved already. It's not just plain old Wicca this year, it's new improved Celtic Wicca; and then it's Celtic shamanic Wicca; and now its Celtic shamanic feng-shui Wicca. (I bet you think I'm making that last one up.) But there's also a place, and maybe more of a place than it's had so far, for old-fashioned magic and Pagan spirituality: spells just like Grandma used to cast.

But there's need for a little caution here. My grandmothers didn't live in pre-Christian Celtic Europe, and you know, I'd be willing to bet that yours didn't either. Nor did any of our grandmothers live in a sort of spiritual vacuum where their only access to occultism and Pagan spirituality was by way of traditions handed down in a totally uncreative, idiot-savant way by rote memory since the beginning of Time. Whether your grandparents lived in this country or elsewhere, they lived in a place and time chock full of a wildly diverse range of occult traditions, Pagan revivals, and spiritual alternatives. That's been true of the entire planet for five centuries now, since the printing press and the first good oceangoing sailing ships dynamited cultural barriers and brought in the early modern world.

Failure to realize this has had some remarkably silly results. All through the nineteenth and early twentieth centuries, for example, there was a running battle between folklore scholars in Britain and the working-class rural people they were studying. The folklore scholars believed in age-old folk traditions passed down from the distant past, and insisted that rural festivals, say, had been done exactly the same way over and over again, with exactly the same songs and so on, since the early Middle Ages if not since prehistoric antiquity. The problem was that this isn't the way rural folk traditionally did them. English farm families had been picking up new songs for centuries; they got them from wandering bards in the Dark Ages; they got them from hand-printed ballad broadsheets during the Elizabethan period; they got record players and radios as soon as they could, and saw nothing wrong with belting out the latest music hall hits over a pint of Boddington's as part of their harvest festivals. This drove the folklore scholars crazy.

Their ideology didn't have room for the fact that borrowing from any source that doesn't run away fast enough is an ancient and very firmly established folk tradition.

The same is emphatically true of magic, occult practices, and alternative religions—including Paganism of various kinds. For example, many of the most famous folk magicians in England in the eighteenth and nineteenth centuries—men and women who made their living taking hexes off cattle and doing marriage divinations for chambermaids—relied on one book above all for their magical techniques. It wasn't a Book of Shadows. It was the 1651 English translation of Henry Cornelius Agrippa's *Three Books of Occult Philosophy*, a classic text of Renaissance high magic. A lot of people in the Pagan scene today don't like to use Agrippa's kind of magic, which is ancestral to the sort of thing used by the Hermetic Order of the Golden Dawn and has large chunks of Cabala and Christian symbolism mixed in with it. Yet we know for a fact that it was used, constantly, two and three hundred years ago, by granny-women and cunning men in villages all over Britain, in Ireland, and in North America as well. A definition of traditional English village witchcraft, say, that leaves Agrippa out of the picture is missing something.

It's missing, among other things, one of the most constant themes in folk magic in the Western world, which is the movement of magical techniques from educated magical circles down into the occult proletariat, the ordinary village wizard or witch who makes a living working spells for common folk. That's been going on since classical times. Ancient Greek folk magicians did a lot of magic with *defixiones*, messages written on sheets of lead and sent to the powers of the underworld by way of cemeteries, wells, caves, and so on. Modem archeologists have found literally thousands of them. One of the most interesting things about them is that very erudite mystical formulae from Orphic religion show up on them, put to use in the most practical forms of magic you can think of. Some Greek village witch gets consulted by someone's maid about a stolen hairpin, writes up a *defixio* to curse the thief, and puts in a chunk of a mystical Orphic invocation to Persephone just to make sure the powers of the underworld will listen up.

Agrippa's handbook of Renaissance high magic followed exactly the same trajectory, and so did many other works of the same period. Historians have been able to trace some very exotic German Rosicrucian magic straight into the repertoire of Pennsylvania hexenmeisters, who used amazing Cabalistic mystical formulae to cure horses of colic and things like that. The connection there is pretty straightforward since there were German Rosicrucian communes in Pennsylvania well before 1700. Up until a few years ago, similarly, you could still get some very potent handbooks of Cabalistic magic from traditional hoodoo supply houses, which provided material for folk magicians in the African-American community. Nowadays some of the same houses carry books by Scott Cunningham; the wheel has come full circle.

But what about Pagan religion? As it happens, Agrippa is a good place to start looking at that and to make sense of the history of Neopaganism in the Western world. Agrippa has a very odd attitude toward Pagan traditions. He cites Pagan authors constantly, and just as constantly disavows his own quotations and presents himself as a good Christian. His chapter on the role of religion in practical magic, Book Three, Chapter Four, explains that by religion he means the true religion, that is, Christianity, whereas all other religions (and particularly Pagan religions) are superstition—but he also says that superstition is absolutely necessary in magical practice. Later in the same chapter he piously asserts that the old Pagan religions are of course damnable idolatry that one must avoid at all costs, but on the other hand the Christian god doesn't completely despise them, or at least not as much as atheism, and they do have a place in magic, and after all he's just quoting things that he finds in other authors. He does an amazing job of talking out of both sides of his mouth.

Now a good deal of this was a matter of plausible deniability, as we'd say nowadays. Agrippa lived at a time when people got burned to death for not being careful enough walking the fine line he was trying to walk. Agrippa himself managed to die of old age, which was an impressive achievement for a very well-known sixteenth-century sorcerer. But there was arguably more to it than that. In his book, *The Pagan Dream of the Renaissance*, Joscelyn Godwin has drawn a compelling picture of the half-Pagan culture of Renaissance Europe, full of people who were fascinated by Paganism but couldn't quite bring themselves to drop Christianity. Agrippa was very much a product of that era and its culture, and his twistings and turnings show the contortions of a brilliant mind trying to embrace two mutually exclusive belief systems at the same time.

But how did that happen in the first place? Once again, we need to look at the astonishing afterlife of Greek Pagan religion.

In its early years, the leaders of mainstream Christianity made a couple of decisions that turned out to be massive mistakes. The first was the adoption of Neoplatonism as the standard basis for Christian theology. Neoplatonism had a lot of advantages: though it isn't monotheistic, it could be wrestled around to look monotheistic with a little bit of mumbling at the right spots, and it had a very impressive reputation, so that Christian theologians who took it up had something to answer the accusation—a very common accusation in ancient times, by the way— that Christianity was strictly for intellectual lightweights. The problem was that Neoplatonism had to be mishandled pretty roughly to make it fit Christian doctrine. It's problematic, for example, to claim that there's this absolute, transcendent ground of being that can't be defined in any way, as Neoplatonism does, and then proceed to define it, as a very concrete, specific person who does things like choosing one small Middle Eastern ethnic group as its Chosen People and sending its son to Earth to redeem humanity from sin. Such claims just don't fit Neoplatonism's own internal logic, and you had better hope that nobody gets their hands on Pagan Neoplatonism, either, because if they do your argument is going to look like absolute nonsense.

So, in hijacking Neoplatonism, the Christian theologians and religious politicians of the fourth and fifth centuries packed the basement of their church with dynamite and left fuses hanging out the windows. But they made an even more serious mistake: they didn't get rid of Pagan literature while they had the chance. In fact, they preserved it, and copied it over and over again through the Dark Ages, because generations of Christian scholars decided that it was only literature, after all, and very good literature, and of course everyone knew that there was only one true religion, so the bits of Paganism in Vergil and Homer and a hundred other writers were harmless, weren't they?

Well, no, actually, not from the perspective of a church organization that wanted to maintain a tight grip on people's beliefs. One of the basic claims of the Christian mainstream was a critique of Paganism that said that Christianity wasn't just the best religion, it was the only good religion. If you make a claim like that, you had better be prepared to live up to it, at least to the extent of following your own moral teachings, and of course organized Christianity failed to do that again and again. And so without intending to, they provided people with an alternative. It's like selling soap; the more time you spend talking about Brand X, even if all you say about it is negative, the more likely it is that people who aren't satisfied with your brand are going to think of Brand X and consider giving it a try.

This same process, incidentally, has been the main driving force behind the rise of organized Satanism over the last six centuries or so. The idea that there are people out there who worship the Christian Devil was an invention of Christian theologians in the Middle Ages and was used to justify the brutal witch hunts of the time. But during the late Middle Ages, the Christianity being practiced wasn't much to boast about, and theologians and Dominican preachers made matters worse by insisting that these alleged Devil worshippers spent all their time feasting, drinking, having lots of hot sex, putting whammies on their enemies, and so on. It's not hard to imagine people hearing this, thinking about it, and deciding that it sounded a lot more interesting than what the theologians and preachers had to offer.

So in the same way in twentieth-century America with the rise of fundamentalism, you had a whole industry of media preachers describing in graphic detail how Satanists were out there fulfilling all their worldly desires and having passionate sex with anything warm when they weren't too busy controlling the world in secret. Of course, some people started thinking that this sounded a lot more interesting than fundamentalism, and if maybe Satan didn't have more to offer than God—or at least more than the caricature of God these televangelists were promoting.

And after a while, as a direct result, you get a guy named Howard Stanton Levey, who renames himself Anton Szandor LaVey, shaves his head, cobbles together a Satanic Bible that's equal parts Aleister Crowley and Ayn Rand, feeds the media a fictional biography that's mostly malarkey but gets published without anyone bothering to check. The end result? He gets Jayne Mansfield to take off her clothes in his living room. Stronger men have succumbed to temptations much less alluring than that.

So, in the same way, the survival of Greek and Roman Pagan literature, in the context of a church that had a very hard time following its own moral teachings, made Pagan revivals inevitable. The files of the Inquisition are full of examples of medieval Pagan cults, most of them worshipping previously unknown goddesses and doing things that don't appear anywhere in pre-Christian Pagan religion. Perhaps the most interesting thing about these Pagan revivals, in fact, is the sheer amount of imagination and creativity that went into them.

The non-Christian beliefs that cropped up all through the Middle Ages weren't simply rehashes of pre-Christian tradition; they had exactly the same sort of impressive creativity that characterizes so much modern Pagan spirituality.

Take a look at the astonishing theological inventiveness of the guy discussed in Carlo Ginzburg's book *The Cheese and the Worms*, who believed that God and the angels grew out of a rotting universe the way that worms grow in old cheese. His name was Menocchio—no relation to the puppet—and he lived in Italy, which was a good thing because the Italian Inquisition was a lot more mellow than its equivalents elsewhere and it actually took them a couple of decades to get around to burning him at the stake.

Menocchio's swiss cheese cosmos full of divine worms was off on a very original tangent all his own. Most medieval Pagan revivals went in a different direction. As I suggested a moment ago, they tended to focus on goddesses. Barbara Newman, in an excellent recent book titled *God and the Goddesses*, has explored the very curious way in which goddesses became much more acceptable than gods in medieval literature. You could get away with using them allegorically, or at least claiming that they were just allegories, where that was a lot harder with gods. Partly that's just a grammatical quirk of Latin, which assigns feminine gender to abstract qualities and concepts—thus Faith, Knowledge, Matter, Rhetoric, Business Administration, are all feminine words in Latin, and if you like to write the kind of learned poetry that medieval scholars liked to write, you can turn all of them into allegorical goddesses who go strolling through your verses displaying their elegant ankles and discoursing on the parts of speech or something like that. But the result was that people all over Europe were thinking in terms of goddesses, even when they considered themselves devout Christians.

And of course, Neoplatonism got into the act again. Some of the most famous literary goddesses in medieval literature are in the writings of Christian Neoplatonist philosophers. One that particularly deserves attention is Bernard Sylvester, who lived in the late twelfth and early thirteenth centuries and at that time was widely considered the most learned man in Europe. He wrote an amazing philosophical poem called *Cosmographia* in which nearly all the characters are goddesses, who go zipping around in near-Earth orbit creating the world and stocking it with life forms with not much more than a nod of permission from the Trinity. Those of you who have read C. S. Lewis' space trilogy would find Bernard Sylvester familiar; that's where Lewis got a lot of his ideas and some of his terminology. The Oyarses, the planetary ruling spirits of Lewis' solar system, are straight out of *Cosmographia.*

Bernard Sylvester was by all accounts a devout Christian. In his time, and for a while thereafter, Neoplatonism in Western Europe was still devoutly Christian; the dynamite was still sifting undisturbed in the church basement. It was about two centuries after his time that someone finally set it off and blew things to kingdom come. The person responsible was a mild-mannered, modest, unassuming Italian scholar named Marsilio Ficino, who worked for Lorenzo de Medici, the ruler of Florence. The Medici family wanted to set up what we'd now call a think tank, and Ficino was a very good scholar of ancient Greek. So quite a bit of Medici money went into buying copies of old Greek manuscripts, which were handed over to Ficino to translate. No problem—except that the manuscripts included a complete copy of the works of Plato, most of which nobody in Western Europe had seen since the fall of Rome, and a copy of the *Corpus Hermeticum,* a collection of mystical tracts heavily influenced by Neoplatonism, entirely non-Christian, and very enthusiastic about astrology and ceremonial magic.

So Ficino, in his modest, unassuming way, translated the lot of it into exquisitely readable Latin and published it, which was pretty much the equivalent of going around that church and flicking his Bic at every available fuse. Over the century and a half that followed, more Pagan Neoplatonist works surfaced: Plotinus, Proclus, Iamblichus, and so on. All of them made a powerful, intellectually compelling case for a Neoplatonist mysticism and religious philosophy that didn't have a trace of Christianity in it. Remember what I said about the impact of Pagan Neoplatonism on people raised on Christian Neoplatonism? That wasn't speculation; it's what happened in the Renaissance right across Europe. It's as though you'd spent your entire life thinking that Budweiser was a good beer, and then someone handed you a craft microbrew. One sip and there's no going back.

Yet a lot of people, including many of the leading figures of Renaissance Neoplatonist occultism, also had a strong emotional attachment to Christianity. A lot of people were also very aware that being burned at the stake hurts. This was the fix that Henry Cornelius Agrippa and many of his contemporaries were in, and it's the fix that Agrippa passed on to future generations of granny-women and cunning men through his famous manual of magic. How to be Pagan and Christian at the same time, because that's what you think magic requires and you want to do magic, was the great challenge facing sorcerers and occultists of every stripe from the middle of the fifteenth century to the middle of the twentieth—from Ficino, one might say, to Gerald Gardner.

Of course, there were alternatives. There were systems of magical practice that stayed entirely Christian; there's a huge tradition of Christian occultism, natural magic and ceremonial magic, something that many modern Pagans don't realize. There were traditions drawn exclusively from Judaism, pursuing one or another kind of Cabalistic magic, and, of course, these were of interest to goyische occultists as well as to Jews. There were also things being imported from other continents from very early on—the first European translations of the I Ching date from the seventeenth century, for example. As Gloria Flaherty documents in her excellent book *Shamanism in the Eighteenth Century*, European scholars were writing learned books about shamanism not much later.

And of course from the beginning of the eighteenth century onwards, in the handful of countries where you could get away with it, there were people who followed the very different direction of John Toland and Thomas Taylor, and simply chucked Christianity altogether in favor of some alternative—usually some sort of Nature worship. But the main current of alternative spirituality for five hundred years in the West focused on this problem of the relationship between Paganism and Christianity. Through a long, awkward, complicated process of redefinition and exploration, this current gradually moved from one end of that spectrum to the other and ended up giving rise to most of today's Paganism.

Now the model I criticized a little while ago has led a lot of people in the modern Pagan scene to dismiss the Pagan traditions that emerged during this process—the Meso-Pagan traditions, in Bonewits' terms—as not really Pagan because they hadn't entirely jettisoned Christianity, or at least didn't say quite as many nasty things about Christianity as Pagans tend to do nowadays. But a lot of these traditions used Christianity in ways that would have made the last of Jerry Falwell's bodily hair fall out on the spot if he'd ever found out about them. Just because someone makes references to Jesus or the Bible in their writings, that doesn't mean their beliefs are anything that Christians would recognize as Christianity.

Redefinition of various kinds played a very important role in the development of Pagan traditions from the Renaissance to the present day.

A lot of people have inherited "family traditions" of various kinds of magic and alternative spirituality. Now of course "fam-trad" stories have been used rather too often as a cover for the invention of something brand new, and they've been used even more often to cover the fact that someone's Pagan roots reach back all the way to a book by Scott Cunningham. But the phenomenon exists; indeed, it's hard to imagine any way it couldn't exist. Since there have been people practicing magic and Pagan spirituality in the Western world for centuries now, and not all of them kept it secret from the children, there are going to be people who are raised in some sort of Pagan or magical tradition.

For example, I know a couple of fam-trad Druids. They've grown up in a Druid family and have been taking part in Druid rituals since before they were born. They're respectively six and three years old, and their parents are members of the Order of Bards Ovates and Druids. Now, I know many people don't consider this a "real" family tradition. But it's hard to say how many generations it takes to make something do the velveteen rabbit trick and become "real." To these two children, their fam-trad is intensely real; it defines the religious context in which they're growing up, and it's hard to see how things would really be that much different if their parents got their Druidry from their parents rather than from the OBOD study course.

But a strange thing often happens with family traditions of magic and alternative religion. A lot of these traditions are mostly practical technique: spells and charms, methods of divination, customs like leaving offerings out for the faeries on certain nights, and so on. Very often these are passed on without much in the way of theoretical background; they're just things one does in certain situations. People grow up with these, and then they go out into the wide world—and that's where they encounter magic or alternative spirituality, not as an assortment of stuff to do, but as a coherent and compelling system of thought and practice that seems to explain the stuff they grew up doing.

So there's a real pull toward using the systems of thought you encounter to explain the practices you inherited. It's particularly strong when the system of thought claims to be a secret tradition passed down through generations, and partly garbled and lost. But that's where redefinition starts happening. You grow up learning a bunch of magic from Grandma, let's say, spells for this, spells for that. Then she dies, you go to college, and you read your first Scott Cunningham book. You may well go, "Aha! Grandma must have been a witch, passing on fragmentary ancient Wiccan traditions she inherited from her granny and so on." But since you now have a book telling you what Wicca is supposed to be, the spells you learned may start migrating toward that new model. Grandma finished all her spells by saying "In Jesus' name, Amen," but you decide that that was a bit of protective cover adopted in the Burning Times, maybe, and end them "in the Goddess' name, so mote it be" on the assumption that that's what it originally was. Or you read about the Sabbats and remember one May Day when you were visiting Grandma and she gathered a lot of flowers and put them all over the house. A Beltane tradition? For you it is.

This isn't a theoretical example; I know people who followed exactly this trajectory from Grandma's folk magic to one form or another of Wicca. Nor is it something restricted to Wicca—far from it. In the first years of the twentieth century exactly the same thing happened with Theosophy. Helena Petrovna Blavatsky, the amazing woman who founded the Theosophical Society, claimed that the astonishingly creative system of spirituality she'd invented was the original primeval wisdom handed down from long, long before the beginning of Time— Theosophists turn up their noses at traditions that are only as old as this universe. A lot of people who had been raised in earlier spiritual and magical traditions read *Isis Unveiled* and *The Secret Doctrine* and decided, like our folk magician turned fam-trad Wiccan, that this was clearly the real esoteric teaching behind what they'd picked up from their Spiritualist grandparents.

In the 1850s and 1860s, Spiritualism and Mesmerism did exactly the same sort of redefinition of even earlier American and European spiritual movements. Antoine Court de Gebelin, Jean-Baptiste Alliette, and Eliphas Lévi reinterpreted the Tarot—which was just a deck of playing cards before their time—and turned it into the most powerful magical and divinatory tool in the entire Western occult tradition. Marsilio Ficino's translation of the *Corpus Hermeticum* redefined the entire literature of medieval magical practice; what had been mostly a tradition of cheap sorcery intended to summon demons for material gain was suddenly reinterpreted as a set of powerful techniques of spiritual transformation, and used accordingly with very good results. And so on.

And there's nothing wrong with this. Quite the contrary, this is how spiritual traditions grow, how they move with the times so that they can meet the needs of each generation. The one way in which it gets problematic is when people don't realize that this is what they're doing; when they think that of course Grandma was a Wiccan, when she may have been a Theosophist, or a Spiritualist, or a Rosicrucian, or any of a hundred other things. This is problematic because you lose touch with the real richness of the history of Pagan spirituality and magic.

Maybe Grandma's Rosicrucian teachers taught her some really innovative stuff they'd worked up—claiming to have gotten it by direct oral transmission from the dawn of Time, of course—stuff that's worth saving. And even if you decide you want to be a Wiccan rather than a Rosicrucian, or a Rosicrucian Wiccan—and remember that by Gerald Gardner's account, Old Dorothy Clutterbuck was a Rosicrucian Wiccan, so that's not exactly an untraditional thing to be—odds are you'll do a better job of reworking Grandma's spells to your own purposes if you understand that that's what you're doing, and if you see twenty-first-century Wicca and mid-twentieth-century Rosicrucianism not as two totally unconnected, isolated traditions but as parts of a much broader social and spiritual phenomenon.

The Rosicrucian movement actually makes a very good model for the way that alternative spiritual traditions develop and propagate in Western society, because its history is pretty well known, and of course that history includes a very important role in Gerald Gardner's account of the origin of Wicca. The group that Dorothy Clutterbuck belonged to—you've probably heard it called the "First Rosicrucian Theatre Company" or something of that sort, but its actual name was the Rosicrucian Order of the Crotona Fellowship, and it was headed by a professional actor named George Alexander Sullivan, who called himself the Master Aureolis. It was a pretty standard early twentieth-century British occult order, with nine degrees of initiation. Sullivan also claimed to have written all of Shakespeare's plays and poetry while he was going by the name of Francis Bacon, so he had an occult theater company to put on his new plays. There were other branches of the ROCF, including an academy that offered correspondence study in occultism. I've read some of the lessons—the content was again pretty standard for early twentieth-century British occult orders.

But "pretty standard for early twentieth-century British occult orders" adds up to an astonishing mix of materials from wildly diverse sources. One important ingredient was Hermeticism, the magical tradition that developed out of the Corpus Hermeticum that Ficino translated back in the fifteenth century, which also had an important place among the sources of the Hermetic Order of the Golden Dawn. Another was Theosophy, the mystical tradition that evolved out of Blavatsky's two massive books and the organization she founded, which was about half Hinduism and the other half cutting-edge nineteenth-century occult thought. Both of these were extremely influential all through the British occult scene just then.

The ROCF also drew a lot of material, and many of its members, from Co-Masonry, which was a branch of the Freemasons that started admitting women in the late nineteenth century and picked up a lot of esoteric material from French occult circles and the Theosophical Society thereafter. There was a lot of overlap between Co-Masonry and the occult scene when the ROCF was active; Dion Fortune started her occult career in the twenties as a member of a Co-Masonic lodge. So one way or another, the ROCF drew on most of the occult currents running around Britain at the time. But why "Rosicrucian"?

There we launch into one of the most amazing stories in the history of Western occultism, which is saying something. The original Rosicrucian movement was a joke. I mean that quite literally. A bunch of college students and professors with occult interests at the University of Wittemberg cooked it up in 1609 or thereabouts as a satire. They wrote this fanciful tale about a mysterious adept called C.R.C. who had founded an equally mysterious brotherhood that had all the answers to everything, and they got it published as an appendix to a translation of this raucous Italian satire in which the god Apollo calls a convention of wise men to solve the problems of the world, listens to their hare-brained schemes, and settles for price controls on cabbages, at which point everyone goes home rejoicing. It was pretty clearly not intended to be taken seriously.

But people took it seriously. Very seriously. All of a sudden people all over Europe were trying to find the Rosicrucian order. A lot of people wanted to join it. A lot of more conservative people wanted to locate its members and burn them at the stake. A second Rosicrucian manifesto surfaced, making nasty comments about the Pope and putting things in a much more serious political vein. It was probably written by different authors; Johann Valentin Andreae, who was part of the first group of merry pranksters and spent most of his career as a very serious, stuffy Lutheran theologian trying to distance himself from his college days, commented in his autobiography that the Rosicrucian comedy, as he put it, had a complete change of cast partway through. And before long there were dozens of books in print claiming to let on the secrets of the Rosicrucians, their spiritual practices, their magical and medical secrets, their organization and bylaws, and so on. Of course, that meant that people who wanted to be Rosicrucians, and somehow couldn't get in touch with the Rosicrucian order, could start one of their own. And of course, they did.

So by the middle of the eighteenth century, you had Rosicrucian orders popping up like mushrooms all over Europe. Where did they get their authentic Rosicrucian teachings? Exactly the same place that modern Pagan traditions get their authentic Pagan teachings. Some of the people who founded Rosicrucian orders were capable scholars and esotericists who assembled the best available package out of what was out there in the occult tradition and in scholarly writings and then filled in the gaps with their own work. Some of them were put-on artists who did exactly the same thing but claimed to get it from untraceable Secret Chiefs—that was their equivalent of the third-degree grandmothers of modern Pagan mythology. Of course, there were also B Team Rosicrucians who came up with less impressive packages. But with each generation, as more of this stuff went into circulation, new Rosicrucian orders had a wider assortment of stuff to choose from, and it reached the point by the late nineteenth or early twentieth century that you could decide to be a Rosicrucian and voila! You basically had a complete package waiting for you.

Of course, the package kept expanding as new things were added to it. Starting in the late eighteenth century, Egypt was fashionable—as fashionable as Druids—and so various Rosicrucian groups from that time on started finding ways to trace their roots back to ancient Egypt, and incorporated bits of Egyptian religion and magic into their teachings. That's why if you go to Rosicrucian Park in San Jose, California, you'll find some very nicely recreated Egyptian architecture—what archeologists are going to think of that two thousand years from now is an interesting question.

But you also had another very interesting thing happening. The first generation or so of Rosicrucian orders could never quite be honest about their origins since they didn't actually have the connection to the supposed real live Rosicrucian order that they claimed. And of course, that same thing kept happening later on. Martinez de Pasqually, who revolutionized French occult and mystical circles at the end of the eighteenth century and launched what eventually became the Martinist movement, founded his magical order on the basis of a blatantly fake charter supposedly signed by Bonnie Prince Charlie as alleged head of all Scottish Freemasonry. The Golden Dawn, probably the most influential magical order in the Western world in the last two centuries, was founded by means of a bunch of forged letters from a non-existent German Rosicrucian adept. But you also have situations, from the eighteenth century on, where people can honestly trace their lineages back to earlier Rosicrucian orders. And so lineage starts to become an issue, not as a piece of public-relations fluff but as a reality, a real connection to real teachings and organizations from the past.

Now, this is often a very good thing. One of the potential drawbacks you face in an innovative scene is that not all the innovations work; not all new ideas are good ideas. So, it's useful to have some idea what you're getting into, to have some link to something that's been proven to work, and that's one of the things that lineage does. If your Rosicrucian teacher was trained in the system of the Orden des Gold-und Rosenkreutz, let's say, by someone who was a member of that Order, you know that what you're getting is a tested system that people have been using long enough to get the bugs out. It only becomes a problem if access to a lineage turns into a power trip or an ego trip: I've got lineage, therefore, I can tell you what to do outside the context of instruction and initiation; or I've got lineage, therefore, I'm a better magician or a better person than you are. Of course, this happened too often, but that's not what lineage has to be about.

So, in the Rosicrucian movement by the early twentieth century, you had an interesting and very complex intersection between innovation and preservation, between the development of new approaches and the continuity of initiatory lineages. The Rosicrucian Order of the Crotona Fellowship was situated right at the nexus of those forces. The background of the Master Aureolis is still not very well known—he ran an earlier magical order before the First World War, the Order of the Twelve; I don't think anybody knows yet where he got his training and initiation, though Co-Masonry is a good bet. But that was only one ingredient in what became the ROCF system, which as we've seen drew from Theosophy, from Hermeticism, from many other sources.

Every other Rosicrucian organization from around the same time is in the same situation. They had a lineage of some sort, a series of initiations their founders went through or a formal charter from some older organization, or simply the personal experiences and insights of the founder, and then they had a much broader field of contemporary theory and practice from which they took anything that looked useful. Like the English rural people at festival time, I mentioned earlier, they weren't averse to creative borrowing, and there's no reason they should have been.

Of course, this is exactly the situation we have now in the Pagan community, and it's a situation we've had now for several hundred years. We have lineages of various kinds that have surfaced from time to time: Druid lineages surfacing at various points from 1700 onwards, Germanic Pagan lineages from around 1900 onwards, Wiccan lineages coming out of the broom closet from 1950 onwards, other Pagan lineages in a flood in the years since then. Some of these lineages claim to go back a long time before the point at which they became public, while others say, look, here's this really excellent system that was invented in 1972, based on X and Y and Z, come be a part of it. And we also have an extraordinarily rich field of theory and practice, some of it evolved within the Pagan and magical communities, some from other cultural traditions of magic, mysticism, shamanism, and religion, and some hauled up from the past by the efforts of archeologists, historians, scholars of comparative religion, and so forth. And it's at the point of intersection between these—between the lineage, the training, and initiation, or the personal experiences of the individual Pagan, on the one hand, and the astonishing wealth of knowledge and technique in the community as a whole—that each tradition and each person operates.

This point of intersection, of course, is the same place occupied by the folk magician turned fam-trad Wiccan we saw earlier, removing Christian prayers from Grandma's spells because that's not what Scott Cunningham's book said should be there. It's the same place occupied by Neoplatonists all over Europe in the middle of the fifteenth century, who took one sip of Marsilio Ficino's strong brew and swore off Neoplatonism Lite for good, and by people of every sort who have found something living, powerful, and meaningful in the Pagan and magical traditions of their own place and time.

And, of course, it's also the place occupied by each of us here today. One of the most important things to realize about the secret history of Neopaganism is that it's not the history of some other group of people a long way off in Space and Time. It's our own history. One of the major problems with the Paleo-Meso-Neo-Pagan model I critiqued earlier is that it makes it very easy to lose sight of that. The tendency to think of

Pagan history as though it's limited to the study of Pagan origins has the same problem. If "real Pagans" are by definition the ones who lived back before the coming of Christianity, and every attempt to revive Paganism from then until last Thursday is mere Meso-Paganism, then it's all too easy to turn modern Pagan spirituality into a sort of Society for Religious Anachronism, in which people pretend to be pre-Christian Celts or something, and practice a religion that has no relevance at all to the lives we actually live or the world we actually inhabit.

If we recognize instead that John Toland, Thomas Taylor, Dorothy Clutterbuck, and each of us here are part of a single historical process, the astonishing history of the rebirth of Pagan spirituality in the West, the world takes on a very different shape; we have a real history, a history of our own, a history from which we can learn and out of which we can draw on a wealth of practical experience. We may not want to use the same approaches that these Pagans of the past did, and there's no reason we have to, just as they transformed what was passed on to them in the light of their own experience and the possibilities available to them in their own place and time.

Now, this way of looking at the history of Neopaganism has quite a few implications in terms of where we are today, and I'd like to touch on one of them in closing. Nearly all of us have tended to underestimate the sheer richness and complexity of that secret history, and seen single threads of connection where we should be seeing ornate tapestries.

For example, Gordon Cooper and I caused some consternation a few years back with an article on the origins of Wicca. We suggested that one of the main sources Gerald Gardner drew on in assembling modern Wicca was an outdoors movement called Woodcraft, which had some very Pagan dimensions, a horned god, an Earth goddess, and an inner initiatory order with three degrees called the Red Lodge. We hypothesized that the Red Lodge had been passed on to the two English offshoots of Woodcraft, the Order of Woodcraft Chivalry and the Kindred of the Kibbo Kift, and ended up in Gardner's hands by way of his contacts with Woodcraft circles through people such as the Druid Ross Nichols, who was a friend of Kibbo Kift founder John Hargrave.

Well, this last summer the rituals for the Kibbo Kift's inner magical order surfaced in a cache of Kin documents, and Gordon and I were in for a surprise. It wasn't the Red Lodge. It was a previously unknown magical order called the Lodge of the Seven Eremites, or the *Ordo Scarabaeus Sacer*—the Order of the Sacred Scarab—into which John

Hargrave had inserted some Woodcraft material. Where did the Lodge of the Seven Eremites come from? So far as I know, nobody has the least idea.

None of that proves that Woodcraft didn't also contribute something to the mix, and, in fact, we now know that it contributed quite a bit to British Druid spirituality. But the point that's clear is that a Wicca-Woodcraft connection, if there was one, can't be seen in isolation. Gardner, like the rest of us, had access to many different traditions and teachings, Woodcraft among them. Was another of them some older form of Wicca? And if so, how much further back in the British Pagan scene did it go as an organized tradition? Was it something Dorothy Clutterbuck and her friends created, and then passed on to Gardner, or did they get it from someone else? All good questions, none of which are easy to answer.

Another example. Pagan scholar Don Frew has been pointing out for a couple of years that Neoplatonism forms the unstated theoretical foundation underlying Wicca. Of course, he's right, and with any luck his comments will inspire Wiccans to study Neoplatonism; maybe someday we'll see Plotinus alongside Ronald Hutton on those First Degree recommended reading lists. But much of the discussion that's followed has focused too tightly on figuring out where a connection between Wicca and Neoplatonism could have come from.

Once again, this is a matter of looking for single threads when we ought to be looking at tapestries because if there's any tradition that pervades spirituality in the British Isles from the Middle Ages to the present, it's Neoplatonism. The first significant philosopher of the Middle Ages was the Irishman John Scotus Erigena, back in the tenth century, and he was a Neoplatonist. All the great English mystics of the high Middle Ages—Julian of Norwich, the anonymous author of *The Cloud of Unknowing*, and so on—were Neoplatonists. The Renaissance occult movement, which was as big in Britain as anywhere, was overwhelmingly Neoplatonist. When the Church of England split from Rome in the sixteenth century, the Catholic Church was getting deeply into Aristotle by way of Thomas Aquinas, and so the Anglicans reacted by making Christian Neoplatonism the basis for their theology. There was a school of Neoplatonism at Cambridge in the seventeenth century, with people such as Henry More and Ralph Cudworth producing some of the best recent works in the tradition, and then by the end of the eighteenth century, you've got Thomas Taylor and the rebirth of a living tradition of Pagan Neoplatonism in Britain.

By the middle of the twentieth century it was all over the place, in a hundred different varieties: Pagan, Hermetic, Anglican, Hellenic, you name it. J. R. R. Tolkien's *Silmarillion* and the novels that grew out of it are up to their eyeballs in it—you've got the One outside of creation, the Valar as divine intelligences within it, everything cascading downwards level by level in the best Neoplatonist style, all of this taking shape in the mind of a devout Christian Englishman creating a personal mythology during the years that Gerald Gardner was studying magic, getting involved in the ROCF and meeting Dorothy Clutterbuck. So the question isn't where a link between Wicca and Neoplatonism could have come from; it could have come from almost anywhere, and it most likely came from many sources at once.

The more important point is that the link is there, and it opens doors to understanding and insight that we can use right now. In the same way, the more important point about all our modern Pagan traditions is simply that here they are: we have them, we have access to teachers and texts, we can do something with them, we can transform ourselves and our world. We are, all of us, part of a movement that has centuries of history behind it, and centuries of momentum: a rising wave amid the tides of history.

By embracing our past in all its richness and complexity, laughing at its follies, learning from its mistakes, drawing on its resources and realizing its potentials, we become part of that momentum, and we can pass on our own traditions to future Pagans, enriched with our own gifts, to help build a Pagan future that may yet be more magnificent than any of us has imagined.

CHAPTER FOUR

Victorian sex magic

One of the pieces of received wisdom about the past that we all get in the course of growing up in modern America is the idea that the Victorian period was very, very, very sexually repressed. To describe attitudes as "Victorian" is to dismiss them as prudish, repressive, and spiritually constipated. Now, of course, each generation before the 1960s believed that it was the first one ever to discover sex, and I think the current notion in popular culture is that sex was discovered once and for all in the back seat of a Chevy convertible in a parking lot near Golden Gate Park in 1965. I hope, though, that I won't be puncturing anyone's faith in Santa Claus or the Easter Bunny if I point out that popular culture pretty often gets things wrong, and rarely so much as in talking about Victorians and sex.

The Victorian era wasn't particularly oversexed, as eras go. But it certainly wasn't particularly undersexed, either. What it was, possibly more than any other culture in recorded history, was caught in a bind between public ideology and private reality. It's popular to dismiss this as a matter of simple hypocrisy, but it was much more complex than that. The Victorians believed intensely in word magic. When Victorians wanted something to be true, they said that it was true, and they expected reality to play along. If it didn't, they got uncomfortable, and said it again, twice as loud. Reality being what it is, they ended up shouting some things at the top of their lungs.

One thing that tends to be overlooked in talking about the Victorian era is that the sexual culture we're discussing was entirely a creation of the English-speaking world—of Britain, America, Canada, Australia and New Zealand, and a few other areas strongly influenced by British culture. It's easy to forget that any degree of sexual repression in England, say, was balanced by the fact that France was not very far away, and France had a completely different attitude toward sex. Or, rather, the French had a different attitude toward word magic, and never managed to achieve the total disregard for reality that reigned on the other side of the channel. The French also profited financially quite a bit from the fact that a remarkable number of British men, and quite a few British women as well, spent their holidays in France, where they could let the word magic lapse for a bit, and refer to the fact that they had genitals and the means, motive, and opportunity to use them.

I've suggested that the Victorians practiced word magic, and that's actually not just a figure of speech. Look closely at the fundamental concepts of modern magic and you'll find some astonishing echoes of Victorian thinking. The concept of the Magical Will, as developed by Eliphas Lévi and the Hermetic Order of the Golden Dawn and popularized by Aleister Crowley, is probably the best example. The Victorians were obsessed by the power of the human will. Go digging in any collection of self-help books from the nineteenth century—if you think we have a lot of self-help books nowadays, take a look at the nineteenth-century literature on the subject and prepare to be amazed. A huge proportion of them focused on developing, strengthening, concentrating the will.

How many of you have read Crowley's *Liber E vel Exercitorum* or *Liber III vel Jugorum*? Those are the books where he discusses methods of will training like dropping the word "I" out of your vocabulary for a day. That exercise, and most of the other things in those essays, were borrowed straight from the Victorian willpower literature. I have a dusty old book by Frank Channing Haddock, copyright 1907, titled *Power of Will*, that contains close to two thousand exercises for giving your willpower a workout; most of them read like classic magical training exercises, and indeed they are—but they're also the sort of thing ordinary Victorians learned in school to build character.

Now, the thought of Aleister Crowley teaching Victorian character-building exercises may make your head spin, but that's exactly what was going on. What makes this irony particularly fine is that one of the major reasons Victorians taught these exercises to young men was that they thought this would help the young men resist the urge to masturbate, while Crowley seems to have taught them in the hope that they would help young men resist the urge not to masturbate.

Of course, masturbation was one of the places where the word magic, I mentioned above, was used most enthusiastically. Serious medical books by physicians and professors insisted that masturbation, or rather self-abuse as it was usually called, was a serious health threat; that only a very small percentage of degenerate young men fell into the awful habit; and that these few were punished with blindness, insanity, and having hair grow on their palms. In all probability every single one of the writers who published these books masturbated regularly, most men do, and I doubt too many of them had to shave their palms or get seeing eye dogs as a result.

I've spoken entirely of young men, you'll notice. Nobody talked about female masturbation back then. Very few people talked about female sexuality at all. The most widely respected medical textbook on human sexuality published in England during Queen Victoria's reign, Dr. William Acton's massive 1857 tome *The Functions and Disorders of the Reproductive Organs*, mentions women twice and vaginas not at all. For Acton, as for most male Victorians, "reproductive organs" meant penises and testicles. Vaginas were utterly taboo. That taboo was so rarely breached that when the scandalous avant-garde painter Gustave Courbet painted a woman's crotch in 1866—just the crotch, filling the picture frame—and titled the painting *The Origin of the World*, the rich private collector who commissioned it kept it in his dressing room with a veil hanging in front of it.

The same Victorian medical establishment that warned of the awful dangers of masturbation also flatly denied the existence of the female orgasm. At most, doctors were willing to admit that a small minority of debauched and depraved women had orgasms but nice women didn't. Nice women had something called a hysterical crisis, which was not an orgasm. It wasn't even sexual, officially speaking, though women who didn't have an outlet for the sexual desires they supposedly didn't have in the first place needed to have a hysterical crisis every so often to stay healthy.

That was the sales pitch for a very popular medical appliance in the latter years of the Victorian period, the electric vibrator. Many middle-class Victorian women had one and used it to give themselves hysterical crises as needed. These aren't the little devices you get nowadays, of course; the motor unit was about the size of a small vacuum cleaner and had a spring-wrapped cable connecting it to the business end. Mind you, for their time, they were marvels of miniaturization, much smaller and handier than the steam-powered vibrators of the mid-nineteenth century, and much more convenient than making an appointment with a doctor to get a hysterical crisis by hand massage—which also happened quite a bit.

All this may suggest that the Victorian sex magic we're going to discuss was hidden away under a layer of euphemisms thicker than Tammy Faye Bakker's makeup. The most amazing thing about Victorian sex magic, though, is that it did nothing of the kind. Crowley was far from the first person to notice that in an age that believes in word magic, speaking the unspeakable can be one of the most powerful magics of all. That's why one of the most influential intellectual movements in the nineteenth century went by the distinctly non-euphemistic name of phallic religion.

That's the theory that human religion started out as the worship of the life force, expressed by its most protuberant symbols. Scandalous though it must have sounded to Victorian ears, it was a very popular theory all through the period. It got started back in the late 1700s when a handful of scholars such as Richard Payne Knight compared ancient Greek and Roman erotic art with the sexual symbolism of Hindu spirituality, which Englishmen were beginning to encounter by way of the British colonial empire in India. Knight and his colleagues were among the first people in the Western world to really grasp the fact that Christianity is nearly alone among the world's religions in being terrified of sexual pleasure. I think it was H. L. Mencken who described Puritanism as the awful, unshakable fear that someone, somewhere, is having a good time. That attitude runs deep in the Protestant churches that dominated Victorian Britain and America, and Knight was one of the first people to wonder out loud why the Christianity of his time suffered from it and nearly all other religions don't.

But Knight and his colleagues went a good deal further than that. They started noticing that a huge amount of Pagan religion, and non-western religion, and in fact every other kind of religion in the world except mainstream Protestant Christianity, has a lot to do with fertility. They noticed that when the Greeks called Zeus "father of gods and men," they weren't talking about his role in the family politics of the gods; they meant "father" in its most robust biological sense—start counting the myths in which Zeus fathers someone on somebody and you'll be busy for a long, long time. They noticed that the classic Hindu symbol of the god Shiva is simply an erect penis. And they ended up arguing that every religion in the world except mainstream Protestant Christianity was nothing more or less than the worship of sex.

It may seem a little odd from our modern perspective to use a one-sided label such as "phallic religion" for these theories, but it's a thoroughly Victorian oddity. Remember that you couldn't even mention the existence of vaginas in public. Thus, learned Britons of the time, or at least learned male Britons, spoke of phallic religion rather than genital religion, and they certainly didn't mention vaginal religion. The remarkable thing is that they found room in their theories of primitive religion for vagina-goddesses as well as penis-gods. This probably explains why books on the sexual dimension of religion were considered pornographic straight through the nineteenth century, not just by moral reformers, but by sellers and buyers of pornography as well. Richard Payne Knight's *A Discourse on the Worship of Priapus*, the 1786 book that launched the phallic religion theory, saw print again in 1865 at the hands of J. C. Hotten, one of the premier publishers of Victorian smut. Plenty of other scholarly eighteenth- and nineteenth-century works on sexual themes in mythology and religion graced the shelves of Victorian London's pornographic bookstores. It was the only way most of them could stay in print at all.

As a talking point among scholars, the theory of phallic religion was scandalous enough, but it didn't stay safely confined in the groves of academe—not by a long shot. And this is where it's time to introduce one of the Victorian sex magicians who are central to our exploration. Those of you who've attended my earlier talks may know this guy because he's been a research topic of mine for a few years now. His name was Owen Morgan; under the title of Archdruid Morien, he presided over the Druid gorsedd of Pontypridd from 1888 until his death in the 1920s. He believed and publicly taught that Christianity is a Pagan sex cult. And he thought this was a good thing.

Morgan was one of the many influential eccentrics of the Druid Revival, the oldest documented continuously active Pagan revival in the world today. The Druid Revival has a reputation nowadays as one of the dowdy branches of Paganism—you know, the kind of people who keep their robes on during the ritual. Several modern Pagan writers have classed them as Meso-Pagans and argued, if I may oversimplify a little, that they're not really Pagans at all, just slightly eccentric Christians in funny outfits. Now, it's true that many of the eighteenth- and nineteenth-century Druid Revivalists had a less hostile attitude toward Christianity than many Pagans do nowadays, and were perfectly willing to swipe appealing ideas from any source, including Christianity. But as we'll see, their version of Christianity was not always exactly the sort of thing that you'll find being preached over at the First Church of Christ this morning. Practiced, quite possibly, but not preached.

The Druid Revival also has a reputation for loopy scholarship, and to be honest, some of that is well earned. Take a look sometime at a forgotten classic of the late eighteenth century, *The Way to Things by Words*, which was written by John Cleland and published in 1766. Cleland was also the author of *Fanny Hill*, the most famous work of pornography in the English language, which is one reason I can't resist bringing him into this discussion, but he was also a big fan of the ancient Druids. He was convinced that the Freemasons were actually surviving Druids. He argued that the Masons got their name, not from being descended from medieval stonemason's guilds, but because they were actually Druids who celebrated Beltane, May Day, as their main festival and so were known as May's sons. Masons. Get it? You can see that the sort of thinking that gave us *The 21 Lessons of Merlin* has a long history behind it.

Owen Morgan came out of this tradition. He also came out of the Welsh branch of the Revival, which means that much of what he taught and did can be traced back to the work of that force of nature Edward Williams, better known by his *nom de barde* Iolo Morganwg. Poet, opium addict, first-rate scholar of medieval Welsh literature, and one of the brightest stars in the glittering firmament of British literary forgery, Iolo burst on the scene in the late eighteenth century and had an immense impact on the culture of the time. He knew a lot of influential people; in fact, George Washington helped fund the publication of his first Druid book. In between stints in debtor's prison, Iolo went around Wales starting bardic gorsedds everywhere anyone wanted one. Pontypridd, a little town in Glamorgan, wanted one, so Iolo gave them a charter, taught them the rituals, and launched them on their journey to the far shores of British religious history.

The Archdruid of the Pontypridd gorsedd was a man named Evan Davies, better known by his bardic name Myfyr Morganwg. Davies started out as a Protestant minister for a small Welsh Methodist sect, small enough that he had to have a day job as a watchmaker. But fate had marked him out for a more interesting career. Sometime in the 1860s, after thirty years of preaching the Christian gospel, Davies abandoned his church and announced that he was reviving the ancient Druid mysteries of his forefathers, with himself as Archdruid. From that time until his death in 1888, he celebrated the solstices and equinoxes beside the Pontypridd rocking stone with a very Pagan version of Iolo's gorsedd ceremonies.

On Davies' death, his mantle passed to Owen Morgan, a writer for the popular press. Morgan quickly turned his literary talents to the Druidic cause, producing a tome entitled *The Light in Britannia*. The scale of this magnum opus of Pontypridd Druidism may be judged by its subtitles: *The Mysteries of Ancient British Druidism Unveiled; The Original Source of Phallic Worship Revealed; The Secrets of the Court of King Arthur Revealed; The Creed of the Stone Age Restored; The Holy Grail Discovered in Wales.* Historian of Druidry James Bonwick called it "among the most candidly expressed books ever printed," and indeed it is. Owen Morgan, you see, had broken the taboo we talked about a little while ago. He talked about vaginas. He did quite a bit of talking about vaginas, in fact, and vaginal religion as well.

Mind you, Morgan began his book with a note warning the unwary reader to expect explicit talk about phallic worship. On the first page, he launched straight into a discussion of the masculine and feminine principles of Nature. A few pages later, Morgan was talking about the vulva of the goddess Venus and outlining the sexual mysteries central, in his opinion, to every religion worth the name. Before long the Sun was revealed as the son of the masculine divine principle Celi; the Earth likewise as Venus, the daughter of the feminine divine principle Ced; and the fertilization of the Earth by the Sun takes place in exactly the way you might expect. Speaking of the feminine principle, Morgan wrote: "Her feet were represented, open like a triangle, toward the Sun rising at the summer solstice and winter solstice respectively; the apex of the fork would be on the equinoctial line, facing the virile Sun in spring rising due east."

In the time of Queen Victoria, this sort of image was startling enough, but Morgan was only just warming up to his theme. When he explained that "Aaron entering into the Holy of Holies and the presence of the Ark of the Covenant, signified the same thing as Noah entering into his Ark," the attentive reader must have guessed pretty quickly that Morgan's phallic theology had thrust its way, so to speak, into the Bible itself. Morgan devotes pages to the task of exposing the Ark of the Covenant as the symbolic vulva of the Earth goddess. One chapter expounds the solar and sexual mysteries of the Tabernacle erected by the Israelites in the wilderness. Another interprets the ritual of the Day of Atonement as a symbolic orgy of astronomy and sex, in which the High Priest enters the Holy Place and is reborn from it, or, in Morgan's own inimitable prose, experiences a new birth "through the hairy eastern outlet of the Virgin of Israel."

And he capped that off by making Jesus a phallic symbol. He did Richard Payne Knight and the phallic religion theorists one better; they thought every religion but Protestant Christianity was sex worship; Morgan saw no reason to exclude Protestant Christianity from the holy truth behind all religions. He was a tolerant man, after all. Now, to be precise, Jesus was more than just a penis in Morgan's theory. He was also a solar symbol, and he was also the historical person Jesus of Nazareth, who came to Britain in his youth, learned the true religion of astronomy and sex from the ancient Druids and proceeded to teach it back home in Judea. So, he wasn't just the Sun and a penis, he was a Druid missionary. At least Morgan didn't make Jesus a Freemason; that had to wait for some of our modern pseudo-historians.

Now I've called Morgan a sex magician, and that may need a little explanation because if he practiced sex magic of the obvious sort no trace of that remains in his books or archives. The sex in his Druidry was all symbolic; Druids, remember, are the ones who keep their robes on in ritual. He invoked the Earth goddess and the Sun god and rejoiced in their lovemaking, but the form that took was watching the rays of the rising Sun caress the Earth on the solstices and equinoxes. But he played a very important role in bringing explicit sexual symbolism into the occult community all through the English-speaking world.

He's obscure today, but his ideas had a very wide influence, and some of the odder bits of early twentieth-century occultism become a good deal less odd when illuminated by *The Light in Britannia*. When one of Aleister Crowley's instructional texts tells the reader to visualize a "solar-phallic hippopotamus," those familiar with Morgan's work will recognize this apparition as a familiar symbol, rather than an unfortunate side effect of too much rat poison on the blotter paper. On a broader scale, Morgan's work is apparently the first systematic account in the modern West of a duotheistic fertility religion, with one god who comprises all other gods, and one goddess who includes all other goddesses. Half a century after Morgan's time, that became the fundamental theology of Wicca. While the Craft certainly had many different sources, I'm convinced that Morgan was one of them.

But his rather rarefied form of sex magic was far from the only one in circulation in the Victorian period. It's at this point that we turn to Thomas Lake Harris, the second of the Victorian sex magicians I mean to discuss today. Harris was an American. He was a little older than Owen Morgan, and quite a bit weirder. He was born in New England in 1823 and had a perfectly conventional childhood, then went to seminary to become a minister. Ah, but there's where he started veering from the straight and narrow because the church he wanted to become a minister in was the Church of the New Jerusalem, better known as the Swedenborgian Church.

Emmanuel Swedenborg, whose writings provided Harris with most of his textbooks in his seminary days, was one of the weirder Christian mystics of the eighteenth century, which is saying something. He was Swedish, one of those gentlemen scholars who contributed so much to science in its early days, and he worked for the government as an inspector of mines. And then just after he turned fifty he started seeing angels; and talking to angels; and having angels explain the true nature of the universe to him, in vast length and immense detail. Being the dedicated scientist that he was, he wrote it all down. To be precise, he wrote over two hundred books on the subject, including his magnum opus, *Arcana Coelestia*, in twelve volumes.

All this output got him a fair amount of attention, and he had one endearing trait that made him very popular among intellectuals at the time. He knew the Bible inside and out and came to the quite sensible conclusion that such a pack of absurdities couldn't possibly be literally true. And so he proceeded to argue that the Bible was a vast collection of metaphors and similes, all of which were simply symbolic ways of expressing the philosophy of Emmanuel Swedenborg. When the Book of Leviticus said "thou shalt not eat bats," that didn't mean you should lay off the Malaysian fruit bat stew; no, bats symbolized something, and eating symbolized something else, and it all ended up in vast detail somewhere in Volume Ten of *Arcana Coelestia*. All of this gave people in the late eighteenth and early nineteenth century an enormous degree of spiritual flexibility. They could claim that they were perfectly good

Christians, study the Bible daily and so on, and still dig into Malaysian fruit bat stew if they had a mind to, because that passage in Leviticus actually meant something else.

Now, some of this may be reminding you of Owen Morgan and Jesus the Penis, but I hasten to reassure you that Swedenborg lacked Morgan's inimitable one-track mind. To Swedenborg, Jesus meant lots of things, and as far as I know—I've only read a small portion of Swedenborg's writings—he never suggested that the best way to find Jesus was to reach into your pants. On the other hand, he did have an attitude toward sex that Richard Payne Knight et al. would have approved of. The stark terror of sex that infected most Christian denominations in his time never seems to have touched him. He read that passage in the gospels where Jesus says that there is neither marrying nor giving in marriage in heaven, and said, well, that makes sense—no marriage, therefore angels are into free love. Got it. And he wrote quite a bit on the love life of angels, and how we all become angels and practice free love as we spiral up through the complexities of the Swedenborgian heaven.

So this is the stuff that poured through the young Thomas Lake Harris' fevered imagination as he studied to become a Swedenborgian minister. Mind you, he still got married and tried to settle into a conventional career running a church, but it just didn't work. Around 1850, he met Andrew Jackson Davis, who deserves a lecture all to himself someday. Davis was called the Poughkeepsie Seer; he was a clairvoyant healer who claimed to have gotten his medical training from the ancient Roman doctor Galen and his spiritual knowledge straight from the ghost of none other than Emmanuel Swedenborg. Davis practiced mesmerism and got onto the Spiritualist bandwagon in its earliest years, and he taught Harris how to put himself into a trance. That was all it took. Within a short time, Harris had friends in heaven. To be precise, he had a *very* special friend in heaven. Her name was Queen Lily of the Conjugial Angels. Not conjugal, mind you, conjugial, though I haven't read enough Swedenborg to be perfectly clear on the difference. Harris and Queen Lily had a very close relationship—close enough that he fathered three baby angels on her. He wrote her reams of syrupy but extremely explicit love poetry; she returned the favor by teaching him all about heaven and how to get there.

The secret of getting there, according to these lectures in bed, was celibacy. Well, to be more precise, physical celibacy. Or to be even more precise, celibacy with partners who were as physical as you were. Once you gave up on sex with other incarnate human beings, you could establish a "counterpartal union" with your angelic soul mate and hop into the ethereal sack on the first date if you wanted to. That was the key to eternal life. Mind you, Queen Lily's lectures covered a good deal more territory than that. She taught Harris to practice a breathing exercise called open breathing, and another exercise called demagnetizing. When you do those regularly, according to Her Conjugial Majesty, the Holy Spirit comes into your body and gets rid of all the negative animal magnetism you've picked up over the years. Once that happens, thousands of happy little fairies show up and take up residence inside your body, scoop up any illnesses you happen to have, and haul them out with the trash. So you become perfectly healthy, not to mention open and demagnetized, and then you're ready to swear off sex with mere human beings and head for the celestial singles bar to look for your angelic soul mate.

Dotty as all this sounds to modern ears, Harris attracted quite a following. Part of that was because the idea of physical celibacy as the ticket to sexual fulfillment on another plane wasn't original to Harris, not by a long shot. The most popular book on the subject straight through the nineteenth century was a remarkable novel titled *Le Comte de Gabalis* by the Abbé Montfaucon de Villars, originally published in 1670. The Abbé was not an occultist, and his book is actually one of the funniest satires on the occult community ever written. His protagonist knows nothing about occultism and wants to learn, so he adopts the plan of claiming to know all about it already—an example that's been copied by a lot of modern beginners in the Pagan scene, of course. He ends up having a conversation with a mysterious nobleman, the Comte de Gabalis, who explains to him the real secret behind Rosicrucian occultism—that it's all about making love with elementals. Lots of elementals. You see, the elementals aren't jealous of each other; they're perfectly happy to cuddle up to the aspiring mage en masse; but they can't stand human rivals. So, if you're going to make it with elementals, you have to swear off less ethereal partners. That's what the Comte explains to our protagonist; it's hard not to glimpse Queen Lily's curvaceous figure peeking out through the veils of the Abbé's raucous prose.

It's a very, very funny book. The only thing funnier is the way it was received by nineteenth- and twentieth-century occultists in Britain and America. They took it seriously. I've got a copy that was published in the first years of the twentieth century by an occult organization calling itself simply "The Brothers." They presented the Abbé's bit of fun as a revelation of the inner teachings of Rosicrucian mysticism, which they read symbolically, of course—much the same way that Swedenborg interpreted the Bible. Now, for all I know, The Brothers were also out there demagnetizing themselves and cuddling up to their angelic counterparts. They might well have been because Thomas Lake Harris was astonishingly influential in the occult scene of the late nineteenth and early twentieth centuries. Those of you who know your Golden Dawn history will remember a Frater Resurgam, mundane name Edward Berridge, a very influential member of the original Golden Dawn. He was also a student of Harris' writings and did a lot of demagnetizing, and he wasn't the only Harris fan in the Golden Dawn scene.

Harris himself established what we'd now call a commune in upstate New York, and then moved to Santa Rosa, California when word got out that at least some of his "counterpartal marriages" were a good deal less ethereal than he claimed. In 1894, he proclaimed that he had become immortal via spiritual union with Queen Lily; they were now one cosmic being, and this having happened, the world was about to end. This somehow failed to happen, and he quietly packed his bags and went to New York City, where he died—much to his own surprise, no doubt—in 1906.

So with Owen Morgan, we have intellectual sex magic; with Thomas Lake Harris, sex magic passes from the realm of the abstract into what Henri Corbin calls the imaginal realm, the world of images and inner experiences. But there's a third Victorian sex magician on the list today, who brought things right down to the physical plane. He was one of the most influential occultists of modern times; a lot of people here today probably don't know his name, but all of you know his ideas. His name was Paschal Beverly Randolph and he was an American original.

Randolph was the first influential African-American Hermeticist, an absolutely brilliant writer and occult theoretician with a gift for original thought that left most of his contemporaries in the dust. If he'd had one additional gift—the ability to get along with anyone, anywhere, for at least five minutes—nobody would remember the Theosophical Society or the Golden Dawn; it'd be all Randolph, all the time. Given that he was a professional sex therapist and a vocal proponent of the female orgasm, I don't think that would have been a bad thing.

He was the illegitimate son of Flora Clark, an African-American woman, and William Beverly Randolph, a white man who Randolph later claimed belonged to the wealthy Randolph family of Tidewater Virginia. He was born and raised in New York's most notorious slum district; he lost his mother by age seven and had to fend for his own thereafter. He worked as a bootblack, begged from door to door, was a cabin boy on a merchant ship, and a barber in upstate New York. But that was before Spiritualism.

It's hard for people nowadays to really grasp the impact that Spiritualism had in the second half of the nineteenth century, especially but not only here in America. For a couple of decades at the height of the movement, it looked as though America might just turn its back on Christianity completely. The story's an instructive one. Three young girls, the Fox sisters, started getting messages from beyond the grave via loud taps that seemed to emanate from the floor of their house. A standard bit of folklore, rooted in common poltergeist phenomena, except that this time it turned into the catalyst for an extraordinary religious movement. America in the late 1840s was full of Swedenborgians and Mesmerists; Andrew Jackson Davis was a leading figure but only one of thousands. Quite a few of them figured out very quickly that they could one-up the Fox sisters by going into trance and having conversations with the dead. Before long millions of Americans believed that you didn't have to take life after death on faith; you could go to a seance and have a conversation with the dear departed Aunt Mildred, find out how she was doing in the Summerland, and so on.

At first glance, none of this had a thing to do with sex, but the spirits had an interesting habit. They didn't stick to the Biblical status quo. They had their own ideas about religion and morality, ideas that had a remarkable amount of similarity to those of the Swedenborgians and Mesmerists who were channeling them, and they also drew on the work of another very strange figure of the time—the French philosopher Charles Fourier.

Fourier was one of those bizarre visionaries who played such an important role in European thought during the nineteenth century. He believed that he personally was the most important person who ever lived, and his teachings formed the boundary between the age of barbarism—the European civilization of his time—and the future age of true civilization. Civilization, you see, is based on the cosmic principle of passional attraction. In a civilized society, people do everything

out of passional attraction, and once people grasped the secret of passional attraction by reading Fourier's philosophy, the entire world
would be transformed. I don't mean just that human society would
be transformed; once people started listening to Fourier, a vast rain of
cosmic citric acid would fall from the heavens and turn the seas to lemonade, four additional moons would come out of hiding and snuggle
up in a close Earth orbit, and so on. And in that future paradise, besides
sipping free lemonade and watching the moons rise, and rise, and rise,
and rise, the most important human activity would be vast amounts of
orgiastic sex.

In Victorian America, this sort of thinking was very popular. Andrew
Jackson Davis drew quite a few of his ideas from Fourier, and so did
a lot of other intellectuals of the time, which is how Fourier got into
Spiritualism. He got into some other traditions of the same era, too. In
there with the cosmic citric acid and the passional attraction, Fourier
proposed that in the society of the future, industry and land would be
owned by the state, not by individuals or companies, and so he appears in
the history books as the inventor of socialism. I'll leave it to you to decide
whether Karl Marx' dictatorship of the proletariat is any more likely
than Fourier's lemonade oceans. For our present purposes, the point
is that Fourier had a major influence on Spiritualism, and Spiritualism
brought many of his ideas to prominence in America and elsewhere.

So, this was the movement that swept Randolph out of his barber-
shop and into the big time. Randolph became a convert to Spiritualism
as soon as he heard of it, and within a few years, he had become one of
the very first African-American Spiritualist mediums. Like most mediums of the time, he studied the whole range of popular occult philosophy. By the early 1850s, he billed himself as a "clairvoyant physician"
specializing in sexual problems, and 1854 saw the publication of his
first book, a novel titled *Waa-gu-Mah*. Great title, but nobody knows
what it was about—it didn't do very well, and no one's been able to
find a copy.

In 1855, he toured England, France, and Germany, holding séances
and meeting with European occultists, and his reception was favorable enough that 1857 saw a second European tour. In 1858, though,
he publicly renounced Spiritualism and spent the next few years on
the anti-Spiritualist lecture circuit, claiming that mediums were the
passive victims of evil spirits. He was always doing flip-flops like
that. Predictably, he ended up picking a fight with the conservative

Christian church that paid for his anti-Spiritualist lecture tours and left the country again. Later on, he claimed that he spent 1861 and 1862 traveling in the Near East, contacted a heretical Islamic sect in Syria he called the "Ansaireh"—they're known now as the al-Nusairi—and got from them the principles of his later occult teachings. Whether this actually happened is anyone's guess, as Randolph's statements about his own biography changed frequently and contradicted one another as often as not.

By the mid-1860s he was back in America, recruiting African-American volunteers for the Union army in the Civil War, and after the war ended, he made a brief and unsuccessful foray into politics. By the end of the decade he was back to writing and occultism, and began to teach the system he called Eulis or the Ansairetic Arcanum, the method of occult philosophy and sexual magic that turned into his real legacy to the occult community. Eulian magic starts with the basic practices of volantia, decretism, and posism. Volantia is calm focused concentration, decretism is the absolute focus on a single act of will, and posism is the mental receptivity that follows the act of will. Once you learn these, you can get started on the magic mirror, the primary magical instrument of Randolph's system, which gives you clairvoyance. Well, actually, it gives you either zorvoyance or aethavoyance, depending on your level of awareness and training; zorvoyance is astral vision, aethavoyance gets you above the astral. All this is a prelude to the art of blending, Randolph's term for the sort of conscious trance where the initiate's consciousness fuses with that of a higher spiritual being.

But the core of the whole system was the mysteries of sex. Randolph was way ahead of his time in his views about sex. Remember that most physicians denied the existence of the female orgasm; Randolph not only believed in it but insisted that orgasmic release was essential to mental and physical health in women as well as men.

What's more, Randolph was also the inventor of the most widely used system of sex magic in modern Western occultism. He's the one who first circulated the idea that intensive concentration on an act of will by both partners at the moment of mutual orgasm is the supreme magical technique. By labeling him the inventor of this method, I'm treading on somewhat speculative ground; in fact, nobody knows whether he made it up or got it from someone else. His own story changed as often, and as drastically, as a punk rocker's hair color. Sometimes he claimed he'd gotten it from ancient Rosicrucian traditions; sometimes he claimed it had been passed onto him by the Ansaireh; sometimes he claimed he'd invented it all himself.

After Randolph's death, a lot of his inventions were borrowed by the Hermetic Brotherhood of Luxor, a magical order which flourished and foundered in the 1880s. The H.B. of L. combined Randolph's teaching with a lot of material from the same underworld of English magical lodges that spawned the Golden Dawn. The H.B. of L. had members in America, Britain, and Europe. For a while, it was the most influential occult order in the Western world, but it had a skeleton in its closet: its secretary had a criminal record for mail fraud. That came out in 1886, and the Theosophists pounced on it—they were in the middle of a war with the H.B. of L. in those days. The H.B. of L. promptly imploded, and its two leaders moved operations to America.

Some British H.B. of L. members ended up in the Druid scene, and as a result, there's quite a bit of H.B. of L. practice in some British Druid orders. In America, the H.B. of L. helped lay the foundations for the Tantrik Order in America, which was launched in 1906 by Pierre Bernard aka Oom the Omnipotent. Yes, that's what he was called. Oom claimed that he'd been trained and initiated in a Tantric ashram in India, but, as far as I know, there's no evidence that he made it any farther west than California. It may not be a coincidence that at the beginning of the last century California was one of the main hotbeds of the H.B. of L.'s successor orders. I wouldn't be surprised to learn that Oom also had connections to William Walker Atkinson, a very important figure in the occult scene of the time, who we'll be discussing in a bit.

Whatever his sources, though, Oom was the first person in America to publicly teach something he claimed was Tantra, and inevitably his version of it—unlike most of the classic Hindu tantras—centered on sex. Members of the lower degrees practiced physical culture exercises; members of the higher degrees did a rather different set of exercises involving two or more participants. Oom got a reputation as the Love Swami, came through several police investigations without serious incident, and ended up with a clientele that included some extremely rich and influential New Yorkers, including at least one member of the Rockefeller family. In the 1920s, his Tantrik Order in America had branches in half a dozen cities, and Oom himself was a public figure of some importance; he was about as respectable as you can get when your business card says, "Tantric sex guru." Things downshifted a bit during the Depression and the Second World War, but the Tantrik Order in America was a going concern until Oom's death in 1955, and I understand it's recently been revived by the modern tantrika Nik Douglas.

Around the time Oom was getting his career underway, though, several members of the H.B. of L. launched orders of their own. One was Sylvester Gould, who led a schism off the Societas Rosicruciana in Anglia—the Masonic parent body of the Golden Dawn—called the Societas Rosicruciana in America, or SRIA, which is still active today. Another was a H.B. of L. initiate in Austria named Karl Kellner. Kellner had the idea of establishing a new quasi-Masonic rite to carry on the H.B. of L. teachings, particularly Randolph's sexual gnosis. Kellner and his friend Theodor Reuss put together this new rite; they called it the Ordo Templi Orientis, and it later attracted the attention of Aleister Crowley, who took over the English-speaking branches of it as a vehicle for his own new religion of Thelema; that's how the Ansairetic Arcanum became one of the trade secrets of today's Thelemites.

One of the things that probably needs to be stressed at this point is that these Victorian occultists weren't isolated voices crying in the wilderness. One of the great misconceptions in the Pagan scene nowadays is the idea that there's anything new about the modern Pagan scene. There isn't. The United States probably had as large a percentage of its population practicing Pagan religion and magic in the 1890s as it does today. The Pagans and occultists of those days did a lot of networking through occult bookstores, as we do now, but they also had a network of magical lodges, occult orders, and public organizations like the Theosophical Society—a much more developed network than most parts of the occult scene have today.

This was a time when African-American hairdressers, who made up most of the hairdressing industry of the time, and made house calls, sold hoodoo preparations as well as beauty products: your husband's not paying enough attention to you? Here's a lip gloss, and a new hairstyle, and here's a mojo bag and some floor wash to keep his cheatin' heart safe at home. That was the business model for hairdressers in those days, and it's the reason why drugstores and beauty supply firms used to be *the* sources for hoodoo supplies.

This was also a time when people who were pumping iron were as often as not practicing magic at the same time. The term for exercise systems in those days was physical culture, and if you read the physical culture literature from the late nineteenth and early twentieth centuries expecting something like you get from today's exercise gurus, you're headed for a big surprise. Some of the most prominent people in physical culture at the time were also occultists. One of the best examples is Joseph Greenstein, stage name The Mighty Atom, one of the last of the old-time strongmen. He weighed about ninety-six pounds soaking wet and could tie a #2 iron horseshoe into an overhand knot with his bare hands. He was also a Jewish Cabalist who did his feats through a mastery of Cabalistic philosophy and esoteric practice. Another great example is Genevieve Stebbins, one of the first exercise teachers for women in America. She learned the Delsarte system of movement exercises in France and taught that. She was also a high-ranking initiate of the H. B. of L. and helped one of its successor orders, the Brotherhood of Light, get started.

There were dozens of people like this, and the old physical culture literature is full of magical exercises. Let's turn back to Crowley again for a moment. One of the other things he had students do in *Liber E*, *Liber III*, and his books on yoga was to hold a single position in perfect stillness for long periods. That wasn't original to him—let's be honest, nothing he taught was original to him—and it wasn't something he got from Hindu yoga. It was out of the willpower literature, which got it from physical culture. Standing motionless in specific poses was an ordinary part of physical training in those days, and people did it for the same reasons Crowley did: it teaches you to recognize and release unnecessary muscular tension in your body. So, the Victorian period, as I suggested earlier, was a time when some of the most fundamental ideas of modern magic were standard practice in all walks of life.

And this is the context in which I want to introduce my last Victorian sex magician, another American, and one of the most interesting of the lot. His name was William Walker Atkinson, but almost nobody knows him by that name anymore, because he was fond of pen names and used a bunch of them. Atkinson was a businessman who worked himself into a nervous breakdown around the beginning of the twentieth century, and recovered by way of New Thought—that's the term that was used for the sort of self-help psychology you still get by the truckload in today's bookstores. After his recovery, he left his old life behind, moved to Chicago, and started a new career as a writer and marketer of books on New Thought, eastern philosophy, and the occult.

Those of you who've spent time in old-fashioned occult bookstores probably remember a line of hardback books with glossy covers, red or blue, no dust jackets, published by an outfit in Chicago calling itself the

Yogi Publication Society; that was Atkinson. You might remember some highly eccentric books on yoga—they're actually about physical culture, but they call it yoga—by a guy calling himself Yogi Ramacharaka; that was Atkinson. You might have seen a book on the secret doctrines of the Rosicrucians by Magus Incognito; that was Atkinson. And if the store in question carried old books on sex magnetism and similar topics, you might just remember some books written by a guy who used the splendid name Theron Q. Dumont, all about mental magnetism and sexual energies and how to get laid by magic; that was also Atkinson.

And probably most of you have seen, if not read, a little blue hardback called the Kybalion, which claims to give the fundamental concepts of Hermetic Philosophy, and was written by three initiates who didn't give their names. All three of those were Atkinson. And one of the seven principles of the Kybalion, the seven most basic concepts of the Hermetic tradition as these three occultists understand it, is the Principle of Gender—the principle that everything has male and female dimensions, everyone has male and female aspects, and every kind of creation comes into being by the sexual interaction of these masculine and feminine principles, however those happen to be expressed in physical form.

So, in the Kybalion, one of the classic works of American occultism, and a book that deserves a lot more attention than it gets these days, everything has sex. The relationship between the Sun and the Earth is sexual, as Owen Morgan suggested; the relationship between living human beings and other-than-human beings has a sexual dimension, as Thomas Lake Harris insisted; and in the sexual union of active and receptive energies, a creative secret of immense power lies hidden, as Paschal Beverly Randolph taught.

The Kybalion's a little late to be strictly Victorian. It was published in 1912, just two years before everything that was left of the Victorian world crashed into ruin in the mud, blood, and trenches of the First World War. That was the end of a world, in a sense I'm not sure many people realize today—not only the end of the Victorian world but the end of the road for the whole Christian, aristocratic, hierarchical society that dominated Europe for a thousand years before then. Josephin Péladan, who was a French occultist, novelist, and art critic and will be getting a lecture of his own one of these days, talked in the decades before the war of *la decadence Latine*, the Latin decadence—and by "Latin" he meant every aspect of European civilization that could trace a meaningful connection back to old Rome. He saw it coming, and his novels—there were twenty-two of them, and those of you who know your French Tarot symbolism already know more about them than most modern literary critics—his novels basically set out to do an autopsy on a dying civilization. But Péladan wasn't a sex magician, so I'll stop there.

When we look back at magical traditions from before 1914, we're looking at the remnants of a world that no longer exists. It's easy to make fun of some of the sillier dimensions of that age, as I hope I've demonstrated; of course, it's also easy to be outraged by habits of thought and action from those days that offend against our modern ideas of decency and propriety. But beyond the laughter and the screams of outrage, there's also the fact that this is the magic of our ancestors. I mean that quite literally. If your great-grandparents lived in America or Europe, odds are that at least one of them, and most likely more than one, belonged to one of the Victorian era's magical secret societies, or practiced the occult disciplines that were part of the old physical culture systems, or got given training exercises for willpower in school, or picked up a mojo bag or some floor wash from the hairdresser to deal with a personal problem. One of them might have studied with Randolph or Oom the Omnipotent, or taken courses from Atkinson, or been shocked out of their socks by Morgan's *The Light in Britannia*.

A lot of people in the Pagan community these days don't like thinking about ancestors in this way. It's very popular to use the term solely for those ancestors who lived far enough in the past that they can be wrapped up in the rose-colored glow of romantic fantasy; and if we don't know a thing about what magic they actually did, so we can project our own ideas back onto them, so much the better. Our own great-grandparents aren't usually so biddable, so unless they've been turned into raw material for grandmother stories and untraceable famtrads, we often don't like to talk about them. Yet, these people, these Victorian great-grandmothers and great-grandfathers, were practicing magic. Some of them were practicing sex magic. Their magic, sexual and otherwise, is still accessible today—and some of those traditions offer resources for our own magic, here and now, that we might do well to draw on.

CHAPTER FIVE

Understanding Renaissance magic

I'd like to start by thanking everybody for coming to today's talk. It's encouraging that so many of you have shown up when you could have gone to something much more fashionable and up-to-date. We're going to talk about a lot of old-fashioned things; about ways of understanding the world and working magic that have very little in common with the ones you may be used to. I've spent around thirty years exploring old-fashioned things of this sort; I'd like to share some of the things I've found with you, and in the process, maybe stretch your conceptions of the world a bit.

Well, actually, I'm going to have to stretch your conceptions of the world more than a bit, because we've all seen the alternative and it doesn't work that well. A few years back, a certain publishing company that will remain nameless published two books by an author that will remain nameless, titled, if I recall correctly, *Celtic Magic* and *Norse Magic*. Read one and then read the other, and the sense of dejá vù might just knock you out of your chair. In large parts of the text, in fact, the only change the author made between the two books was to run a search-and-replace and swap out about a dozen words in Old Norse, and about as many Norse gods and goddesses, with a dozen words in Old Irish and about as many Irish gods and goddesses.

87

What's more, the theory of magic, the practices, and the spells in both books weren't Norse; they weren't Irish; they were generic late twentieth-century American Neopaganism dolled up in Norse or Irish decor, looking about as convincing in their new role as a drag queen with a handlebar mustache. I think we've all seen plenty of equivalents in recent magical literature: books that claim to offer some unique and distinctive teaching that turn out to be nothing more than another rehash of currently popular magical practice with a little bit of exotic bric-a-brac to make it look more interesting. Mind you, there's nothing wrong with that; for that matter, my friends who are into drag tell me that there's a place in the scene for drag queens with mustaches. As the song says, though, "you are what you are and you ain't what you ain't", and if you're looking for something other than one more rehash of currently popular magical practice you can look forward to plenty of disappointments in your local magical bookstore.

There are a number of reasons for this. Part of it, of course, is the simple and understandable desire to make a quick buck from the occult book trade by riding the wave of some currently fashionable ancient culture, or coming up with a rehash nobody else has thought of yet; the options are getting a bit thin these days, though there's still room on the bookshelves for another round or two of magical fusion cuisine. Still, there's another dimension to the problem—subtler, deeper, and harder to avoid. That's the awkward fact that modern magic, and the ways of thinking about the world that underlie it, don't actually have all that much in common with the magic and the worldviews of other societies and other periods in history.

The past is a foreign country. When we think about people in the past, we imagine ourselves in funny clothing in a world that's basically the same as the one we know. We're encouraged to do that by generations of historical novels that portray ancient people as though they had the same hopes, fears, and outlook on life as modern people do. Yet, when we do that, we're wrong. It's as simple as that. The past is a foreign country; not only do they talk funny there, and wear funny clothes, and do things in ways we don't understand, they don't experience the universe in the same way we do; in some sense, they don't live in the same universe we do.

I'll borrow an example from C. S. Lewis' excellent study *The Discarded Image*. Most people nowadays remember Lewis as the author of the Narnia books, but he was a brilliant scholar of medieval literature and understood the worldview of the Middle Ages and Renaissance to a depth that few other modern scholars have done. Here's his example. None of the languages of the Western world in ancient or medieval times had a word for our concept of Space—the idea of space as an infinite empty continuum in which everything exists simply wasn't there. *Spatium*, the Latin word from which our word "space" comes, meant the gap between two objects. *Locus*, another Latin word, means place, the spot where something is. *Vacuum*, another, means "emptiness"; if there's anything in it, from an atom to a planet, it's not a vacuum, and most ancient scientists agreed with Aristotle that an actual vacuum, a space with nothing at all in it, could not exist in the universe. The universe was a body, and every bit of it was full of some kind of matter.

The concept of infinite empty space did not exist for people in the ancient and medieval worlds. Yet, that concept is fundamental to our modern way of thinking about literally everything. Hold up your hands and put them about a foot apart. What's between them? If your first, automatic thought is "empty space," or "nothing," you're like most people nowadays—and you're also wrong. What's between my two hands? Air. Lots of it. Fourteen pounds of air pressure per square inch. If you had fourteen pounds pressing down on each square inch of one hand, you'd notice it. This room is packed full of matter, the kind of matter we call air; that's how an ancient or medieval person would have thought of it; but we're so deeply in love with the image of infinite empty space that we've all grown up ignoring the tons of matter filling this room and thinking of it as empty.

What color is the universe, by the way? To the modern mind, it's black: an infinite black abyss reaching away into eternal darkness in all directions. To the Renaissance mind, the universe was full of light. The only reason the night sky looks black, they believed, was that the Earth's shadow darkened the portion of it into which we're looking at night. Think about the difference between a universe of empty darkness and a universe full of substance and light, and you can begin to get a sense of the way the universe changed at the birth of the modern world.

The transition between the Renaissance and the early modern period was when that change took place—when people stopped thinking of the universe as a luminous body, a shape of matter filled with light, and started thinking of it as infinite empty blackness with chunks of matter bobbing around here and there through the eternal dark. That change didn't happen at the same time everywhere or all at once. It was a slow, wrenching process, and it affected every dimension of the way people thought about their world. The German historian Oswald Spengler argued almost a century ago that the way a culture conceives of space is the keystone for everything else in that culture's worldview, and he's got a point.

When the universe stopped being a finite material body and turned into an infinite void sprinkled with chunks of stuff, everything was up for grabs. Our concept of the Individual, of who we are, is a concept of Space. Here you are, lump of matter A; here I am, lump of matter B, separated from you by a certain amount of space—physical space, emotional space, personal space, and so on; we may interact in one way or another, but the only connection between us is that we happen to be in nearby regions of space just now. That sort of thinking seems like common sense to modern people. As far as I know, no other human culture in all of history conceptualized individual identity like that.

The worldview that went into history's dumpster at the end of the Renaissance certainly didn't. In that way of thinking, you and I and all the other human beings in this room are parts of a series of nested wholes— this event; this country; the human race; the world of the elements; the universe. Without participation in a larger whole, we wouldn't exist at all; our relationships define us and create us. In the modern worldview, by contrast, relationships are optional; what defines us is the space that separates us from every other being in the universe.

The shift from the universe as body to the universe as space affected magic, too. The change took a while to get there because magic is usually one of the most conservative things in any society. For a working magician, what's important about magic is that it works, and the way to be sure you've got something that works is to get something that's been used successfully for a long, long time. That's why you find medieval German Cabalistic incantations in twentieth-century Pennsylvania Dutch pow-wow magic, and why you had Renaissance sorcerers scrounging their incantations out of classical Greek sources such as the Orphic hymns and the Corpus Hermeticum. It's also why you find the medieval cosmos, with the Earth at the center of the planetary spheres reaching up to the Primum Mobile, in the version of the Cabalistic Tree of Life used by almost all magicians today, who one and all believe that the Earth moves around the Sun and the stars are scattered through infinite space.

But, the new way of looking at things did redefine magic in its own likeness eventually, and the person who finally succeeded in creating a magic of space was Alphonse Louis Constant, aka Eliphas Lévi. Lévi, as we might as well call him, was a close student of the magical traditions of the Renaissance, and quotes names in his magical writings that I suspect most of his modern readers have never heard of—people like Guillaume Postel and Ramon Lull. For all that, though, he was a man of his own time, a time when steam power was revolutionizing transportation and the electric telegraph was creating the world's first internet—a time when it was easy to think about hidden forces and energies that might be harnessed to human purposes by people clever enough to do so. He was also, like a lot of his contemporaries, a fan of the German philosopher Arthur Schopenhauer, whose philosophy centers on the concepts of will and representation. Rename the second half of the equation *imagination* and you have a very familiar formula.

Thus Schopenhauer's philosophy—the world as will and representation—became Lévi's formula for occult powers—magic as will and imagination. This latter is still the central formula for most kinds of magic in the Western world today, because Lévi basically invented modern magic, and for the last century and a half, the vast majority of magical writers in the Western world have either borrowed from Lévi, or borrowed from people who borrowed from Lévi, or—like Aleister Crowley—claimed to have been Lévi in a previous life. Very few people read his book *Doctrine and Ritual of High Magic* any more; it's written in a style that was carried off to the cemetery about the same time as Queen Victoria, and it suffered the horrible fate of being translated into English by Arthur Edward Waite, whose prose has all the grace and elegance of a rhinoceros with diarrhea. His translation, I'm sorry to say, is still the only one in print, mistitled *Transcendental Magic*—Waite never could settle for a good title when he could find a boring one to use instead.*

So Lévi created the approach to magic that still defines most magical thinking and practice today. He wasn't the first person to try to craft a magic appropriate to the modern worldview, though he did a much better job of it than his predecessors. There were any number of these; if you've read Joscelyn Godwin's useful book *The Theosophical*

---

*Fortunately this is no longer the case; a new translation by Mark Anthony Mikituk and me, titled *The Doctrine and Ritual of High Magic*, was published by Tarcher/Perigee in 2017.

Enlightenment, you know about some of them, but the first wave happened long before the beginning of the period Godwin covers. It emerged right about the time the ancient worldview gave way to the modern one, in the seventeenth century, and its creators were the mostly anonymous authors of the grimoires.

For those of you who don't know the term, these are famous magical handbooks—the *Goetia*, the *Black Pullet*, the *Grimoire of Honorius*, the *Petit Albert*, and many more—detailing the art of summoning demons from Hell to cater to your desires. Grimoire literally means "grammar"; the books present themselves as the ABC's of evoking fallen angels. For a variety of reasons they got mislabeled as medieval magic in the nineteenth century, and to this day, when modern people try to imagine the sort of magic that medieval people practiced, the grimoires are usually what come to mind; it's a trap I fell into myself, once upon a time, and in print, too, which makes it even more embarrassing.

But the magic of the grimoires is a magic of space. Look inside their covers and you'll find an attitude toward magic that is all but indistinguishable from the sort of debased sorcery that makes so much money nowadays in the form of books like *The Secret*. It's basically what that book calls the Law of Attraction—that is, I want it, and therefore the universe ought to give it to me. Most of the grimoires are cookbooks teaching you how to browbeat demons in order to get rich, get laid, and get various neat toys you won't find in the Sharper Image catalog just yet. The isolated individual magician stands at the center of a magical circle, separated from the hordes of Hell by a protective barrier of space.

The grimoires do borrow some ideas from older traditions of magic, for reasons we've already discussed, and many of them backdate their own origins to the Middle Ages in ways that will doubtless be very familiar to those of you who've watched some of today's Pagan traditions try to cover up their own dates of manufacture. Still, the more popular grimoires are modern—early modern, but modern—and that's the reason so many modern magicians find them so congenial.

And that's also the reason for this possibly overlong introduction. To encounter the magic of the Renaissance on its own terms, it's necessary to step outside our modern assumptions about magic, and about the universe in which magic operates. You can't get there by doing a search-and-replace on modern Wicca, or modern Hermetic magic, or modern anything else, in the fashion of those books I mentioned back at the start of this talk. You can't get there via the grimoires, either; they contain the first tentative, clumsy attempts at the magic of infinite space, not the magic of the universe that came before ours. You have to step into that universe, at least for a moment, and glimpse the kind of magic that works there.

So imagine for a moment that we're sitting outside on a starry night, and look up. You're not looking out at an abyss of black emptiness with lumps of rock and blobs of incandescent hydrogen scattered all anyhow across the face of the void. No. You're not looking out at all; you're looking up, at a structure—and you're looking at it from the inside.

High up above you, and surrounding you on every side, is the second biggest thing that has ever existed or will ever exist: the sphere of the fixed stars. It's so far away that if you could look down from it, the Earth would be smaller than a pinpoint. The only thing bigger than it is the sphere just outside it, the Primum Mobile or sphere of first motion. Both those spheres, and everything else down to the orbit of the Moon, are made of a kind of matter that only exists in the flasks of alchemists down here on Earth: the quintessence or fifth element, perfectly transparent, brighter than fire and subtler than air.

The planets are made of the quintessence—more precisely, the bodies of the planets are made of the quintessence. The planets themselves are conscious living beings. In the technical language of the time, they are intelligences: in the great chain of being that reaches from the lowest forms of matter to the throne of deity, they rank below the angels, above the spirits, and a good deal further above humanity. If you're a Pagan, they're the younger generation of gods; you know which ones; they still have the same names. If you're a Christian or a Jew, they're mighty spiritual beings created by God and given charge over certain aspects of the cosmos.

Below the circle of the Moon, things are different. Now we're in the realm of the four elements. Fire is outermost, reaching from the top of the atmosphere up to the Moon's orbit. This is pure fire, not the muddled, impure fire we see down here: it's transparent, luminous and formless. The reason fire down here always rises upwards is that it's trying to get to its proper place in the universe. Earth falls, water pours downwards, and air bubbles up for the same reason: each thing has its assigned place, and though things are all mixed up down here below the Moon, the elements are always trying to sort themselves out. Earth goes at the bottom, or almost; water surrounds it, air finds its place above water, and fire is above all, reaching right up to the Moon.

Below the element of Earth is something that didn't have to exist, and won't exist after a certain point in the future. The universe is all there is, and there's nowhere outside it, so when certain parts of creation went completely awry, a place had to be found for them in the structure. That's Hell: the trash can of creation, tucked away at the very bottom of existence at the center of the Earth. Fallen angels end up there, and so do fallen humans. Pagans in the Renaissance believe in that just as much as Christians and Jews: the Chaldean Oracles, one of the most popular works of Greek Pagan spirituality in the Renaissance, talks about it at length, and a lot of Pagan writings about Hades were reinterpreted along the same lines. Sooner or later, everyone pretty much agrees, the trash will be disposed of, but until then, the apple of the world has a worm at its center, and things occasionally creep out from the depths to make trouble and have to be sent back there.

The world is round, by the way. You learned that in grammar school, and if you go on to college you can listen to learned professors explain the evidence that proves it. They'll also prove to you that the Moon is smaller than the Earth, that the Sun is much, much larger, and the stars are so far away you can't even imagine the distance. They can explain how eclipses happen, and they're right. They can tell you how big the Earth is, too, and their figure is within a few hundred miles of the right one; that's why every geographer in Europe knew that Christopher Columbus was nuts when he said he could sail across the ocean to the Indies. They were right then, too; he and all his crew would have starved to death months before they could have reached China. It's just that neither they, nor Columbus, nor anybody else except a few bedraggled descendants of Vikings in Iceland had any clue that there were a couple of unknown continents in the way.

Those same professors can tell you a lot more. They'll explain to you that humanity isn't the pinnacle of existence by a long shot; instead, it occupies the middle rung on the great ladder of creation. Below us are animals, plants, stones, elements, and raw unformed matter itself. Above us are spirits, intelligences, and the nine choirs of angels rising up rank on rank to the foot of the divine throne. They may get into an argument with one another if you ask them about faeries; everybody knows that those exist, along with fauns, satyrs, dwarfs, and the like. Some scholars argue that they are a distinct order of being all their own, either slightly above or slightly below humanity; others have other opinions, but their exact place in the great chain of being is a matter of lively debate.

Nobody doubts that they have a place, though, because everything does; nothing in the universe is random. Whether you're Pagan,

Christian, Jewish, or some mixture thereof—and there were plenty of mixtures thereof all through the Renaissance—you know that the universe didn't just happen. It was created. It's an artifact, and it was shaped by powers that are so far beyond merely superhuman the word's hardly worth saying. You've read Plato's *Timaeus*—*everybody* read Plato's *Timaeus*—and so you know that the divine power that made the universe made it as perfect as anything of matter can possibly be.

Whether you're Pagan, Christian or Jew, you probably believe that sometime in the distant past the whole elemental realm below the Moon was purified with water, and you probably believe that sometime in the future everything below the Moon will be consecrated with fire and transmuted into something new and even more perfect. Above the Moon, no such changes have ever happened or will ever happen; the planets and the sphere of the stars turn in their everlasting cycles. Beyond that is—what? Not space; space doesn't exist; the universe is a single body of matter without a vacuum in it anywhere. Beyond it is the Empyrean, the realm of pure spirit, in which there is no place and no time: the realm of the divine unity and the angels.

That's where the power and wisdom that guide the whole vast structure comes from. They don't come all in a lump; there are specific currents and patterns—the technical term is "influences." That word has been watered down into perfect vagueness in English, but in Latin it's still *in-fluere*, flowing inward, like great waterfalls of force cascading down from the Empyrean through the spheres of the stars and planets into the realm of the elements. Everything here below the Moon exists because some particular current of influence brings it into existence and keeps it going. Everybody knows that; most people use it in little ways, making charms and medicines out of particular herbs and stones to cure an illness or bring a blessing because those herbs and stones participate in some particular influence.

But the magicians of the Renaissance don't limit themselves to little ways. They study the influences that descend through the heavens from the timeless and spaceless light of the Empyrean. They know that the movements of the planets against the backdrop of the stars reveal the way those influences ebb and flow, harmonize and struggle, create and destroy. They know that particular material things receive and collect different influences; that particular colors, shapes, musical modes, geometrical patterns, words, and names resonate with each influence. They know that magic is just our name for the process that creates and sustains the entire cosmos at every moment, and their books tell them how to step into the flow of that process, shape the dance of creative power, and accomplish wonders in the world.

That's why you won't see them summoning demons from Hell, in the manner of the grimoires; they don't need to waste their time with failed powers that have fallen right out of the great chain of being into the trash can of the cosmos. That's also why you won't see them trying to make things happen by using will and imagination; they have much mightier powers to work with. You won't see them raising cones of power, or grounding and centering; the forces they direct come from above; they don't need to be called down, either, and, for that matter, it would be a waste of time to try. They're not subject to human control, any more than winds or waves—but just as the sailor or the surfer can ride the wind or the wave and go where he wants to go, the magician surfs the influences of the cosmos.

It's at this point that we get to the most fundamental branch of practical occult knowledge in Renaissance magic, which is astrology. In today's magic, astrology is simply one kind of divination, and not an especially popular one, either. Peter Carroll's *Liber Null and Psychonaut*, one of the most popular books on Chaos magic, tells the student to take up some form of divination, and then turns around and says, "not astrology." While it's a bit funny to see a book on Chaos magic setting out rules and prohibitions, there's a point to the exclusion. Chaos magic is probably the most extreme form so far of the magic of infinite empty space, and astrology comes from the age when space didn't exist yet; even in its modern forms, it embodies ways of looking at the world that are by no means in harmony with the universe of space.

From the perspective of the older tradition, though, astrology isn't just a form of divination. It's the key to the magic of the universe before ours. Once again, magical power comes from the Empyrean, out there past the stars, and cascades down through the visible heavens to reach us here below the Moon. The planets, as they circle through the skies, each receive a particular current of influence and pour it out onto the Earth. Look at an astrological chart for a particular moment in time, and you're looking at the equivalent of a flowchart or a circuit diagram that allows you to see at a glance what influences are flowing at that moment, where they're going, and what you can use them to accomplish.

One word of caution, though. You won't be able to do this with the kind of astrology you'll learn from modern astrological books.

Modern astrology, like modern magic, had to come to terms with the new universe of infinite space, and so what you get in the vast majority of current astrological books is humanistic, person-centered astrology—that is, astrology that takes the isolated individual human being as its main, or even its only, focus. Natal astrology—that is, astrology that concentrates on interpreting personality on the basis of somebody's birth chart—is tolerably well suited to this sort of approach, which is why natal astrology is nearly the only form of astrology practiced these days. Many people today don't know that there's any other kind.

The astrology of the Renaissance, by contrast, wasn't humanistic and it wasn't person-centered. It was cosmos-centered. You didn't cast an astrological chart to find out who you were; you cast an astrological chart to find out what the cosmos was doing. If you cast the chart for the moment of your birth, you could indeed learn some things about yourself, though the Renaissance astrologer would be more likely to tell you how long you would live, what diseases you had to watch out for, what sort of profession you would find suitable, and what kind of person you would marry, than the sort of psychological analysis that plays a central role in so much modern natal astrology. Still, that was only one possible application of astrology and a fairly specialized one; the rules of natal astrology can't just be applied across the board to the rest of the art.

It was also something of a latecomer to the astrological toolkit. The oldest forms of astrology belong to the branch of the art called mundane astrology. I know, that sounds dull, but "mundane" is another word that's lost a lot of its meaning over the centuries. It literally means "of the mundus"—that is, of the world—and mundane astrology is the astrology of world events, the rise and fall of nations and their rulers. Go take a look at the surviving astrological records of ancient Sumer and Babylon—if you can read cuneiform writing, that is—and that's what you'll find: "A halo around the Moon, and Mars within it: the King of Elam shall die." That sort of thing. Natal astrology came into existence out of mundane astrology, when the old astrologer-priests started keeping notes of what the heavens were doing when the children of kings were born and noticed that you could predict some things about the life and destiny of the child from the position of the heavens at the moment of birth.

Long before then, though, those same priests had already begun using their knowledge in another way. If you want things to go a particular way, and you know how to read the heavens, you can time your actions to move in concert with the stars. That's called electional astrology, from the Latin word *electio*, "choice." An election in the political sense is when we choose our leaders—at least in theory. An election in an astrological sense is a time chosen because a particular influence that you want to work with is strong, balanced, and moving in the direction you want to go. That's the crucial kind of astrology for Renaissance magic because it allows you to time your magical workings to take advantage of the winds and waves of the heavens.

There's also horary astrology. Horary—the word comes from Latin *horarius*, "of the hour"—is divination pure and simple. You ask a question and then cast a chart for the exact moment when the question was asked, and you find the answer to the question in the state of the heavens at that moment. It's an elegant and very precise system of divination, but it's not too popular right now because it actually gives hard and fast answers. You ask it "will I get my heart's desire?" and it may just tell you "no." Worse, it may well be right. The people who bought umpteen million copies of *The Secret* do *not* want to hear that. You'll notice that the kinds of divination that have been most popular since the end of the Renaissance are all things that give the diviner, and the querent, as much wiggle room as possible—and wiggle room, after all, is just another kind of space.

But the kinds of divination that were popular in the Renaissance didn't offer wiggle room. You could ask a straight question and get a straight answer. Horary astrology thrived in that sort of market. So did geomancy, the poor man's astrology. Geomancy probably has its roots in sub-Saharan Africa; it uses sixteen patterns of single and double points, generated in various random ways, to construct a chart that the geomancer interprets; and it's just as hardnosed as horary astrology. It won't waffle, or talk about your personality, or give you some sort of vague encouragement that doesn't actually amount to anything; it won't even say "reply hazy, ask again later." It'll give you a straight-up answer, and if the answer is no, that's what you get. That's what people in the Renaissance wanted; they took their divination seriously and wanted to know the facts. In my experience, at least, when you cast a geomantic chart or erect a horary divination, that's what you get.

Electional astrology has the same sort of cut and dried approach, and that's especially true when you're looking for an election for magic. Henry Cornelius Agrippa, whose *Three Books of Occult Philosophy* is one of the most accessible sources for the old magic, gives the basic rules in Book II, Chapter Twenty-nine. In most cases, you start out by choosing one of the seven planets, because they govern the seven most accessible currents of influence in the heavens. Then you find a time, as Agrippa puts it, when the planet is "in its dignities, fortunate and powerful, and ruling in the day, hour, and figure of the heaven."

What on Earth, or above it, does that mean? This is where we start getting into the differences between the old astrology and the modern version. Each planet has certain signs of the zodiac, and certain portions of the signs of the zodiac, where the influence that comes through it has extra power; those are its dignities. It also has certain signs, and certain portions of the signs, where the influence is weak; when you're doing magic, most of the time, you stay away from those. So, if you're planning a working that draws on the influence that comes through Jupiter, you need to find a time when Jupiter is in one of the signs it rules—Sagittarius or Pisces—or the sign of its exaltation, Cancer. If you can't find a suitable time, there are also less important dignities—the terms, which are uneven sections of each sign assigned to the planets, and the faces or decans, which are one-third of a sign and are also assigned to the planets; for example, the first six degrees of Aries are one of the terms of Jupiter, and the middle ten degrees of Leo are one of the faces of Jupiter, but those are weak dignities and you use them only when you can't find anything better.

But that's just the start. Those are the essential dignities of the planets. There are also the accidental dignities of the planets, which come out of the ways they relate to the other planets at any given moment. For any given kind of spell, there are certain planets you want to be associated with the planet you've chosen, by certain specific kinds of relationship, and certain others you don't want to have anywhere in reach. You always have to pay attention to the Moon, which needs to be dignified either essentially or accidentally. It's good to have your planet in a favorable aspect to the Moon—the favorable aspects are trine and sextile, which are angles of 120 and sixty degrees respectively. A conjunction, when your planet and the Moon are in the same degree of the zodiac, is just as good.

If you can get them, for most kinds of magic, you want Venus and Jupiter related to your planet by favorable aspect or conjunction, too. Jupiter and Venus were called the greater and lesser fortunes respectively, and, in most cases, you want them on your side. Another thing you want, when you can get it, is Mercury in favorable aspect to one of the two fortunes, since Mercury is the planet ruling magic.

Then there are the unfavorable aspects. If your planet is within eight and a half degrees of the Sun, unless it's the Sun itself, of course, its influence will be drowned out by the solar rays; if you can get a sextile or trine with the Sun, on the other hand, that's good. What really ruins a chart is an unfavorable aspect—a square of ninety degrees or an opposition of 180 degrees—between your planet and Mars or Saturn. Saturn and Mars are the greater and lesser infortunes, and except in very specialized situations, you do *not* want them hostile to your working. You also don't want Mercury in aspect to one of the infortunes, because as Agrippa says, Mercury takes his character from the company he keeps.

In each of these aspects, mind you, the planets need to be approaching the point where the aspect is exact. In astrological jargon, the planets need to be applying to the aspect, not separating from it. That's one of the differences between electional astrology and natal astrology. In a natal chart, a trine is a trine; if it's separating, it's a bit weaker than if it's applying, but it still has its usual influence. In an electional chart, once the moment of the exact aspect is past, the aspect is over with; haul it out with the trash.

So you need a time when the planet you've chosen is in one of its essential dignities, and when the Moon is also in an essential dignity or in a favorable aspect to one of the fortunes, and when neither the planet nor the Moon is in an unfavorable aspect to the infortunes, or too close to the Sun; and you want to have your planet in a favorable aspect to the fortunes and the Moon, Mercury applying to the fortunes, and the Sun trine or sextile your planet. Quite a shopping list. But we're not done yet, because Agrippa also reminds us that all this has to happen in the day and hour of the planet.

I think most people know that each of the seven days of the week corresponds to one of the seven planets; that's why we have weeks with seven days, after all. Not so many people are aware that each hour of the day is associated with one of the planets. Old books on magic include tables of the planetary hours, and they also teach you how to calculate their length—and you have to do that; the planetary hours are not clock hours; they're each one-twelfth of the period from sunrise to sunset, or from sunset to sunrise, and that means they change length depending on your latitude and the season of the year. So if you want to do a magical working with the influence of Jupiter, you find an hour of Jupiter on a Thursday—that's Jupiter's day—when Jupiter is in one of his dignities and all the other details are in place.

Now all this takes work, and it also takes a very solid knowledge of traditional astrology. The good thing about all this, though, is that if you can catch that influence at the right time, and use the right substance and form, you can make a container for the influence; you can store it up like electricity in a battery and keep using it long after the heavens have stopped being favorable to that one influence. The battery in question is called a talisman. Well, actually, it's either a talisman or a gamahe, and just to add to the fun, what most occultists nowadays call a talisman—a piece of parchment, wax, metal, or what have you carved with words of power and weird geometrical symbols—is what magicians in the Renaissance called a gamahe. A talisman, to them, was a statue, painting, or drawing that symbolized the magical force it contained. Sometimes those were crude little things of wax, parchment, or metal; sometimes, as we'll see in a bit, they were quite a bit more impressive.

The talisman or gamahe was usually made of a substance that resonated with the influence you want to attract, or in a color that resonated with that influence, and it was carved or painted or drawn with names, images, and geometrical forms that also resonated with that influence. The form is crucial. Medieval and Renaissance physics distinguished between the form of a thing and its substance; the influences of the heavens are forms—in modern terms, they're not energy or matter, they're information, and they communicate themselves to whatever resonates with them. Agrippa explains that you can make a very effective talisman by simply creating an image of whatever it is you want to bring about. That's the logic behind poppet spells: you take the male poppet and the female poppet and bind them together face to face as though they're doing the nasty, and the man and the woman you're using the poppets to represent are drawn into the same somewhat undignified position. Agrippa, though, is saying that you can do that with anything because a form that resonates with a celestial influence will attract that influence.

In Renaissance magic, talismans and gamahes are the name of the game. The influences of the seven planets weren't the only option, either, though they seem to have been the most popular. You can do the same sort of thing with the energies of the fixed stars; there are fifteen stars, in particular, the Behenian stars, that were used very often to make talismans. You can work with the mansions of the Moon—the twenty-eight stations of the lunar zodiac, each of which has its own distinctive magical influences. Each of the geomantic figures has its own governing influence, and there's a whole set of geomantic symbols used to make gamahes at the right planetary day and hour. There's much more. Everything in the Renaissance cosmos is packed to the bursting point with influences from the heavens, and if you know how, you can use them.

Making talismans and gamahes doesn't always have to be as complex as I've outlined, by the way. When you only need to apply a modest magical shove to a situation, you can make a talisman or a gamahe any time it's the right planetary day and hour, so long as the planet itself isn't afflicted and the Moon is favorable. Making them can also be much more complex than I've outlined. Turn the pages of some of the classic texts of astrological magic, such as the *Picatrix* or Thabit ibn Qurra's *On Images*, and you'll find recipes that make Agrippa's instructions look like child's play.

Here's an example from Thabit ibn Qurra, a working to enable somebody to become rich by his own efforts. You start by casting the natal horoscope of the person in question. Find their ascendant—that's the sign of the Zodiac that was rising on the eastern horizon at the moment of birth; then find a time when that same sign is rising, when that sign, and the planet that rules it, are both dignified, essentially or accidentally; when the sign in the tenth house of the chart, and the planet that rules *it*, are both dignified essentially or accidentally; when the Moon and the planet ruling the sign the Moon is in are both dignified essentially or accidentally.

But that's not all. You also need to have the planet ruling the second house making a trine or sextile aspect with the planet ruling the ascendant, and one of those two planets either in a sign that the other planet rules, or the sign of its exaltation. And if you can—Thabit doesn't require these last few points, but he highly recommends them—make sure that the signs in the eleventh and eighth houses, and the ruler of the eleventh, are dignified essentially or accidentally, and that the Part of Fortune—that's a point in the horoscope that's calculated from the positions of the Sun, the Moon, and the ascendant—is on the ascendant or in the tenth house.

Then—at that exact time—you make your talisman, your magical image, and it stores up just about every possible influence from the heavens that could favor somebody getting rich by his own efforts. You give it to the person for whom you've made the talisman, and it's as though that particular arrangement of the heavens is constantly beaming those influences down on that person; they've got the momentum of the entire universe on their side when it comes to making a good living, and that overwhelms whatever factors have been keeping them poor.

The magicians of the Renaissance would have said that a different way. To them, wealth and poverty could be read in the natal horoscope; when you're born, the position of the heavens allots you your destiny, and there you are; your second house is unfortunate, you're going to be poor. Magic, from that perspective, is the art of horoscope repair. Somebody comes to you with a bad second house, you figure out what astrological influence can fix that, and make them a talisman that gives them the favorable influences their natal chart doesn't have.

You can do the same thing to a city, or a kingdom. Everything that comes into being down here below the Moon has a birth chart; everything starts out with a certain set of influences given it by the heavens, and if those are unfortunate, well, tough—except that magic can fix that. There's a great deal of what might be called mundane magic, magic to help shape the affairs of kings and nations. Not all of this is the sort of beneficial magic I've been describing up to this point. For example, the old texts give workings that are meant to destroy a city. Basically, you stand all the usual rules for electional astrology on their head, and choose a time when the influences of the heavens are in a really ugly mood, Mars and Saturn are applying to squares or oppositions to the planet ruling the city, and so on. You make a talisman at that time, and bury it somewhere in the city, and everything starts going horribly wrong. Accidents happen, the economy goes south, sooner or later war or plague or famine drives most of the population away, and, eventually, you have one more crumbling ruin.

Of course there may well be a magician in the city who can cast a counter-talisman; there may be somebody who can use geomancy or horary astrology to figure out where your talisman is buried, dig it up, and destroy it; there may also be somebody who can make a similar talisman aimed at your city, or you personally, and you find that things start going horribly wrong for you. It could turn into quite a magical arms race. It's not impossible that this sort of thing had a significant impact on history. In the twelfth century, quite a bit of what's now Iraq and Syria went from settled farm country dotted with cities to desert wasteland inhabited mostly by sand fleas. Historians argue about the reasons—soil salinization, climate change, and so on—but all those factors had been in play for a long time previously. I sometimes wonder if what happened was that a magical arms race of the sort I've described spun out of control.

The attitude of the old magical handbooks to this sort of thing was very different from the way ethical issues are handled in modern magic. Our magical handbooks are public; you can get 'em at your local occult bookstore any day of the week; and so the standard ethical response— the one I use in my own books—is to give instructions for beneficial magic, stay strictly away from the malefic stuff, and point out as clearly as possible that malefic magic is a very bad idea anyway. That's a valid approach, but it's a response to current conditions; different conditions, different responses.

In the Middle Ages and the Renaissance, moral philosophy was something every educated person studied; you didn't have to spoonfeed people with simplistic rules of thumb like the law of threefold return, you could just allude to some passage in Aristotle's *Nicomachean Ethics* and everybody would know what you were talking about; and the magical handbooks weren't public. You couldn't walk into a bookstore and buy a copy of the *Picatrix*; you had to know somebody who had one, and know that they had it, and convince them that you wouldn't misuse the information. This was the nuclear physics of the Renaissance, and these things were kept secret for exactly the same reason that build-your-own nuclear-warhead recipes aren't exactly easy to find today.

Does this suggest that every serious Renaissance magician was expected to be a moral philosopher? You bet. Magic in those days was not the sort of hole-and-corner subculture it's become in our age; it was something that attracted the attention of the top minds, the rocket scientists and nuclear physicists, of the Renaissance. To do it, and do it well, requires mastering a very extensive body of knowledge. You have to know astrology inside and out; you have to know the lore of natural magic, which tells you which plants and stones and other substances correspond to which planets; you have to know a huge amount of symbolism. You have to pick up a working knowledge of philosophy, mathematics, botany, and half a dozen other subjects. You have to tackle a course of study not noticeably less demanding than the one you'd take on today to get a Ph.D.

This is a lot of work. The magicians of the Renaissance had ways to make it easier, though. They borrowed an old Greek system of memory training that became popular in the late Middle Ages and turned it into the ars memorativa, the Renaissance Art Of Memory. The basic form of the Art of Memory can be learned—yes, memorized—in about five minutes. You visit a building, someplace with lots of nooks and crannies, often enough that you can imagine yourself walking through the whole thing, room by room, with enough of the details in place that you know where you are. You then put mental images in your imagined building.

Do you want to remember your grocery list? Put each of the items in it in their places in one room of the building, in order—the flour, the sugar, the milk, and so on. Do you want to remember the stones that correspond to Saturn in the lore of natural magic? Another room, with Saturn himself in the middle, old and gray, leaning on his scythe; around the room go images that remind you of the names and properties of each stone. Here's a piece of jet; since this is a modern memory palace, you make a jet airplane out of the stone. You have a guy pouring a bucket of water on the jet because jet also corresponds to the zodiacal sign Aquarius, and you have a demon cowering in fear nearby because the magical virtue of jet is that it banishes evil spirits. Then it's on to the next stone.

That's the basic form. There were plenty of very, very unbasic forms. The far end of the spectrum, the Thabit ibn Qurra of the Art of Memory, was Giordano Bruno, who was burned at the stake for heresy in 1600. His memory methods are so complex that you have to learn the basic Art of Memory first, so you can remember what to do! But his memory system is also a system of magic, which may help explain why the Inquisition made him the guest of honor at one of their barbecues. Remember, a form that resonates with a celestial influence attracts that influence; according to Renaissance philosophy, that's true whether the form is impressed on wax, or metal, or the subtle substance of thought. So Bruno used memory images to attract the influences of the heavens. Most of his stuff has never been translated out of Latin; Frances Yates' books *The Art of Memory* and *Giordano Bruno and the Hermetic Tradition* are good places to start making sense of his work.

There was another approach, though it's one even more poorly documented today than the Art of Memory. If everything here below the Moon comes from the heavens, then the sort of talent that gives some people a natural gift for some particular field of knowledge comes from the heavens, right? And the influences of the heavens can be attracted by proper forms, right? That's the basis for what was called the Notory Art or Ars Notoria—that's N O T O R Y, by the way, not notary as in notary public. It was designed for people who weren't magicians yet, so the methods were a bit different. A book on the notory art would give you a complicated diagram; you'd draw that out yourself on parchment, and then once a day, concentrate it while repeating an incantation.

There was a different diagram for each subject, sometimes more than one, and they all had to be drawn just so, so as you can imagine, it was a complicated process. Unfortunately, the only readily available book on the notory art, the seventeenth-century English translation by Robert Turner, simplifies the whole process considerably by leaving out all the diagrams. Someday, somebody is going to have to go over to London or Paris or one of the other big European libraries, find a good ars notoria book, and translate it out of Latin with the diagrams intact; then, and only then, we'll be able to revive that very useful magical art.

Now, of course, that implies that there's a point to reviving these old magical arts, and that raises questions that have to be dealt with before we can wrap this up and plunge back into the familiar universe of infinite space. After all, we all know that the Earth isn't at the center of the cosmos; we all know that space is, well, space and that there's no sphere of the fixed stars arching overhead, sending down influences from the Empyrean through the planetary spheres to the sublunary world of the elements. We know that.

Don't we?

That's where we start getting into the deepest and most difficult issues raised by the comparisons we've been exploring for the last hour or so. Every culture is convinced that its own vision of the universe is the simple, straightforward truth about things. So far, every culture has been wrong. A lot of people nowadays think that modern industrial society is exempt from the common rule, but you know, if there was any chance I'd be around to collect on the bet, I'd put money on the suggestion that in five hundred or a thousand years, people will look back on the ideas we have about the universe and giggle.

Our culture doesn't have a monopoly on the truth. We just have our own way of thinking about the world, a way that's just as dependent on mythic narratives and emotionally compelling images as any other culture's worldview. Our way of looking at the world has enabled us to accomplish some things other cultures never managed, but the same is true of other cultures. Nothing in the modern industrial worldview could have led to the discovery of acupuncture; that took the traditional Chinese way of looking at the world. And of course, nothing in the modern industrial worldview would lead anyone to create the astrological magic of the Renaissance—itself an extraordinary achievement, and one that works very well in practice.

Yes, I said that out loud. Renaissance magic works. So does modern magic, Eliphas Lévi's magic, the magic of space that uses will and imagination to shape the astral light and cause a change in conformity with will. So, for that matter, does Taoist magic, which draws its meaning and its ground rules from a completely different universe, the universe of classical Taoism, which is at least as different from either the Renaissance or the Modern universe as each of these are from each other. So do many other kinds of magic, from many different universes.

And this is important to keep in mind just now, at this moment in history, because right now it's not impossible that we're moving out of the universe of infinite empty space, into some new universe that nobody really has a handle on yet. The universe of space has taken us just about as far as it can go. Talk to people on the cutting edge of several contemporary sciences and you'll find that the data they're dealing with is getting increasingly hard to interpret in terms of a universe of atoms bumping into each other in the void. Look at the environmental crisis that takes up so much space on the front pages of newspapers these days and you see the logical result of a set of ideas about the universe that places humanity at the summit of creation and deny that any of us has any responsibility to the larger unity in which, from another perspective, each of us has a part.

For that matter, look at the magic we practice. Even the magic of space has had to lead a hole-and-corner existence in the modern world because magic—any kind of magic—challenges the universe of empty space to its core. Something's going on that goes beyond atoms bumping into each other in the void: something that plays mumbledy-peg with our current notions of Space, Time, and Causality, something that has deep linkages with Consciousness, Meaning, and Spirit—factors that the metaphysics of space can't really cope with at all. I don't think it's accidental that just as the modern worldview started showing its first really visible cracks—as physics began wrestling with the preposterous realities of the quantum realm, and the first great wave of ecological

crises served notice on the industrial world that it ignored the consequences of its own actions at its very real peril—that magic came boiling up out of the broom closets and, for the first time in a very long time,
became something approaching a mass phenomenon.

We need magic now. It's not the only tool we need in our toolkit at
the end of the age of space, not by a long shot, but it's a tool we can't
very well do without; and I suggest that just now the old, proud, starry
magic of the Renaissance may be particularly well suited to some of
the needs of the time before us. Many other kinds of magic have their
place; we can't afford to do without any of the available options, not if
we're to make it through the difficult years ahead of us with some of the
heritage of our time intact. Still, one thing we need very badly is a magic
that reaches beyond the individual, a magic that's not afraid to attempt
great things, and we also might just learn something crucial about ourselves and our world by embracing a magic that sees humanity as one
small part of a greater whole. Thank you.

CHAPTER SIX

Magic, metapolitics, and reality

We're here tonight to talk about magic, metapolitics, and the decline and fall of industrial society. Not the most popular topics these days! They're among our culture's taboos, and, in fact, taboos are the first thing we need to talk about. Now, of course, this is a modern, rational, industrial society, and we don't have taboos; there are just things we don't talk about, things we hedge around with doubletalk and euphemisms and a well-trained refusal to look them in the eye. Sex is one of our taboos. Death is one of our taboos—and isn't it interesting that the rock-bottom realities of human life are among the things we just don't want to talk about. But the taboo subject I'd like to talk about here is magic.

That's one of our biggest taboos, by the way. Most people in our society get uncomfortable when the raw realities of sex or death intrude on their comfortable middle-class existence, but I don't know a lot of people who insist that sex doesn't actually exist, or that people who die are just faking it. Magic is different. Not only do Americans not want to see it, but they also don't want to think it exists at all, and when it intrudes on their lives, as it often does, a good many of them either shut their eyes and hope it goes away, or just go quietly nuts.

Anthropologists will tell you that in tribal cultures, every taboo has its exception. If it's taboo to eat bananas, then there's a festival once a year where people are supposed to eat bananas or something like that. In American society, the exception to our taboos is the media. We shy away from actual sex and actual death, but the media is packed to the bursting point with people making love and getting killed. Magic is the same way. Americans pay millions of dollars to watch some kid actor in a Harry Potter movie wave his hand, spout some bad Latin, and have special effects come spewing out of the end of a wand. But if you want to bring a conversation about Harry Potter to a screeching halt, try suggesting that there might be something to that magic stuff in what we fondly call the real world.

Our taboo on magic is a very strange thing when you look at it. Every human society on Earth has magical traditions; every human society on Earth, including ours, actually practices magic. It's as much a universal of human culture as, well, sex or death. Like sex and death, magic is something nearly all societies surround with various customs and restrictions, but again, like sex and death, it's an everyday part of life. In hunter-gatherer societies, hunters use magic to help them find and kill their prey, and gatherers use magic to maintain good relationships with food plants. In agricultural societies, people use magic to ward off blights and bad weather and encourage the crops to grow. In urban societies outside the modern industrial West, people use magic for a thousand different reasons, from love to politics to horse racing.

In fact, people in the modern industrial West use magic too; they just don't do it in public, and everyone else turns their back and pretends it's not happening. Like sex; like death.

Of course, during our school days, we're all taught the reason for this very strange taboo. We're taught that about 350 years ago, for the first time in all the million-year sweep of human history, a handful of men actually noticed what the world is really like. That small group of men—and they were all men; white men; middle-class white men with college degrees and a set of very specific political and religious opinions—realized that everything everyone else had always believed about the world was completely wrong and that all the great thinkers of the past were perfect idiots; that magic obviously doesn't work and gods clearly aren't real; that the only things that actually exist in the world are little particles of dead matter bumping together in a lot of empty space. And of course, once they saw that, well! Modern industrial society was the inevitable result.

That's what we call the Scientific Revolution. Now I've taken the usual rhetoric of popular history about that period and pushed it a little further than it usually goes, to make a point. The point is that if you believe in the standard account of the Scientific Revolution, you have to accept some very strange ideas about history, and about humanity. You have to believe that nobody until 1650 ever noticed things that were perfectly obvious in that year, and have been perfectly obvious ever since. You have to believe that all through human history, people lived their lives in blithe disregard of the most self-evident facts about the world until the first scientists came along to tell them how wrong they were. It's like one of those Native American tales where the people are going along doing things in the worst possible way until Coyote or somebody comes along and sets them straight.

It's precisely like one of those tales, because, of course, what we are talking about is a myth: the origin myth of the modern world; the foundation myth of the most popular and least discussed religion in the modern world.

But, of course, we don't have myths, any more than we have taboos. Only what we like to call primitive societies have myths, right? In fact, it's a common trope of modern thought—you'll find it repeated endlessly in popular nonfiction and cocktail-party chatter—that myths are a thing of the past: our culture has left myths behind, we no longer have myths of our own. Mind you, this isn't necessarily presented as a good thing. The same thinkers who proclaim the death of myth far and wide have, as often as not, mourned its absence. You'll even run across the term "amythia," the pathological lack of myths, which the punditocracy points out from time to time as the root of various modern problems.

But, at this point, we're deep into irony. While the rising spiral of problems facing industrial society has plenty of sources, a myth shortage is not one of them. It's true, of course, that most educated people in the modern West don't believe the central myths of Christianity and Judaism anymore, but that didn't happen because people just stopped believing in myths. It happened because those older myths were shoved aside to make room for a new and more appealing myth, a myth that seized the collective imagination of the West and remains dominant today.

The myth we're talking about is the myth of progress. Most people nowadays—even most of those who cling to symbols borrowed from older mythologies—believe that all of human history is one vast upward movement from the ignorant squalor of a primitive past to the Promethean grandeur of a Star Trek future. Most of us assume that newer opinions are more true and newer practices more effective than older ones, just because they're new; most of us believe that the older an idea is, the more certain it is to be wrong. Many of us assume, without thinking about it, that our grandchildren must have better lives than we do, and most of us have better lives than our grandparents because that's progress; that's what happens.

The irony doesn't stop there, because a lot of the people who believe in this intensely mythic narrative insist that it's nothing but plain sober fact, and claim to be completely free of myth—even suffering, pathetically or heroically depending on their rhetoric of choice, from abandoning the comforts of myth for the cold realities of the world as it actually is. We've stood the tale of the emperor's new clothes on its head: the modern emperor is convinced of his own perfect nudity, as he trips and stumbles over the gorgeously embroidered robes he's convinced himself he's too wise to be wearing.

Half the trouble here is caused by confusion about what myths are. A lot of people use the word "myth" to mean a story that's not true— you know, touching toads will give you warts, the Moon is made of green cheese, Social Security will be there when you retire, and so on. That's not what the word actually means. Myths are the stories we tell ourselves to give meaning to the world. Every culture and every person has myths. Some of them have goddesses and heroes and get told in epic poetry. The myth of progress has *Homo sapiens* as its hero and textbook prose as its literary medium, which doesn't speak very well of modern taste.

So it won't work to say that something can't be a myth because it's true. Some of you may have had exactly this reaction when I described progress as a myth: progress has happened; therefore it can't be a myth. Quite the contrary. It's precisely because a myth is true in some sense, at least some of the time, that it's a myth at all.

But the fact that a myth has been true for part of the past doesn't mean that it must be true forever. We live at the crest of a wave of technological progress around three centuries old. Those three centuries have seen a lot of changes, and, of course, we all learned in school that all those changes were for the best—that everything tossed into the trash cans of history in the course of progress belonged there, and everything that was brought in as a replacement must have been better because it was newer; magic was chucked aside, therefore it's nonsense. Because that's progress, that's what happens.

But we go on to make the easy assumption that the next three centuries will see even more progress, and so will the three centuries after that, and so on. That's where history gives way to fantasy, because from where we now stand it's becoming increasingly clear that the next three centuries aren't going to see anything of the kind.

The claim that progress has been going on throughout human history is another bit of fantasy. Progress as we know it is a very recent thing. Over the last 350 years, the world has been utterly reshaped by the discovery of fossil fuels. A handful of nations in Western Europe, and a few of their overseas colonies, hit the ultimate economic jackpot—a fantastically abundant source of concentrated energy that was very nearly free for the taking. That's what gave birth to industrial society and the modern world: what ecologist William Catton calls the Age of Exuberance.

If you look back to the year 1650 and see what the past looked like from that standpoint, you won't see the rising curve of technological progress our history textbooks like to imagine these days. Looking back from the standpoint of 1650, human history looks like a sine wave, not a rocket launch. Between the Agricultural Revolution and the Industrial Revolution, in fact, very little changed in terms of everyday human life. Technological advances happened now and then during all those centuries, of course, but the new technologies had a very modest impact on life; the gains from the invention of the moldboard plow, say, or the water wheel were pretty much canceled out within a few generations by the depletion of soil fertility and the effects of population pressure. Technological decline also happened, as mechanical toys of various kinds turned out to be too expensive to maintain, or civilizations broke apart and knowledge got lost in the process. Until 1650, that was the way the world worked.

What makes this fascinating is that almost everything necessary for industrial society was invented many centuries before the Industrial Revolution. Renewable energy sources? People were using wind power, water power, and biomass millennia ago. Scientific knowledge? The laws of mechanics were worked out in ancient times, and a Greek scientist named Hero of Alexandria even invented a working steam turbine before the birth of Christ. Human ingenuity? People in past ages were just as ingenious as we are. The Byzantine empire in the early

Middle Ages even had a petroleum industry; they used it to supply flamethrowers for their navy—you may have heard of Greek fire; that's what it was.

The one thing nobody had before the Industrial Revolution was an effective method to turn fossil fuels into commercially useful energy. And that's the one thing that made all the difference. Very few people these days realize just how much energy is packed into fossil fuels. Take a moment to do a little thought experiment. Imagine that you put a medium sized car into neutral, left the engine off, and pushed the car for thirty-two miles. Think about how much muscle power that would take. That much power is in one gallon of gasoline—well, actually, the gallon of gas has more, since I don't think anyone in this room can push a car at seventy miles an hour.

That kind of energy, locked up in coal, oil, and natural gas, is what made the Age of Exuberance possible; it's what makes our lifestyles possible. And of course, that's now become one of the main ingredients in that rising spiral of problems I mentioned a little while back, because coal, oil, and natural gas are finite resources, and we've been using them all at an astonishing pace. Oil, especially. It's the hydrocarbon lifeblood of industrial society, it has more energy per unit volume than any other fossil fuel, and yields more net energy than anything else, period—and the world pumps more than eighty-four million barrels of it out of the ground every single day.

This is a problem, because there's only so much of it in the ground, and there are hard geological limits to how fast you can pump it out. Right now, with world oil production around thirty billion barrels a year, we're running flat out at what will probably turn out to be close to the all-time peak of world oil production. Most of the big oil fields that have been the backbone of production for the last couple of decades are running down, and the new fields coming on line right now aren't big enough to make up the difference. That's the nasty secret hidden inside those innocuous words "peak oil."

Now we could talk about peak oil for hours, and argue about it for much longer. Bring in natural gas and coal, and we'd be here for days. I'd encourage everyone here to learn as much about it as they can, and not be satisfied either with the facile handwaving of the establishment types who insist that somebody will pull a high-octane rabbit out of a hat so we can have business as usual forever, or with the Hollywood fantasies of survivalists who never got over the fact that Y2K didn't happen and they didn't get to live out their fantasy of blasting away on full auto at rampaging mobs. We're facing a long, difficult, extremely challenging transition to a world very few of us will recognize.

Peak oil isn't the only factor pushing us in that direction. It's only one of a dozen or so symptoms that industrial society is running up against hard planetary limits. We've got a global climate system that's spinning out of control, we've got a world population that's at least three times what the planet can support, we've got looming shortages of everything from grain to fresh water to fish stocks to topsoil, we've got a dozen different forms of ecological blowback sawing away at the limb our civilization is perched on, and the list goes on.

Back in the early 1970s, a research team sponsored by the Club of Rome coined the term "the limits to growth" for this. Their book of the same title predicted that once you push economic growth past the point of diminishing returns, the costs of growth rise faster than the benefits until finally the sheer economic burden of economic expansion overwhelms growth itself and forces the economy to its knees. That's actually what *The Limits to Growth* predicted, but you won't find that out by reading anything from the media furor that broke over the research team's heads when they published their findings. They broke the taboo; they spoke the unspeakable—that progress might not be all it's cracked up to be; that the god our civilization worships, the god of progress, might not be omnipotent, might actually turn into his own nemesis and bring about his own Ragnarok.

That's also the message of the Hubbert curve, which some of you probably know about. The Hubbert curve is a tool used by petroleum geologists all over the world. It tracks production over time for any oil reserve, from a single oil well to a planet. It's a bell-shaped curve: oil flows slowly at first, rises to peak production, then falls gradually to zero. The peak arrives when roughly half the oil is gone. When Hubbert first applied the curve to the oil reserves in the continental US back in 1956 and announced to the world that US oil production would peak in 1970, people had a fit. He was denounced as a complete crackpot. Unfortunately, he was right on the money, and US oil production has been declining steadily since 1970. We're still producing a lot of oil; in fact, the US is the second largest oil producer in the world, right after Saudi Arabia. The problem is that there's less of it every year.

To misquote T. S. Eliot, this is the way the oil ends, not with a bang but a trickle. And the rest of the world? Same story. More than half the oil-producing regions on Earth are already past their own Hubbert peaks. Hubbert predicted in 1970 that the entire world would peak in 2000. We have better numbers now, and the best current estimates are that the world peak is sometime between 2004 and 2008: in other words, right about now. Other fossil fuels and nuclear fuels are headed the same way; they all have their own Hubbert peaks, and those come a lot sooner once they have to make up for declining oil production. For example, you have to dig three tons of coal to get the same amount of energy as you get from four barrels of oil, and at that rate even huge coal reserves start running down fast.

Renewable energy sources are more complex. They have some big advantages; they can keep on going forever, or close enough, but there are hard limits of scale and net energy to cope with. Net energy is how much energy you have left after you subtract the energy you have to use to get energy in the first place. It's the joker in the deck; a lot of so-called energy resources have zero net energy or even negative net energy—you have to use up the equivalent of one and a half barrels of oil, for example, to extract one barrel of oil from kerogen shale, which is why half a dozen oil companies started building huge kerogen shale plants in Wyoming in the 70s and then just shut them down and walked away. Renewables have fairly modest net energy and serious problems with scale and reliability. That doesn't mean we shouldn't pursue them; they're the only thing we'll have left when oil becomes too expensive to burn, but if we launched a crash program today on all the renewables— solar, wind, water, biodiesel, the lot—we'd end up being able to replace maybe 15% of America's current energy needs, maybe less.

Now 15% is a lot better than nothing. The problem we face isn't having no energy at all. It's having to make do with less and less each year until, finally, we get down to levels that can be sustained indefinitely.

That's the framework for Dr. Richard Duncan's Olduvai Theory. Rich Duncan is a retired professor of engineering up at the University of Washington who's been setting people's teeth on edge for the last decade by asking hard questions about the long-term future of industrial society. His Olduvai Theory—he calls it that because he came up with it after a visit to Olduvai Gorge in Kenya—has been published in peer-reviewed human ecology journals. He starts out from White's Law, which is one of the basic rules of human ecology: economic development is a function of energy per capita. Pretty straightforward: total energy divided by population gives you a good general measure of development.

Map it onto history, and you get pretty much the image of the past I outlined a little while ago. Until 1750, energy per capita was very modest, fluctuating up and down with the cycles of history. After that, you get a ballistic curve upwards to about 1925, the peak of coal energy; a slump from there until the Second World War; and another upward curve to 1979.

That was the all-time peak of energy per capita worldwide. Since then, it's been stuck in a plateau. A little up, a little down, but not going the way it's supposed to go, not climbing endlessly upwards the way the myth of eternal progress says it has to.

That's where Duncan's model moves into prediction. The decline in global energy per capita after 1979 was caused by population growth outstripping the very small annual increase in total energy resources. As the Hubbert curve peaks and other fossil fuels start running short, that decline goes into overdrive, because then you have a growing world population competing for slices of a shrinking pie. Follow the curve, and by 2030 or so, global energy per capita is where it was in 1930, around a third of its 1979 value. Duncan argues that the industrial age is what engineers call a *pulse waveform*, a single, bell-shaped, nonrepeating curve. Since renewable energy resources can provide only a fraction of the fantastic amounts of energy we're squandering right now, Duncan predicts that the thousands of years of low-tech cultures before the industrial pulse, when nobody knew about all the free energy locked up in fossil fuels, will be balanced by thousands of years of low-tech cultures after the industrial pulse, when the treasure will be gone forever.

If Duncan's right, in other words, you can kiss your Star Trek future goodbye. What he's saying is that the future we've got coming our way isn't the sort of vista of endless progress our national religion promises. It's a slow and difficult return to the world as it was before 1750, a world dependent on renewable energy and the ordinary cycles of Nature, where Sun, Wind, Water, and muscle provide the energy to do whatever is going to get done.

But at this point, we're deep into taboo territory. The idea that progress can give way to regress, seriously, over the long term, is something most people in today's industrial cultures can't grasp at all. It's not even forbidden; it's unthinkable. Take a moment to try to fit your head around it, and see if you can. Imagine industrial civilization winding down, most of our technologies gradually abandoned because nobody can afford to keep on shelling out the huge amounts of energy and raw materials needed to keep them in use, most of modern science turned into trivia because nobody has any use for subatomic physics or biochemical engineering anymore. Imagine crumbling nation-states and resurgent local cultures burning through the last reserves of fossil fuels to cushion the way down into a new Middle Ages, as most people return to subsistence farming, craft work, or manual labor to support themselves, and what's left of the intellectual class tries to market its knowledge to anyone who will keep it fed and clothed. Imagine the footprints on the Moon fading into legend. Imagine the stars forever out of reach.

What's your reaction to that vision of the future? That it can't possibly happen? That somebody, somewhere, someday, will somehow manage to get progress moving again? That there's no way the world can become what it was for ten thousand years before 1750? That's how a lot of people react. That's why I call the belief in progress a religion, our established religion, the dominant faith of the Age of Exuberance. People believe it at a gut level; they don't reason about it. To suggest to most people nowadays that progress was a temporary condition caused by a 250-year glut of fossil fuels is like suggesting to a medieval peasant that the Sun doesn't move around the Earth.

That's the power of myth. Myths are the stories we tell ourselves to give meaning to the world, and when myth and reality part company too far, the world becomes meaningless and people go crazy. In case you haven't noticed, the world is pretty crazy right now. Duncan's numbers may be the reason why. According to White's Law, which again is one of the basic rules of human ecology, we haven't been progressing since 1979, and people have had to avoid noticing that, to look away from the broken taboo.

That craziness is one of the things that makes politics so toxic right now. All the power centers and voting blocs that make up our allegedly two-party system are committed to the religion of progress. Every candidate stumps for votes by saying that he can create jobs, bring prosperity, get economic growth back on track, and so on. Of course, none of them can do any of it, and if you correct for the real rate of inflation and take out the effect of a half dozen speculative bubbles, the American economy has been contracting steadily since 1979—curious coincidence, that. But that's what everyone wants to hear, and when it doesn't happen people start looking for scapegoats. Everyone has a different scapegoat. To the right, it's the left. To the left, it's the right. Or it's the Arabs, or the environmentalists, or the big corporations, or the rascals in power, or the rascals out of power—you name it, someone's pointing a finger.

And we get angrier and angrier. Listen to the tone of political dialogue these days—well, actually it's inaccurate to call it political dialogue; it's not a dialogue when everyone's shouting so much nobody can hear what anyone else is saying. Self-righteous anger and a passion for finding scapegoats is a bad recipe for a constructive future, but it's common enough when a myth is coming apart at the seams.

Our problem is that we're stuck in politics, and what we need is metapolitics. What do I mean by that? Politics literally means community affairs; *polis* is Greek for community, *politike* is what pertains to the community, community affairs. You can't have politics if you don't have a community, which is to say that you can't have politics unless you have a functioning, shared myth, because that's what makes a community. People become a community when they tell the same story to themselves and each other, when they give the world a meaning in a common way.

Metapolitics is what happens when you don't have a common myth. It's the process of making a new myth—weaving it by consensus, imposing it by force, or anything in between. Think of it as the politics of reality. Where ordinary politics deals with who makes the decisions, who gets the benefits, who pays the costs, metapolitics deals with what's meaningful, what's possible, what exists to make decisions about in the first place. Outside the United States, the entire twentieth century was a bare-knuckle, no holds barred metapolitical brawl, and it's not over yet. Inside the United States, we've had two big outbreaks of metapolitics, one right after the First World War and one in the 1960s, but, in both cases, the forces of the status quo managed to marginalize the alternatives. Maybe you've noticed that America doesn't seem to inhabit the same planet as the rest of the world; that's a measure of the gap between the old myth our country is still clinging to, and the new myths that are surging to life in the wild world outside our borders.

The idea of metapolitics is the klieg light we need to illuminate something I've already mentioned, the Scientific Revolution—the turning point that launched us on our 250-year binge of progress. Look past the mythology we all got in school and it becomes the final move in one of the great metapolitical struggles of all time, the reality wars of the Renaissance. From 1463, when the great Italian scholar Marsilio Ficino translated an old book of magic called the *Corpus Hermeticum* and blew the hinges off the old world of the Middle Ages, to 1661, when the founding of the Royal Society in England set the seal on the triumph of the new scientific worldview, everything was up for grabs.

The same schoolroom mythology we've already discussed presents the Renaissance as a face-off between heroic early scientists and the powers of superstitious obscurantism, but that's a partisan view and a simpleminded one at that. Renaissance Europe was a boiling cauldron of myths, of alternative visions of reality. One of them won the metapolitical struggle, and that's the one that's cracking around us today. The taboo on magic I mentioned a little while back came out of that process. In fact, it was essential to that process, because there's a skeleton in the closet of the Scientific Revolution, and it wears a tall pointy hat covered with moons and stars.

The hard fact is that some of the most important figures of the Scientific Revolution were occultists. Isaac Newton, who was the poster child of the new science in the late seventeenth century, practiced alchemy and studied the Cabala. Robert Hooke, the founder of modern chemistry, was an alchemist. Sir Robert Moray, the Scottish Freemason who did more than anyone else to found the Royal Society and get it supported by the English government, was basically a wizard—there wasn't much in the way of Renaissance magic he didn't at least dabble in. And the list goes on. These men who supposedly abandoned magic and superstition for science were practicing magic while they were kickstarting the Scientific Revolution.

Look a little further back in the history of early science and things get even weirder. The first detailed account of the scientific method is in a book by John Dee, Queen Elizabeth's court astrologer and one of the most accomplished sorcerers of his time. Until the seventeenth century, in fact, if you look for scientists what you mostly find are wizards who included science and technology as part of their bag of tricks.

That's the skeleton in the lab closet of science. Science and magic weren't two different things until after the Scientific Revolution. Science was part of magic, one particular branch of it, what John Dee called archemastry: the art of figuring out what powers natural things had in themselves, and using them to accomplish marvelous things. Already in the Middle Ages people had been talking about what this sort of natural magic could do, given half a chance; the alchemist Roger Bacon back in the thirteenth century wrote about wagons that could go by themselves without oxen to pull them, boats that could sail underwater, craft that could fly through the air. That's how the founders and publicists of the Scientific Revolution sold the new science: this is the real magic, this is the stuff that will actually do what magic has claimed to do for all these years. That was one of their big weapons in the metapolitics of the time. And of course, you see that same rhetoric today, right up to the kid actor in the Harry Potter movie with his Industrial Light and Magic incantations.

But that rhetoric, that set of claims, involved a massive misrepresentation of what magic is about. I've avoided giving a definition of magic so far, and I'll keep on avoiding it for a little while yet. But archemastry was only one branch of magic, one of the tools in the operative magician's toolkit. It wasn't the whole thing, not by a long shot. And the sort of archemastry that Newton and Boyle were pioneering, and their scientific successors have done ever since, was not the sort of archemastry that John Dee would have recognized. There's a major difference, and the difference, curiously enough, is ethical.

Magic has its own traditional ethics. You'll find them discussed in great detail in the old books, and in a lot of more recent books as well. The main ethical issue in magic isn't whether it helps people or hurts people, though you might think that if your main exposure to magic is via modern fantasy fiction. The main ethical issue in magic is the relation between the magician and the rest of the universe: in the language of magical philosophy, between the microcosm—the little universe, you and me—and the macrocosm, the big universe that surrounds us. In traditional magical ethics, good magic, the magic of light, is magic that takes the macrocosm into account. To practice the magic of light is to always keep an eye on how what you're doing affects the rest of the universe, and how the rest of the universe affects you.

The other kind of magic, what the old books call cacomagic, ignores the macrocosm. The ethical magician says, "How does this intention of mine affect the universe around me?" The unethical magician, the cacomagus, says "I want this, and that's the only thing that matters." Put another way, ethical magic is about participation in the dance of cosmic powers, while unethical magic is about manipulation, domination, control.

The kind of archemastry that became modern science is cacomagic. How does the scientific method work? You take something and isolate it, cut it off from the rest of the universe, and see what you can make it do. You control every variable but one, and then tweak that one until you get a response. That's why the number one scientific virtue is objectivity—which means the maximum possible distance between the experimenter and the experiment, the manipulator and the manipulated.

Our modern industrial system is cacomagic. We want what we want, and to hell with the rest of the universe. We've pumped a trillion barrels of oil out of the depths of the Earth, burnt most of it and turned the rest into plastic and asphalt, because we wanted to, and it never occurred to anyone until the last few decades that maybe we should think about how all that smoke and plastic and asphalt would affect the rest of the world—the world that we, along with all other living creatures, have to live in. And of course, that's the problem with cacomagic and the reason that the old books of magic warn over and over again that it's a very bad idea. What goes around comes around; you can only piss in your own bed so often before you end up having to sleep in a wet spot. That's one of the fundamental laws of magic, by the way, though the old books usually put it in a more genteel language.

Now there's another detail about cacomagic, and that's one of the few things the fantasy writers get right. True magic, the magic of light, empowers everyone and everything it touches because when you participate in the dance of cosmic energies the energies flow more freely, the whole world becomes a little more luminous. Cacomagic empowers the cacomagus and nobody else. Actually, in the long run, it doesn't even empower the cacomagus. He becomes a tool in the hands of his own distorted desires and the machinery he builds to fulfill them. But it's the lure of exclusive power—the lure of domination and control, of having power yourself by taking it from everyone else—that tempts people down that path. That's another dimension of cacomagic that's present and accounted for in modern science and the industrial system. For all the talk about science and technology empowering people, notice that you and I don't actually get more power; the machines get more power and the people who own them get more power. And you and I? We get to share in a little bit of that power, in exchange for giving up something else. Usually a lot of something else.

Back in the 1960s, there was a group of radical philosophers in France called the Situationists, who paid a lot of attention to issues like this. They argued that the way the system works is that people are lured into giving up their own abilities and talents and potential, so they could be convinced to buy shoddy technological imitations of those abilities and talents and potentials at an inflated price. It's a powerful analysis, and it cuts to the core of what I'm exploring here. Look anywhere in a modern industrial country and you'll see this sort of bait and switch at work. Instead of learning how to bake bread, we buy bread machines. Instead of learning how to use our memory, we buy palm pilots. Instead of using our own imaginations we turn on the TV. We live in a pros-thetic society, where the technology that surrounds us doesn't give us anything we don't have already; it just replaces our own power with a power we can only get by obeying. We become cogs in the machine—and so do the people who own the machines.

That's the trap of cacomagic; the cacomagus gets sucked into his own spell, he becomes just another cog in his own machinery. Tell a story often enough, and you end up believing it yourself. If it's a story that heals and empowers, you gain by it. If it's a story that controls and dominates—well, you do the math.

That's a definition of magic, by the way. Magic is a kind of storytell-ing. The magus tells a story, to herself or to other people, and tells it so powerfully, so seductively, that the listeners are drawn out of the stories they're used to, and become characters in the new story. It becomes their story, and the meaning it gives to their world *becomes* their world. The difference between true magic and cacomagic is that the true magus, the practitioner of the magic of light, tells a story that's always at least a little about learning how to tell stories because that's the story the true magus is always telling herself. That's the story of magical initia-tion, the story of how you learn to tell stories. But the cacomagus tells a story that's always at least a little about losing the ability to tell stories, about being dominated and controlled by stories, because he wants his listeners to be snared in his story and lose the ability to tell different stories of their own. And that's why he ends up getting sucked into his own story and trapped there alongside his victims.

There's a little more to it than that because the magic of light is always about finding the power within the self. I talked a moment ago about the Situationists and their analysis of the system. To the magus of light, the first place to look for a solution to any problem is within the self. Instead of buying a bread machine, learn to bake bread—and learn to take part in the dance of it, sharing in the life of grain and yeast and water, until what comes out of the oven isn't simply a lump of food but a work of alchemy. Instead of hauling around a palm pilot, learn how to remember. There's an entire branch of magic called the Art of Memory; it starts with a set of very subtle, powerful techniques for using the memory effectively, and went from there to grasp what memory is and how its powers can be used to shape and reshape the universe of our experience. That's how true magic works. And that's something we're going to need very badly as we slide down the back slope of the Hubbert curve because the powers and potentials that are inside us don't need petrochemicals; they don't need to be plugged in. In an age of technological regress, human skills trump machines because they don't have to be plugged in or gassed up. Do you remember Frank Herbert's grand ecological science fiction novel *Dune*, with its Mentats and Bene Gesserit witches, people who mastered human potential in a way that we can barely imagine? That's the shape of our future.

That's the weakness of cacomagic. Cacomagic turns away from the self and looks for tools, and inevitably the cacomagus becomes the slave of his tools. That's the lesson hidden in the old story of Doctor Faustus, the guy who bargained with demons for seven years of absolute power. Faustus would have been fine if he'd relied on his own power; everything he wanted was already inside himself. But he didn't see it that way. He wanted to dominate, not to participate, and the demonic powers of his own pride and fear and craving finally turned on him and devoured him. The cacomagi of industry have done exactly the same thing, and the demons are showing up on schedule: demons named climate change, energy shortages, economic decline, and war.

That's why true magic, the magic of light, is so crucial nowadays. The founders and early publicists of the Scientific Revolution knew what they were doing. They had excellent intentions—cacomagi very often have good intentions at first. They wanted to give humanity power over Nature, take the old dreams of wagons that went without oxen and boats that didn't need sails and make them a reality, banish hunger and disease and so on. All they had to do was take that one little step, stop worrying about the big picture—after all, they said, questions about the big picture are for theologians to bicker about—and get down to the business of making Nature obey them so that humanity could progress. It was a very seductive story, that story of progress—so seductive that the people who came after them never realized it was a story, never imagined that things had ever been any other way. And the founders of the Scientific Revolution did their level best to make sure people never imagined the world in a different way by slamming the door on the old magical traditions that taught people how to tell their own stories, how to join the dance of living powers and find new meanings for the world.

They could never quite get rid of magic. One of these days we may all realize how much we owe to that. They could force it underground, make magic one of the biggest taboos in the Western world, create a world where even today believing in the reality of magic is listed in DSM-IV, the standard psychological diagnostic handbook, as prima facie evidence that you're stark staring nuts. They couldn't get rid of it, because the coming of the Scientific Revolution was also the beginning of the golden age of secret societies in the Western world, and that's where the old magic stayed alive.

Now, of course, that's not the story you hear on talk radio, and it's not the story you read in the books you'll find in your average American bookstore. No, the story you get there is that secret societies are responsible for just about everything that's wrong with the world. They're out to take over the world, or they already control the world, or both at once—I've never quite been sure how that works; read the current literature on the New World Order and see if you can figure it out. And somehow it never occurs to anyone to ask why, if secret societies are so powerful and so malevolent, people who denounce them get million-dollar contracts from big publishing houses, and hours of airtime on corporate radio stations. And when's the last time you saw something positive about secret societies in the mass media?

But people don't ask those questions, because secret societies are the scapegoat du jour. Remember what I said earlier, about people turning to scapegoats when their myths break down? For the last hundred years, secret societies have been prime fodder for that process. There's a huge amount of money to be made by spreading weird claims about secret societies, and the weirder it gets, the more money rolls in. In the process, the fairly modest reality of the Western world's secret societies has been stretched and twisted like saltwater taffy when it hasn't been papered over with sheer fantasy.

Now, I have to admit to a personal bias on this subject. I'm a 32nd degree Freemason, and I belong to several other secret societies as well. According to some people these days, that makes me an evil space lizard from another dimension who's only pretending to be human. Does anyone else remember a TV show from the early 80s called "V", with reptiles from space who dressed up in human masks and red jumpsuits and took over the world? That's a very popular idea of reality in some circles these days, and according to those circles, Freemasons are all evil space lizards.

Actually, you'd be amazed how many details of contemporary conspiracy theory were lifted from movies and TV. When a myth breaks apart, people start clutching at any story they can find. When the mythology of German invincibility broke down in 1918, a lot of Germans ended up clutching at ugly old antisemitic myths from the Middle Ages, as retailed by a crackpot with a Charlie Chaplin mustache named Adolf Hitler. We've seen where that leads. There are some uncomfortable parallels to the present case, since Hitler's favorite antisemitic screed—a forgery called *The Protocols of the Elders of Zion*, which was whipped up by the Russian secret police in the 1890s—is being reprinted again in current conspiracy literature.

But behind the scapegoating and the recycled science fiction movies is a reality almost nobody outside the surviving secret societies knows anymore. Just before the Scientific Revolution took off, people interested in the old magic started to join the old builder's guilds, or as they called themselves, lodges of Freemasons. That wasn't as strange as it sounds. The builder's guilds were the people who made the Gothic cathedrals; they understood quite a bit about symbolism and sacred geometry—they had to, it was part of their trade. They preserved that when everyone else abandoned it. And because it kept the old traditions more or less intact, and because the old tradition of not talking about lodge business outside of lodge made it a safe zone for people with unpopular opinions, that's where a very large number of men who were interested in magic ended up over the next 350 years.

Then, once people figured out how the lodge system worked, how to write new initiation rituals, and what were the best ways to pass on magical teachings in a lodge setting, new secret societies started to appear, offering instruction in different systems of magic, alchemy, all the old occult sciences. Well, actually, new secret societies started springing up for every purpose you can imagine. In 1920, there were more than 3,500 different, independent secret societies in the United States alone, and half the adult population of the country belonged to at least one secret society. In the Western world as a whole, there were maybe ten thousand, maybe more. I spent most of a year writing an encyclopedia of secret societies almost a thousand pages long, and, even so, I could only cover the most important ones. There were political secret societies, fraternal secret societies, ethnic secret societies, religious secret societies, you name it.

We can talk about those some other time. The point that needs making here is that the secret societies were a place where different stories got told. Not all of them were empowering stories; not all magical orders kept to the magic of light, and some of the nonmagical secret societies slid into various abuses of their own, but a surprising number of secret societies of all kinds, and some of the most popular and influential, stayed true to their ideals. Once the lodge doors click shut, you can let go of the official story; you can tell a different story. If you're a Freemason you can say, "I am not just a consumer, an employee, a cog in the machine. I am a builder, heir to the great builders of the cathedrals, and what I am building is myself." And if you're an initiate of the Golden Dawn or some other magical secret society, you can say, "I am becoming a storyteller, and I know that there's more than one story in the world—I know that there's more than one story I can tell."

Both of those are stories the world needs very badly right now; because the old story, the grand mythology of progress, is cracking apart around us. Magic is everywhere, like sex and death, and we can either embrace it—embrace our power to tell a new story, to take part in the dance of living powers that weaves creation into being—or we can run away from it, and cling to the old myth until it drags us down with it.

Do you need to belong to a secret society in order to learn how to tell stories—or in less metaphoric language, to learn how to work magic? Of course not. Do you need to study the old traditional magic? No. I've chosen both of those, made them central to my own life, and made a career about writing and teaching about them; that's my path, and in the language of a very different school of mysticism, it's a path with heart. But there are plenty of other options. Any path that teaches people to look within themselves for the power to change the world, instead of surrendering their own power to the machine, is a path with heart; it's a path through the present crisis toward the new world that, like it or not, we're all going to live in—and that we might as well start building now.

CHAPTER SEVEN

Alchemical initiation

For more than a quarter century now I've been a student of the
Western mystery tradition, and like many of you, I'm sure, I've
pursued my studies through a variety of initiatory orders and traditions. That's had certain advantages—besides filling my ritual closet
with a good collection of funny hats, that is. Just as it's easier to figure
out the shape of a mountain when you look at it from several different
angles, there are dimensions of the Mysteries that can best be understood when they're approached by more than one path.

The old parable of the blind men and the elephant has a special relevance for those of us who try to follow the path of the mysteries in the
modern world. To borrow a phrase from Plato, the Mysteries in their
totality are a pattern laid up in heaven. What we have down here in the
sphere of Malkuth, the world of manifestation in matter, consists of scattered glimpses and reflections of a unity that none of us, no matter how
highly initiated we are, can grasp as a whole. Each tradition, each mystery school, and indeed each student of the esoteric traditions weaves
together a collection of glimpses and reflections into something that
works, some set of practices and concepts that gets the feet of the Seeker
solidly placed onto the path of the Mysteries—a path that ultimately is
different for every person who travels it all the way to its end.

129

Making sense of the traditions we've inherited, in other words, requires a wider vision, and that's not always the easiest thing to achieve. In most dimensions of the mystery teachings, the main obstacle these days is a profoundly debased idea of what esoteric study and practice can accomplish, a debasement that has its root in the rejection of the Mysteries by the triumphant materialism of the Scientific Revolution, and the adoption of that materialism as the established religion of the modern world.

We've all seen high magic prostituted into cheap sorcery; we've all seen the oracles of the gods—that's what the word "divination" literally means, after all—turned into a confidence trick or a party game for the entertainment of the perpetually bored middle classes. I suspect most of us have been at our share of rituals where the participants would most likely have wet themselves right there in the circle if the powers they were invoking actually bothered to show up. The debasement factor has also played a role in obscuring the possibilities of alchemy, but there's at least one more factor at work—a widespread confusion about just what alchemy is.

For quite a while now, since Jung made it possible for modern people to mention the word "alchemy" in polite company, students of alchemy have been squabbling over this point. You can still find plenty of people who buy into the conventional wisdom of modern materialism, and insist that alchemy was the rightly discarded predecessor of modern chemistry that, because it was burdened with all kinds of irrational beliefs about the nature of matter, wasted centuries in a foredoomed attempt to turn lead into gold by inadequate means. You can find plenty of people who have adopted a simpleminded misinterpretation of Jung's take on alchemy and see alchemy as a primitive form of depth psychology which the alchemists themselves, through sheer lack of psychological sophistication, mistakenly projected onto the contents of their retorts and alembics—and of course these two groups quarrel with one another constantly.

Move out from the materialist mainstream into the fringe areas of contemporary culture, where most of the people who actually practice alchemy these days find their natural home, and the disagreements multiply as enthusiastically as rabbits. We've got our spagyrists, who use alchemical methods to extract healing substances from plants and minerals—there are some who dabble in the opus animalis, but most of those keep noticeably quiet about it. We've got our practitioners of the old alchemy of metals, for whom lead is lead, gold is gold, and turning one into the other by way of the confection of the Red Tincture—or some particular operation at the very least—is the name of the game.

Then we've got our practitioners of sexual alchemy, who take the cohabitation of the Red King and the White Queen a little more literally than most of the rest of us do. We've got our practitioners of psychedelic alchemy, for whom alchemy involves taking large doses of mind-altering substances and surfing the resulting trips. We've got our practitioners of internal alchemy, for whom it involves disciplines that circulate currents of subtle energy within the body—most of those come out of the East Asian alchemical traditions, but by no means all. We've got people for whom alchemy is a method of psychological transformation and healing, whether via a Jungian approach or some other. We've got people who follow Jakob Böhme's lead and practice an alchemical mysticism in which the one matter, one vessel, and one fire of the old alchemical texts are all aspects of the soul, and the philosopher's stone is the unio mystica in which the soul dissolves in God—and these are just a sample of what's out there.

It's still fairly common to hear practitioners of one kind of alchemy insist that other kinds aren't real alchemy. One of the orders in which I've received initiation is called the Order of Spiritual Alchemy; it was founded back in the 1920s, though it draws on older sources; it teaches a system of inner work that starts by clearing away emotional and psychological messes and works up from there into a path of Hermetic alchemical mysticism. It still fields hate mail now and then from people who do some other kind of alchemy and insist that because the OSA doesn't use the same definition of alchemy they do, it must be a bunch of frauds.

All this is rooted in what philosophers call a category error. It starts from the assumption that alchemy is a single discipline, equivalent to, say, chemistry, or psychology, or mysticism. Yet, if we take a hard look at the surviving literature on alchemy from the Middle Ages and the Renaissance, that assumption can only be called a spectacular oversimplification. Most of the forms of alchemy I've just listed can be found solidly documented in alchemical writings from the days when alchemy was in flower, and any interpretation of alchemy that fails to embrace the whole spectrum of alchemical work gives a misleading picture of the tradition.

The alchemy of minerals and metals, to begin with, was clearly a major branch of the tradition, but even there it covered more ground than many modern interpretations ever get around to noticing. The

Great Work of confecting the philosopher's stone was central to mineral alchemy, but there again it wasn't the only game in town. There were also, at least in theory, particular operations that turned a fixed quantity of base metals into silver or gold without yielding the Stone of the Wise; there were also processes to turn ordinary stones into gems and to make a form of glass that was flexible and malleable.

Spagyric alchemy, the art of creating alchemical medicines from natural substances, is also very solidly documented, and, of course, it's still very much practiced today. Closely allied to it were medical traditions, Galenic and Paracelsian, that understood the living body in alchemical terms and embraced anatomy, physiology, diagnosis, and treatment, using diet, exercise, and lifestyle issues as well as spagyric medicines to free the body from the waste products and imbalances that cause disease.

But the list doesn't stop there. Even in the modern alchemical community, for example, not too many people realize that alchemical agriculture was once a very well-developed system. Adam McLean's late and much-lamented *Hermetic Journal* in one of its later issues published a very good alchemical recipe for organic fertilizer. Look in Kirchweger's *Aurea Catena Homeri* and you'll find the theory to match, a very canny analysis of what we'd now call nutrient cycles, in which the cyclical interplay of niter and salt makes a great deal of sense of the way chemical nutrients from the atmosphere and the soil work together to foster plant growth.

These similarities to current ecological thought aren't accidental, by the way. If you trace the history of the modern science of ecology you'll find that it has its roots in the German *Naturphilosophie* movement of the eighteenth century, and that evolved out of exactly the same late alchemical traditions that Kirchweger or, say, Michael Sendivogius exemplify so well. When the old alchemists talk about harmony with Nature, in other words, there's a reason they sound like members of some Renaissance version of the Green Party.

Alchemical practice is also well documented in the arts and crafts. I think most of you have heard of the astonishing red and blue stained glass of medieval Gothic cathedrals, which can't be duplicated by any method known to modern chemists. René Schwaller de Lubicz used to insist that the medieval glassmakers did it by infusing the spirit of metals directly into the glass, and since he could duplicate it, I'm inclined to think he knew what he was talking about. The Renaissance Italian artist and writer Giorgio Vasari wouldn't have argued; in his handbook of art technique, the best surviving source on the actual methods used by Renaissance painters, he's constantly mentioning that you can get this pigment or that medium from your local alchemist.

Those artists and craftspersons in need of a little liquid inspiration could also rely on alchemy—there's an elegant little late medieval English alchemical text called *The Boke of the Quintessence*, which gives a very fine alchemical recipe for distilling your own booze. I'm not sure how many moonshiners back in West Virginia know that they're part of the alchemical tradition, but there you are. Once you're sufficiently befuddled on their fine product, you might try a shot of the alchemical economics of Renaissance intellectuals like Gerrard Winstanley, the chief theoretician of the Diggers during the English Civil War, who used the language and ideas of alchemy to make sense of the circulation of wealth and authority in society.

The spiritual dimension is also very solidly documented in the old alchemical literature. Read Jakob Böhme or the early Rosicrucians and you'll find that they make it very clear that the gold they manufacture counts as currency only in the bank of heaven. As the *Fama Fraternitatis* says, the Rosicrucian alchemist rejoices not because he can make gold, but because he sees the heavens open, the angels ascending and descending, and his name written in the Book of Life. Along these same lines, you can find the alchemical interpretation of Christian theology, in which Christ is the transmuting Stone of the Wise and the Last Judgment takes the form of an act of calcination in which the world will be purified from its dross by fire and transformed into the crystal stone of the New Jerusalem.

All this is confusing enough if you want to insist that alchemy is a single field of study and practice, like chemistry, or psychology, or mysticism. But it gets worse because there are also traditional alchemical works that use two or more of these fields to make sense of one another. The DOMA manuscript, a Rosicrucian document from the late seventeenth century that the late and great Manly Palmer Hall reprinted a while back, is the poster child here. The DOMA manuscript is about metallic alchemy, and it's also about Christian Rosicrucian mysticism; it proposes that the process that leads the unregenerate soul to salvation is exactly parallel, point for point, with the process that transmutes the prima materia into the philosopher's stone. From the metaphysical theory, the manuscript says, flows the physical practice—and in the process, that flow sweeps away any last justification for the common but mistaken claim that alchemy is about one specific field of theory and practice.

That's the category error. Alchemy isn't a specific field of study like chemistry, or psychology, or mysticism. It's a universal method, like science. The parallels between alchemy and science are exact. Just as there's a scientific method, there's an alchemical method: *solve et coagula*: find the prima materia, separate it gently into its components, the subtle from the gross; purify and transform them in their separated condition; then reunite them to produce something with the properties of the original at a higher level of vibration. Just as you can apply the scientific method to just about anything and get a particular science, you can apply the alchemical method to just about anything and get a particular alchemy.

This realization has at least two advantages. The first is that we can get past the old and pointless quarrel about which of the particular alchemies I've listed is real alchemy; they all are; they all have a place in the broad toolkit of alchemical approaches to the cosmos. The second, though, is that if we're not stuck on the idea that real alchemy is about metals, or archetypes, or whatever else you prefer, we may just notice that there have been other alchemies going on all along that were never noticed as such.

That's what I intend to do this morning. As I mentioned earlier, my own pilgrimage into the Mysteries has taken me into, and occasionally out of, a variety of Western initiatory orders. There isn't necessarily a great deal of common ground among those orders; again, everybody has a different fragment of the whole system, and some of those fragments don't seem to have much to do with one another. Nearly all of these initiatory orders, however, share a specific set of practices centering on the art of initiation.

Now there's probably been more nonsense written about initiation than any other single subject in the field of occultism, with the possible exception of the lost continent of Atlantis. Plenty of occult entrepreneurs over the years have claimed that they've gotten the real thing straight from the Unseen Masters, and will pass it on to you for some very considerable chunk of change. Plenty of others have claimed that they've gotten the same thing from the same source, and won't give it to you— you just get to listen to their teachings for, again, some stratospheric fee. The inevitable backlash has had its own unproductive results, in the form of people insisting that rituals of initiation are a pompous waste of time and the whole thing ought to be chucked.

Behind all the hucksterism and hoopla, though, is an elegant and very carefully crafted toolkit for transforming individual consciousness. Some of the hammers and wrenches in that toolkit will likely be familiar to most everybody in this room; others may be a little less so, and so it might be useful just now to walk through the basic structure of a standard initiation ritual in the Western esoteric tradition and get some sense of what makes it tick. For the sake of clarity, we'll focus on the first initiation of any initiatory system; there are complexities later on in the process because the later degrees will riff off that first one in a variety of ways.

Let's start with the obvious. An occult lodge—there are a dizzying array of terms used for occult and non-occult lodges alike, but we'll stick with the basic label for now—is a part-time operation. Many occult teaching orders don't have the funds to afford their own buildings, and even those that do rarely have meetings more than once a week. The sort of constant flow of ritual and practice that you can find in an Asian monastery or an ancient temple is a very rare thing in Western occult circles, and that's been true for many centuries now. That imposed two requirements for initiatory lodges. First, they had to be able to use a fairly generic space for their purposes; second, they had to be able to turn that generic space into fully charged and activated sacred space in short order whenever they wanted to do an initiation or any other kind of ritual.

Those requirements had a profound impact on the structure of initiation, because people realized very quickly that the same processes that allow you to turn an empty lodge room into a magically charged sacred space in a single ritual working will also allow you to turn an ordinary candidate into a magically empowered initiate in a single ritual working. Thus, you'll find that in the great majority of initiation rituals in our Western tradition, the opening ritual for each degree has very close structural similarities to the initiation ritual of that degree.

This led the occult lodge tradition into very deep waters. I don't imagine I'll have to spend much time explaining to anybody in this room the Hermetic doctrine of macrocosm and microcosm, the mirroring of the universe in the individual human being and vice versa. What students of the occult lodge tradition realized, though, is that those are two terms of a three-term relationship. Between the macrocosm and the microcosm, the universe and the individual, stands the mesocosm—literally, the middle universe—which reflects both the macrocosm and the microcosm. That's what the lodge becomes when it's ritually opened. It's a mirror of the macrocosm, representing the entire universe in miniature. It's also a mirror of the microcosm, representing every aspect of the individual in expanded form.

The advantage there is the advantage you always get in magic by moving from a twofold to a threefold relationship. Put any two things in relationship with one another and they polarize; they become a pair of opposites; and that opposition, that polarization, fixes the volatile. If you want to go on and build on that foundation, you have to bring in a third factor. It's with the triad, Binah the Great Mother, that creation happens. In the same way, macrocosm and microcosm can polarize one another, but there's always the risk of fixation, of stuckness. Bring in the mesocosm and things start to move; having fixed the volatile, you volatilize the fixed, and transmutation becomes possible on many different levels.

Now, this actually happens in any form of magical work. One of the great discoveries that came out of the evolution of the occult lodge tradition is precisely that occult adepts had been working with mesocosms all along. Consider the early modern sorcerer in his magic circle, blasting trident in one hand and grimoire in the other, conjuring the demons of the pit by the mighty names of God. The magic circle is a mesocosm; it represents the entire universe in symbolic form, with its four-quarters, its divine names and the working tools of the art representing the powers of the cosmos, and chaos and old night pressing close around the periphery; it also represents the sorcerer himself, the four-quarters and innate powers of his own body, mind, and spirit.

This is how magic works. The macrocosm reflects the microcosm and vice versa, but when you create a mesocosm between them, reflection becomes a process that allows magical changes to occur. You start with the mesocosm reflecting the macrocosm and microcosm, but then the macrocosm and the microcosm reflect the mesocosm; when you change things in the mesocosm, the corresponding changes reflect outward to the macrocosm, and inward to the microcosm. You constellate a planetary influence, let's say the energies of Jupiter, in a talisman through a ritual in your magical mesocosm; that same calm expansive influence reflects in both directions and constellates itself in your inner and outer life. As between, so above, and so below. That's also the way initiation works, as we'll see shortly.

Now the first step in an initiation ritual is the preparation of the space, the formulation of the mesocosm on outer and inner levels alike. The vast majority of Western initiation rituals are designed to be performed in a completely generic space; if you've ever been inside anybody's lodge hall, from the Masons to the Elks to the Woodmen of the World to the Concatenated Order of Hoo-Hoo—and yes, that's a real order, by the way—you know the design. A rectangular space with chairs along the sides, a seat for the presiding officer on one end, a door, and an officer to guard it on the other, an anteroom outside, and an altar that can be put at the center of the space: that's the basic kit.

Everything that goes on in an initiation takes place in that setting. In some rituals—quite a few of them, in fact—you use the generic lodge hall as is, and the variation consists of the robes and ornaments of the officers, the altar furnishings and other symbolic items in the space, and the words and actions of the ritual. Sometimes you bring in additional furniture—anything from candlesticks to pillars to veils crossing the room to what have you. Sometimes you set up a smaller enclosed space—a chamber, a vault, the tomb of Hermes or Christian Rosycross—somewhere in the lodge hall, and the ritual focuses around it; but unless you've got a lodge with enough resources to afford a building of its own, and these are very much an exception, the whole kit and caboodle is designed to be set up before the ritual and taken down afterward.

You set up the space physically, and then you set it up ritually and energetically. The procedure here is pretty much fixed. The presiding officer makes sure that the doors are closed and everyone present is already an initiate; there's a litany recounting the symbolism of the degree and the names and duties of the officers; there's an invocation of whatever spiritual force presides over the working; then the lodge is formally declared open. Ritual designers have plugged almost every conceivable variation into this framework, but it still amounts to the same process. First, the mesocosm is set apart from the world around it; second, the symbolic patterns and stations are established and reinforced in the collective consciousness of the lodge and in the minds and wills of each person present; third, a spiritual force is called down into the waiting receptacle; finally, by an act of will the mesocosm is made complete and the work begins.

In an ordinary fraternal lodge, this is done in an entirely exoteric way. That can be powerful all by itself, because the symbolism and the psychological effectiveness of the ritual doesn't depend on the magical prowess of the initiators, and of course it also happens that people who've been doing lodge ritual for long enough end up practicing magic without ever quite realizing that that's what they're doing. I've been astonished more than once by the amount of magical steam some old men and women without a trace of occult training can build up when they're working a fraternal lodge ritual they love, and doing it for the three thousandth time.

In an occult lodge, though, you can do the same thing consciously, and bring whatever set of inner tools your tradition provides you to bear on the work of initiation. Remember that the lodge as mesocosm represents the universe, and it also represents the candidate. The presiding officer of the lodge represents the divine power presiding over the universe, and also represents the higher self or guardian angel of the candidate, the reflection of the divine in the sphere of the self. Each of the other officers of the lodge represents a different power of the cosmos and a different factor in the candidate's psyche. Each piece of lodge furnishing represents an aspect of the universe and of the self. When the officers take on their roles consciously and mediate the energies they represent, the initiation tends to have a much greater impact, and the more skilled they are at handling magical energies, the more pyrotechnic the results can be.

The lodge space itself also undergoes a transformation in this process, from a blank slate to a map of the cosmos and the self. Every traditional initiation ritual divides up the lodge hall into areas corresponding to different aspects of the universe, which are also different aspects of the candidate. For example, you might have the lodge divided up into five zones—there are the four material elements in the four-quarters and the element of spirit in the center. You might divide it into two zones of darkness and light, with the place of balance at the central altar. You might map the whole Cabalistic Tree of Life on it or some part of the Tree of Life. As the opening ritual proceeds, each section of the lodge room is charged with the appropriate energy; the officers begin mediating the appropriate forces; and you're ready to go.

It's interesting to note that from the candidate's side, the process of opening the lodge has a distinctive effect as well. This is especially important in the first initiation, the one that candidates receive at the very beginning of their initiatory career. While the lodge is being opened, the candidate is sitting out in the anteroom, or in a chamber of reflection not far away. She may be just sitting there, or there may be some subject for contemplation—it used to be very common to have something melodramatic like a skull, a candle and an open book on a black-draped altar. Corny though that sounds, it works; the candidate spends maybe five minutes thinking that it's corny, and then very often the mask of phony sophistication that we all get taught to wear in this society starts to slip, and it sinks in that the skull used to have some living person's brain in it, and the book and candle stop being props and start meaning something.

Even without that, the experience of sitting in the anteroom is a more important part of that first ritual of initiation than I used to think. Those of you who've been through traditional initiation ceremonies know what this is like. You're sitting there, waiting, and you can hear just enough going on in the echoing space on the far side of the door to know that something is happening there that you don't know about—yet. And it goes on, and on, and on, for what seems like an appreciable fraction of eternity, and just when you've started to wonder if they're going to get to the business of initiating you during this age of the world, somebody raps on the door and you jump out of your skin.

The point of this exercise in suspense is that it puts you in an altered state of consciousness. There's an old saying that Bulwer-Lytton quotes in *Zanoni*—"man's first initiation is in trance." As we've learned from some of the better hypnotherapists in recent years, that word "trance" covers a lot more territory than people used to think. It doesn't necessarily mean eyes rolling back in the head, saliva dribbling, and some entity named Tofu or something starts speaking through your lips. Any time you get sufficiently off center that the ego loses control over the structure of your experience, you're in one form or another of trance. It can be very subtle or very drastic, but one way or another, it's necessary in order for the process of initiation to work.

So your candidate has been sitting out in the chamber of preparation, looking at the skull, the candle, and the book, feeling nervous and excited and a little scared, and completely out of her element. Then somebody knocks on the door. Somebody blindfolds her and ties a cord around her, and the door opens. Unable to see a thing, guided by unknown hands into a space whose dimensions are a complete mystery, with voices coming out of darkness in various directions, the candidate loses her bearings completely. It's a very good way to get somebody into an altered state, and that's exactly the point.

Or part of the point, because one of the advantages of the lodge toolkit is that every part of it has many uses. Another aspect of those circumambulations in darkness and the candidate's encounters with the different lodge officers is that she's being given a guided tour of the mesocosm of the lodge, which of course amounts to a guided tour of the universe and of the inside of her own head. Each officer, remember, represents one of the great powers of the cosmos and one of the aspects of the initiate's own self, and the different sections of the lodge room are the different realms of the cosmos and the self. The speeches of the officers and the magical energies that impact her give her a set of handles for the reflections of the mesocosm in herself and the universe alike, and the blindfold and the other confusing factors make sure that she's not likely to be able to rationalize and discount the experience; the ego has been temporarily displaced from its job as doorkeeper of the soul, and the whole troop of divine archetypes comes marching in.

Finally, the long journey in darkness and confusion guarantees that whatever the candidate sees when the blindfold first comes off is going to be burnt into her mind and memory for keeps. Most rituals of initiation focus everything around that moment and the first couple of minutes afterward, when the receptive state of awareness is still at its peak. If you've got a well-designed ritual and competent lodge officers, you can raise the blindfold for just a moment, lower it again, and then go around the lodge room in darkness a few more times; then repeat the process one or more times, and finally take the blindfold off for good—but if you do that, the glimpses need to be short and disorienting, and the final scene when the blindfold finally goes away needs to be visually and dramatically powerful enough to make up for a less intense altered state.

One way or another, two things happen in the course of these journeys through the darkness, one before the blindfold comes off, and the other immediately afterward. What comes before is the taking of the obligations of initiation—the oath or promise that binds the initiate to keep the initiation secret, and to accept whatever other requirements the lodge places on initiates of that grade. Oaths of secrecy have come in for some rough handling in the occult community over the last century or so; Aleister Crowley made quite a famous fuss about his experience with the Golden Dawn Neophyte grade, where he pledged himself to secrecy with terrific oaths and then found himself entrusted with the Hebrew alphabet and the symbols of the planets.

Now to some extent, this was just Uncle Al blowing off steam. To some extent, it shows his own high opinion of himself; after all, it makes perfect sense for an initiatory order in possession of some serious magical chops to find out, before entrusting them to some brand-new initiate, if he can be trusted to keep his mouth shut about something a little less important. But there are deeper dimensions to the practice of secrecy. It's the exact equivalent of the sealing of the lodge at the beginning of the opening ritual; it defines a part of the universe of your experience as a separate reality, cut off from the collective consciousness of society as a whole—and since the collective consciousness of society as a whole is one of the main things you want to transcend if you want to follow the path of self-transformation, that's not a minor thing.

The irony here is that it doesn't matter what the secret is. It can be something completely bland, or completely silly. It can even be something that anybody can look up on the internet. It's not secret because it's important; it's important because, and only because, you keep it secret. Keeping your mouth shut about some silly password can become one of the most potent tools of self-discovery and self-discipline in the entire Western esoteric tradition because you can't keep a secret if you just let yourself drift on the tides of collective consciousness. You have to be aware of what you're saying and what you're not saying, and to whom. You establish a boundary and keep it, and, in the process, you learn how boundaries work, and how to keep yourself within due bounds even when the pressures of the passions, or the subconscious, or collective consciousness itself are trying to push you outside them. And the boundary of secrecy, the boundary that divides what you can talk about from what you can't, is the boundary of the mesocosm.

So the obligation is the first of the two things I mentioned a moment ago, the one that happens just before the blindfold comes off. The second, the one that happens right afterward, is the transmission of the password, grip, and sign of the degree. These have a very direct connection with the obligation of secrecy because they're the things that are most often kept secret. Here again, there are many levels. To some extent this is simply state of the art security technology from, oh, around the year 1600; you have to know these things to get into the lodge. But they're conferred right after the blindfold comes off, when the altered state of consciousness is at its height. Why? Because they're somatic keys to the ritual itself.

Remember that the candidate has been brought into the lodge in a receptive state, and a variety of things have been done to keep her in that receptive state. What is she receiving? The spiritual and energetic patterns that were created in the lodge in the opening ritual, and reinforced by the intensive inner work done by the members during the early sections of the initiation. With the ego knocked off kilter and unable to keep its usual grip on the structures of experience, those patterns reshape the way the candidate experiences her world and herself. When that experience is still at its height, the candidate gets a peculiar way of shaking hands, a set of strange gestures, and a word she's probably never going to encounter outside of a lodge setting.

Those are triggers for state-dependent memory. Every time she does the handshake, makes the gestures, and whispers the password, she's going to slip back at least a little into the mental and emotional state she was in at the peak of the initiation ceremony. So she's got the keys to the mesocosm. In any occult lodge worth its salt, she's taught how to use those keys in at least two ways. First, she's encouraged to attend initiations and other lodge activities in her grade, where she can get used to the opening and closing ceremonies, repeat the handshake, signs, and password on a regular basis, and reinforce her contact with the pattern of energy she's received. Second, she's taught some basic ritual that riffs off those energies in one way or another.

The resemblance may not be obvious. The basic ritual may work with the core energy pattern of the initiation without copying its forms, the way that the Lesser Ritual of the Pentagram borrows its cosmology from the Neophyte Grade without borrowing anything else from it; that was very traditional in the days when people took secrecy more seriously. In other cases, the initiate may be taught a simplified version of the opening and closing ritual and set to practice it daily. That has advantages, not least because anybody who seriously pursues the lodge's system of training ends up being able to open and close a full lodge in their sleep. But to each their own.

After the communication of the secrets of the grade, there's usually a bit more symbolic drama, and then in the standard type of first initiation, the candidate goes to a seat on the sidelines and gets lectured. This is partly because the lingering traces of the altered state of consciousness make this a good time to get important teachings firmly fixed in the candidate's head, and partly to talk her down from the altered state so she doesn't leave the lodge hall floating six inches off the ground. Finally, the lodge is closed, using a ritual that typically echoes the core elements of the opening ceremony.

Now let's stop and look at what's happened here. You've taken a candidate, an ordinary person who is suited for magical training and initiation but hasn't yet contacted the wellsprings of magical force in the macrocosm or the microcosm. You prepared the candidate for the process in various ways that open her to the effects of the initiation. You then placed the candidate in a sealed container and circulated her around the container, exposing her to different energies and influences in the process. You brought the process to its culmination, during which the candidate changes from one state of being to another—from candidate to initiate, from interested outsider to member of the lodge, and hopefully to a practitioner of occult disciplines as well. Then you cooled the container and the candidate back down before unsealing the container and proceeding from there.

That is to say, you've just performed an alchemical operation. By putting the candidate into a mild trance, you've done the *solve*—you've separated the ego just a bit from the rest of the self, so that change can take place, and you've used that separation to help the candidate project the contents of her own self onto the lodge officers for the duration of the ritual, so that each part of the self can speak its piece and come back together in a different way. Then, purified and consecrated, the candidate returns to something more like ordinary consciousness; you've done the *coagula*, and the end product is noticeably different from the beginning.

Alongside all the other alchemies, in other words, we need to make room for the art of initiatory alchemy. If alchemy is a universal method, as I suggested a little while ago, it can be applied to almost anything to produce a particular alchemical art. Now it's possible to take this as saying that the alchemical method can be applied to initiatory ritual, but that's actually not what I'm saying. What I'm saying is that it has already been done; that the initiation rituals that have come down to us in the Western mystery tradition are alchemical rituals, designed by people who knew their alchemy inside and out, and applied alchemical ways of thinking to older and less effective rituals to create the elegant toolkit of lodge ritual we have today.

To support that claim in historical terms it's going to be necessary to get into some potentially controversial territory, so I want to apologize in advance to anybody who takes offense at what's going to follow. The history of the Western esoteric tradition is a complex and emotionally loaded subject, not least because it used to be an essential bit of marketing for esoteric lodges to claim ancient roots. Quite a few modern traditions have inherited those claims, and it can be a wrench to admit that the family trees of our initiatory schools have roots about as steady as those of Birnam Wood. Still, it has to be faced, and there's much to be gained by facing it; in exchange for dreams of Egyptian mystery temples or what have you, we gain roots and filiations that can actually teach us something.

Here's an example. Earlier in this talk, I mentioned the Order of Spiritual Alchemy, one of the esoteric schools in which I've been initiated. It has a foundation legend that traces its origin back to medieval France in the twelfth century. It wasn't founded in medieval France in the twelfth century; it was founded in America in the early twentieth century, and if you really work at tracing its lineage back as far as possible you might just be able to get to late seventeenth-century traditions that emerged in response to the spiritual vacuum left by the triumph of rationalist materialism in the Western world at the time of the Scientific Revolution. It has a very specific toolkit of methods for transforming consciousness by applying alchemical principles to the emotions and the psychological dimensions of life. Those are very effective, but there's often much to be gained with a system like that by fleshing it out with parallel techniques from related systems.

If you look for related systems in twelfth-century France, though, you're going to look for a long time and find very little. Look instead for related systems in late nineteenth and early twentieth-century America and Great Britain and you've got your pick of dozens of closely related systems of inner work, with philosophies and practices that very closely complement the material you find in the OSA knowledge lectures. What you lose in bragging rights, in other words, you gain in access to resources that can add measurably to the breadth and intensity of your inner work.

The same is true across the board. The Golden Dawn system gains immeasurably once you recognize that its origins lie in the Victorian underworld of magical lodges that Ellic Howe chronicled so crabbily a few years back; you can follow any number of loose ends back to their sources and find yourself equipped with knowledge and skills that are forgotten today but that every Golden Dawn initiate already had, because they were universal in the British magical community of that time.

The system of magical lodge work we've inherited in the Western esoteric tradition is no different. In the usual way, it claims to date back to the dawn of Time, or more precisely to the mystery temples of ancient Egypt. Its actual origin is in seventeenth-century England, and its roots can be traced straight back to a single distinctive source: the Most Worshipful Brotherhood of Free and Accepted Masons, which started the seventeenth century as a medieval guild of stoneworkers and ended it as one of the weirdest hybrids in the history of esoteric spirituality, part gentlemen's club, part school of morality veiled in symbols, and part Hermetic initiatory school for those who have eyes to see.

It's not often realized that the rituals now practiced among the Freemasons are entirely a product of the seventeenth century. Before then, as you can find from the early Mason's catechisms, they were pretty much the standard sort of "brothering" ritual found in every craft guild in medieval Europe—you gather in an upstairs room at the local pub, bring the candidate in blindfolded, subject him to various forms of horseplay, then declare him a member, give him the secret password that keeps nonmembers from getting the guild's trade secrets, and expect him to buy drinks for everybody present. There were only two degrees, Apprentice and Fellow, and neither one of them were particularly inspiring in their original form.

But the Masons also had secrets of sacred geometry and esoteric symbolism that descended from the cathedral builders of the Middle Ages, and that made the horseplay and bar tab worth putting up with to the scholarly gentlemen who made their way into Masonry over the course of the seventeenth century. And it's interesting, to use no stronger word, that a good proportion of the first wave of these gentlemen were deeply involved in alchemy. One of the first known Accepted Masons in England, for example, was none other than Elias Ashmole, one of the greatest alchemists of his generation, a man whose collection of British alchemical literature brought Thomas Norton and George Ripley to the attention of alchemists across Europe. One of the first in Scotland was Sir Robert Moray, a capable alchemist and one of the most respected Hermeticists in the British Isles.

Now maybe it was a coincidence that within a generation of the time that these major figures in the alchemical community became part of Freemasonry, the noticeably crude rituals of the old stonemasons guild suddenly took a quantum leap in sophistication and depth, added a Master Masons degree packed to the bursting point with Hermetic symbolism, and evolved into something not far from the rituals we perform in the Craft today. Maybe—but I wouldn't bet on it. It seems a good deal more likely that the alchemical structure that runs through Masonic initiation got there because a group of well documented seventeenth-century alchemists put it there.

And once there, it spread into the rituals of every esoteric system in the Western world, for two good reasons. First, esotericism is pragmatic. It's not there to be decorative, or to preen itself on the purity of its family tree; it's there to accomplish things, to lead its initiates step by step along a path of transmutation to the fulfillment of the highest dimensions of human potential. Anything that helps that process along is fair game for an esoteric school, and accordingly one of the oldest and most deeply revered traditions in esotericism is the tradition of stealing anything that's not nailed down—and bringing a crowbar along for the things that *are* nailed down. So once Masonic initiation evolved into the pattern I've outlined, every other esoteric tradition in the Western world borrowed as much of it as suited their fancy.

And they could do this with great facility because until around 1950 or so, practically every male alchemist and occultist in the Western world had been initiated into Freemasonry, and a great many of the female alchemists and occultists had been initiated into either an order that borrowed these traditions of initiation from Freemasonry, or one of the schismatic offshoots of Freemasonry that admit women as well as men. A great many common features spread through the esoteric community by the same route. A lot of things that today's Hermeticists sometimes use to trace their traditions back to the dawn of Time actually show just how lively and creative the esoteric community was in the late nineteenth and early twentieth centuries when most of the systems we have today took shape.

So, we have an alchemy of initiation—an alchemy that centers on the magical empowerment and transmutation of the human individual through ritual means. It's not the be-all and end-all of alchemy, and, in fact, one of the consequences of seeing alchemy as a universal method rather than a particular science is that there is no be-all and end-all of alchemy. There are simply different alchemies, applying the same method to a different subject. Some alchemies may be more important from a given standpoint, but that judgment changes as standpoints change; alchemical fertilizer may not seem like a big deal if you're trying for the Great Work, but if you need to make sure there'll be meals on the table and the resources you have to hand are farm tools and a field, I promise you the alchemy of agriculture takes on quite a bit of importance.

The alchemy of initiation has traditionally been practiced in esoteric lodges, and that's still a wholly valid place to practice it. It can also be practiced individually, or by working groups outside a formal lodge structure; I've worked in all three contexts with good results. It can be combined with other forms of alchemy, and with other, non-alchemical forms of esoteric work—yes, there are several different methods in esotericism, all of them mutually compatible but each with its own strengths and particular applications. And all of them can be applied, must be applied, to the transformation of the individual self and the world in the great transitions of the present age, when the self and the world stand so much in need of the help that esoteric spirituality can bring.

CHAPTER EIGHT

Healing through the elements

As students of occult teachings in the twenty-first century, we all occupy something of a strange position in the long history of occultism. Most of us, perhaps all of us, have built our own personal work on teachings and traditions handed down from the past, and some of us are very proud of what we've inherited. At the same time, if we look back further into the past, it's clear that what we've inherited, unless it's of very recent vintage, is simply the collected fragments of something that was once much bigger, much more intricate, and capable of many more things than alchemists and occultists generally do today.

One way to get a sense of the differences I'm discussing is to compare what we have available in Western occultism with the body of knowledge available to esoteric spiritual traditions in other parts of the world. We'll take Taoism as an example since it's fairly well documented in Western languages these days. Like your common or garden-variety Western occultist—or at least those common and garden-variety Western occultists who have done their homework—a properly trained Taoist initiate has learned an abstruse system of mystical philosophy, at least one method of meditation, some magical rituals, some useful methods of divination, and a bit of alchemy.

So far, so good; the Taoist and the Western occultist are pretty much on a par. But this is where the Taoist shifts into overdrive and leaves the occultist in the dust because the list I've given barely touches the surface of the things the Taoist has to hand. To start with, the alchemy he's learning didn't have to be reconstructed from obscure texts; the teacher who taught it to him normally has a lineage going back to the T'ang dynasty or thereabouts. The Taoist also gets to learn systems of physical and energetic exercise—qigong and neigong—and those very often shade over into one or another style of gongfu, the Chinese martial arts—this can be the very subtle and philosophical kind, such as t'ai chi, or it can be the hard styles that teach you to kick the other guy's gonads out through the top of his skull. Taoism includes both, and even the soft styles are not as fluffy as Americans like to think, but that's a topic for another talk.

Feng-shui, the art of spatial arrangement, is another commonplace of Taoist study, and so is a range of religious rituals done for the community, more or less along the lines of the sacraments of Western faiths such as Christianity. Our Taoist also probably knows how to play at least one of the instruments used in the music for those rituals; yes, they're all set to music, and we're talking classical Chinese music here, very complex, formal, ornate stuff. Finally, he almost certainly spends a lot of time learning healing arts, and by this I don't simply mean that he knows a little bit of herbalism or some version of laying on of hands. He's likely studied acupuncture, acupressure, moxibustion, Chinese herbal medicine, massage, and also—and crucially—the very subtle and effective philosophy and theory of Chinese medicine, which allows him to make accurate diagnoses and prescribe the right treatment for ailments.

That sounds like a lot. Look at other traditions of esoteric spirituality, though, and you find the same sort of thing. Many of the older Sufi orders teach their own complex systems of healing and divination, and though they don't talk about it much, I've been told that the old astrological magic of the Brethren of Purity and the Picatrix still gets handed down privately by shaykhs to their more promising students. Tibetan Buddhism—gods, I don't even want to start talking about the stuff that Tibetan Buddhism has available; we'd be here all night. The Hindu tradition would keep us here even longer. Many shamanic traditions in tribal cultures, for that matter, have the same sort of extended knowledge base: it's not just a few chants, a few trance techniques, some funny mushrooms and away you go. Typically there's an extensive body of drumming and other music technique, lots of it, with the music theory to go with it; there's poetry, by which I don't mean the modern habit of vapid self-expression in free verse but rather an entire corpus of traditional poetry in formal verse that has to be memorized, and then recited during ritual performances; there's a lot of practical healing techniques, an encyclopedic knowledge of local plants, sacred geography of this world and a dozen or more otherworlds, and much more.

We used to have the equivalent in the Western esoteric traditions. We still have scraps of it. Still, "scraps" is the operative word. Compare Western occult medicine, for example, with traditional Chinese medicine; we've got a decent grasp of practical herbalism, some elegant spagyric methods, some techniques of energy healing, and a few other things, but there's so much more in the Chinese system and most of it has no surviving equivalents in our tradition.

That didn't happen by accident. As inheritors of the Western occult traditions in the modern age, we are basically picking up pieces after a catastrophe. The catastrophe was the Scientific Revolution: two hundred years, roughly speaking from 1650 to 1850, when the whole immense heritage of Western occultism that the Renaissance inherited and enriched was tossed into the dumpster to make room for newborn materialist science. The people who founded the modern occult movement—Eliphas Lévi, first of all; Blavatsky, of course; the adepts of the Golden Dawn, and their successors such as Dion Fortune and William Gray; the great French occultists of the same period, Josephin Péladan, Papus, St. Yves d'Alveydre, and so on; Central European adepti such as Franz Bardon; here in America, P. B. Randolph, William Walker Atkinson, Manly P. Hall, and others—were all engaged in an immense salvage operation. They went dumpster diving among the bare ruined choirs of the Renaissance, and what they salvaged is most of what we've had to go on ever since.

To borrow an image from the novelist John Crowley, it's as though some great machine of glass and gleaming bronze had been smashed to flinders and flung out into the streets to be trampled by passersby, and the occultists of today are picking the fragments out of the gutter and trying to piece them together without benefit of blueprints or even, in many cases, a clear idea of what the machine looked like or what its purpose was. Much of the difference between occult schools is simply that they've gotten different pieces, and very often gotten them working, but then mistaken that part for the whole. It's understandable; the whole machine is so much bigger than any of the pieces, and so much more complicated, that the imagination staggers beneath the effort of trying to envision it all.

Now, I don't propose to offer a glimpse at the whole; I think we're still a couple of centuries of hard work away from even being able to make an attempt at that, though we're getting a very good idea of how some of the parts work and the principles of one or two of the main assemblies may well be within our grasp. The last few decades have seen some very promising work; alchemical studies have taken a major leap forward, and every year, primary sources that people would have killed to get a century ago show up on the bookshelves. We've still got a long way to go, but every time somebody pulls something new out of the wreckage, rinses away the muck, and starts the process of figuring out how it works, we make progress.

That's what I'm hoping to do today. I'd like to discuss one of the parts that has gone unnoticed by most of the occult dumpster divers of the last century and a half. It's specifically one of the bits that I mentioned a moment ago when comparing traditional Chinese medicine to what's left of the old Western magical art of healing: the core of the system, the philosophy, and theory that underlies all the different practical techniques. The irony, and it's a rich one, is that I've heard—I think many of us have heard—occult healers and Western herbalists bewailing the absence of such a philosophy and theory. If only we had something like the Chinese system of yin and yang and the five elements, or the tridosha, the three principles of Ayurveda!

This is why occultists need to learn more about their own history. Their real history, not the pseudohistorical mythology full of untraceable Fraulein Sprengels and identical third-degree grandmothers churned out by some granny factory in the New Forest, and secret teachings dating back unchanged to the mystery temples of Egypt that just happen to quote Aleister Crowley on every other page. You still hear people insisting that the word "Tarot" comes from the Egyptian *tar rosh*, "royal road," even though *tar* and *rosh* aren't Egyptian words at all and the Egyptian for "royal road" is *w3t nesw*.

For that matter, you still hear people insisting that the Tarot comes from ancient Egypt, even though Italian art historians showed decades ago that it was invented in Milan between 1414 and 1418 by Marziano da Tortona, secretary to the Duke of Milan. That matters, too, because once you ditch the fantasies about Egypt and Fez and ancient Atlantis and realize that we're dealing with one of the great creative products of the Italian Renaissance, the deck's images are put back into their original context; you can see how they relate to the Renaissance Art of Memory, traditions of emblems and images, and the rich philosophical background of Renaissance Neoplatonism, all of which had a potent influence on the design and use of the deck and adds immeasurable richness to the work you can do with it.

We're in exactly the same situation with healing. We don't have to come up with some pastiche of modern notions about health and claim that it's been handed down by a long line of sea priestesses from ancient Atlantis—though somebody will probably do that anyway, and make a medium sized fortune in the process; it's always a lucrative racket to teach people what they already believe under the pretense that it's ancient wisdom. Still, I'll leave that to somebody else, because the philosophy and practice of healing that underlay every branch of Western esoteric medicine five hundred years ago is still around. You all know about it, at least in outline, although you may not know that it relates to healing, much less how to apply it to issues of health and disease. That's what we're going to discuss this evening. By the time you stagger out of this lecture an hour from now, you're going to have learned the basic principles of an entire system of medicine based on one of the most fundamental conceptual structures of Western occult teaching: the four elements.

I have a handout here that summarizes what we're going to cover.* Right on top, you'll find a diagram that most of you have probably seen so often you could draw it in your sleep. I got it early in my occult training, like the rest of you, and you probably noticed, as I did, that nobody paid a lot of attention to those adjectives at the corners of the small square: hot, cold, moist, dry. That's where the healing application of the elements starts from, though. The elements are not separate things; they're conditions of the One Thing discussed in the Emerald Tablet, and what defines them is the four qualities I just named. When the One Thing becomes hot and moist, it becomes Air; when it becomes hot and dry, you get Fire; when it becomes cold and moist, Water is the result, and when it becomes cold and dry, why, then "its power is integral if it be turned to Earth."

---

*The handout follows the text of this talk.

But the One Thing which is all things is also the human body, which can become hot or cold, moist or dry. In the early days of the elemental system, the four elements were associated with four fluids that are produced by the body—blood, yellow bile, phlegm, and black bile; in Latin those are called humors—literally, "moistures," from the same root as "humid"—and the old authors treated them as physical substances that were in the body, in excess or deficiency. You'll find that in the works of Galen, the Roman author and physician who played a central role in putting this system together; you'll find it in the works of Avicenna, the great Arab physician and philosopher, whose books are generally considered the zenith of the art, and in many of the later practitioners as well. Still, that doesn't work as well as seeing them as elemental patterns; you can have a very cold and moist condition, for example, and not produce all that much phlegm.

Now that implies that you can have different degrees of these elemental patterns, and indeed you can. In fact, you can have different degrees of all of the four qualities; a little hot and very dry is not the same thing as very hot and a little dry, and the two need to be treated differently. There are traditionally four degrees of each quality. The First Degree is mild; the Second Degree is moderate; the Third Degree is strong, but not so strong that it's dangerous; the Fourth Degree is really strong, strong enough to harm the body if it isn't balanced by something else. The human body overall is normally warm and moist in the First Degree; really strong poisons like deadly nightshade are cold and dry in the Fourth Degree. Herbs, foods, medicines, and so on, by the way, are defined by what they do to a living body—thus if you take deadly nightshade your body becomes very, very cold and dry, or in other words, dead. Pretty straightforward.

You also have herbs, foods, and the like that are "temperate" along one or both axis—that is neither hot nor cold, or neither dry nor moist. Look in the old herbals and you'll find the author commenting that such and such an herb is hot and dry in the Third Degree, or hot in the first and moist in the Second Degree, or temperate and dry in the First Degree. That's the technical jargon of the elemental healer.

This is what's called temperament, and it's one of the four things you need to know about any medicine, herbal or otherwise. Temperament refers to the balance of elements—for example, "hot and dry in the Third Degree." You need to know that, but you can't stop there. You also need to know its appropriation, which refers to the part of the body influenced. You need to know the property, which refers to general effects on the body or particular systems. Finally, you need to know the virtue, which means the effects of the herb on particular illnesses or conditions. You have to know all of these things to choose an herb or anything else to treat an illness or prevent one. Temperament isn't enough by itself.

If you've got a chest cold, for example, and it's cold and moist, not every hot and dry herb will help you; it might make your bladder or your skin hot and dry, but do nothing for your lungs. You need to choose a hot and dry herb that is a pectoral—that is, its appropriation is to the human chest. You need to choose one that is an expectorant—that is, its property is to clear mucus from the respiratory system. And you need to choose one whose virtue is that it's specific for chest colds. You can find all these things in the old herbals; for example, elecampane is hot and dry in the Third Degree; it's a pectoral; it's an expectorant; and it's specific for chest colds. So there you are.

But the temperaments, appropriations, properties, and virtues of medicines are only one side of the picture. The other side, and it's the more important of the two sides, is the person that you're treating, whether that's yourself or anyone else. One of the biggest sources of screwups in today's allegedly scientific medicine is that very often, it treats illnesses rather than patients; as a result, the illness gets better, but the patient doesn't. The old elemental healing art, like its equivalents in China, India, and elsewhere, treats the patient first and foremost, and that requires a clear sense of the patient's own state of health—in elemental terms, his or her temperament. Each body has a place of balance among the four qualities; it's not the same for everybody. It's by finding and keeping close to that place of balance that the individual remains healthy; it's by getting back to that place of balance, wherever it is, that we get healthy when we've been sick.

There are four factors, according to the old elemental medicine, that come together to define the current state of an individual's body: constitution, habit, lifestyle, and illness. Get used to four of this and four of that, by the way—most of the system is structured in fours, which is partly to make it convenient for the Art of Memory, the old medieval and Renaissance system that gives you the memory of one of Frank Herbert's Mentats. You can build your imaginal memory palace so that most of the rooms have four loci or places for memory images, and you're good to go—but again, that's raw material for another talk.

Okay. The first factor that determines the state of your health is constitution. I'll probably date myself fatally in this crowd if I mention that no, you can't get that by rolling three D6. Constitution refers to what we'd call heredity—it's the pattern of elemental balance you inherited from your parents. You can't change it, but you can use habit, lifestyle, and medicine to mitigate its effects if it happens to predispose you to some state of ill health. Habit refers to the long-term effects your lifestyle has on your temperament. You can change it the same way you get it, by changing your lifestyle, but that takes time; in the short term you can balance it out with lifestyle changes and medicine.

Lifestyle refers to what the way you are living right now is doing to your temperament. It can be changed by changing your behavior and your surroundings, and its negative effects can be balanced over the short term by medicines. Illness, finally, refers to the specific health condition that's unbalancing your temperament right now. You've been unbalanced in the cold and moist direction by getting caught in a rain shower, and by running yourself ragged at work so your internal heat is weak; that's temperament. When the cold and moisture concentrates in your chest and gives you a chest cold, that's an illness. Once that happens, you need medicine.

Still, lifestyle's really the crucial issue in getting and staying healthy. The elemental healer of the Middle Ages and Renaissance wasn't interested in keeping people on medicines all the time, like doctors these days; his job was to keep people healthy; much of his income came from what we'd consider health coaching, and he usually made his own medicines at his own expense, so he didn't have the mercenary motive that leads so many doctors nowadays to turn into pill pushers. Medicines were there as a backup for treating acute illness when there wasn't time for lifestyle changes to have the necessary effect on health.

The old books list six factors in a person's lifestyle that could be changed to affect their state of health; these were called the Six Externals. The first was Air, by which they meant the purity, temperature, and humidity of the air the patient habitually breathed. Here, that's hot and dry outdoors, cold and dry indoors, and not too clean wherever you are; the old doctors would have shaken their heads in dismay at our willingness to tolerate air pollution. Air, according to the old lore, doesn't simply affect your lungs; since the lungs are the bellows that fan the inner digestive fire that Paracelsus called the archeus, the quality of air affects your digestion, and since every system in the body depends on receiving nourishment, any part of the body can be negatively influenced by bad air—or dry air, or moist air, or what have you.

The second is food and drink, which includes the type, purity, and elemental balance of everything you swallow. We'll talk more about this a bit later on. The third is sleep and waking—how much you sleep, how long you stay awake, and where your sleep period falls in the cycle of the day. Sleep moistens you, waking dries you out, and sleeping at different times in the daily cycle can affect your balance of heat and cold.

Number four is exercise and rest. There was a whole medieval literature on exercise that I don't think anybody, but a few specialists, remember these days. The healing literature discusses it in some detail as well. For something to count as exercise, it had to make you break a sweat— depending on your state of health, the right exercise might bring you just a bit of damp on your brow, or it might be the sort of all-out exertion that soaks your exercise clothes to the dripping point. As for rest, it isn't the same thing as sleep; it's much closer to the modern notions of leisure or relaxation time, and according to the old books, you need that just as much as sleep. Exercise dries you, rest moistens you, and either one, depending on details, can heat or cool you.

Fullness and emptiness are number five. This refers to food and drink, again, in terms of their quantity, their quality, and how fast they move through your system. Eating too much, eating too little, long or short spaces between meals, how often your bowels and bladder do their job—all this falls under this category. So does menstruation. The old medical lore insisted that women were naturally healthier than men, by the way, because menstruation clears toxins from the body.

The last of the Six Externals is the affections of the mind—that includes everything we'd consider mental, emotional, and spiritual. The modern notion that you can draw a hard and fast line between body and mind would have had medieval healers either giggling helplessly or absolutely aghast. It's not simply that your thoughts, feelings, memories, intentions, and so on affect your body; your mind and your body are not two separate things, but two aspects of a single thing. Thus your thoughts and feelings affect your state of physical health, and your state of physical health affects your thoughts and feelings; to get rid of a depressed mood, which is cold and dry, it's often very effective to use warming and moistening treatments.

All of the Six Externals must be in balance in order to produce good health. That means you've got a constantly moving target, because the balance of Nature is always changing, and you need to change with it. Each time of day, each phase of the Moon, each season of the year, each direction of the wind, and each place on the Earth's surface has its own temperament. The healer pays attention to all of these. Back in the Middle Ages and Renaissance, so did everyone else; there are old handbooks of health for the use of ordinary people, talking about how to adjust your diet and habits in accordance with the seasons and the daily and lunar cycle.

All these environmental factors, though, affect different people differently, and so it's crucial to start with a clear sense of your own temperament. There are four basic temperaments, corresponding to the four elements: the sanguine, which is hot and moist; the choleric, which is hot and dry; the phlegmatic, which is cold and moist; and the melancholic, which is cold and dry. Those four words are still in circulation; it took a long time for scientific thought to chase them out of psychology, and when that happened they holed up in literature like a band of desperadoes in a box canyon and have been holding off the posse there ever since.

The sanguine temperament includes what we'd consider a body type and an emotional type—once again, to the traditional mind, these aren't two different things. The sanguine person has a relatively fleshy body, not fat but not hard. Skin is pink and soft to the touch; veins and arteries are large, and you can find the pulse with no difficulty. The sanguine person sleeps like a baby and has generally pleasant dreams; when the dreams turn agitated or vague or frightening, you know that they're out of their ordinary balance. Digestion's good, excretion's good, urine tends to be a bit reddish—examination of urine played a major role in diagnosis. The emotional life is mostly upbeat but changeable—sudden transports of delight, equally sudden tears, falls in love easily and often. You know the type; about a quarter of you *are* the type.

The choleric temperament is something else again. The body type is lean and muscular; your extreme choleric type has abs you could break a two-by-four across. Skin is sallow. The veins and arteries are average size but feel hard, and the pulse is strong and fast. The choleric person gets by on not much sleep, thrashes around in bed, and has active, even violent dreams. The digestion is good as long as there's enough roughage in the diet; otherwise, all that internal heat produces excess dryness in the bowels, and you can figure out the rest from there. Urine is yellow and clear. Emotionally, the choleric person has a hot temper—think about that phrase a bit and you'll see how many traces the old system of temperaments has left in our language; the voice is sharp, and the opinions are definite and often extreme.

Next is the phlegmatic. The body type here is plump and soft, the skin is pale, compared to others of the same ethnicity, and often moist, and the veins and arteries are narrow, with a slow soft pulse. The phlegmatic person sleeps long but not deep, with vague diffuse dreams. Digestion is not good; there's not enough heat to digest the more difficult foods, so stomach troubles are common, and the phlegmatic person can usually tell you all about the foods he or she shouldn't eat. Urine is pale and denser than water. The phlegmatic person lives a rich emotional life but a lot of it stays inside; when it bursts out, no matter what bursts out—joy, anger, sorrow, you name it—expect tears.

Finally, we've got the melancholic. The body type is bony, thin, and angular, the skin tends to be rough and dry; the veins and arteries are small and hard, and you'll have to work at getting a pulse. The melancholic person tends toward insomnia and has frightening dreams. You know those nightmares where everything is pitch black and you're fighting for your life against an enemy you can't hurt? That's a classic melancholic dream. The digestion is weak, the urine thin and watery, and the emotional life—well, it's legendary. Renaissance healers from Marsilio Ficino to Robert Burton wrote whole books about the melancholic type: somber, moody, introspective, eccentric, prone to delusions and obsessions and bursts of brilliance. It's the temperament of geniuses and of dangerous raving maniacs in padded cells.

In using these there are two things you have to keep in mind. First, these are ideal types. Most people fall somewhere closer to the middle—sanguine with a bit of choleric, melancholic tending toward phlegmatic, or what have you. A few people have constitutions dead in the middle. Second, and even more important, your basic temperament is part of your constitution, and whatever it is, that's your state of health. This is very hard for modern people to get their heads around. If you have a phlegmatic constitution, "healthy" for you means plump; you're never going to look like a model, and trying to make yourself look like a model can wreck your health. It's that simple; there is no one definition of "healthy" that fits everyone, and trying to force yourself into a definition that doesn't suit your constitution is a good way to get sick.

I think most people nowadays have noticed that weight loss programs don't work for most people, and this is why. In elemental terms, if your constitution is choleric or melancholic but habit and lifestyle have unbalanced you in a phlegmatic direction, you may well be able to get your body back to its natural shape by diet, exercise, and so on. If your body is naturally phlegmatic, all the diet and exercise in the world will simply make you a fat person who's very strong and hungry all the time. One size does not fit all. In particular, today's popular fashions in body shape do not make a useful guide to health. These things go in cycles; a hundred years ago, it's worth remembering, a woman who'd be considered attractively thin today would have been begging her doctor for a diet to help her gain weight and become pleasingly plump.

Okay, so you have your constitution, your habit, and your lifestyle. If these are in balance, you're healthy. If they're not in balance, you get sick. The basic cause of illness, according to the traditional lore, is an unbalanced temperament, caused by one or more of the Six Externals. The imbalance, again, is always relative to the body's normal state: what is normal and healthy for a hot and moist sanguine type can be badly imbalanced for a cold and dry melancholy type, and so on. That's why you have to have some sense of a patient's natural temperament before you start trying to make changes. I don't happen to know the medieval Latin translation for "if it ain't broke, don't fix it," but I'm sure it's to be found in the old books.

The basic rule is that if one of the externals pushes you out of your natural temperament, you get sick. Thus you can get sick in four ways. If you're moderately sanguine, let's say, something can weaken your heat and push you in the phlegmatic direction; something can weaken your moisture and push you in the choleric direction; something can weaken both, and push you in a melancholic direction; or something can strengthen one or the other, or both, and make you more sanguine than your body can handle being. In any of these cases, you get sick.

Any of the elements can also become *adust*, that is, inflamed; symbolically, the humor catches fire. This produces symptoms of inflammation and apparent heat, no matter what the underlying elemental balance is. This is trouble; adust conditions are generally much more problematic than simple imbalances, and you have to deal with the inflammation and the underlying imbalance at the same time. The best way to keep an imbalance from becoming adust is to treat it early on, because conditions become adust when they're left untreated too long.

The relationship between temperament and disease can be complex. There isn't a one-to-one correspondence between them; for example, colds can be hot and moist—that gives you a running cold with fever. They can be hot and dry—that gives you a stuffy cold with fever. They can be cold and moist—that's a running cold with chills; they can be cold and dry—that's a stuffy cold with chills. Equally, you can get many different illnesses out of a single temperament, depending on the fine details of the imbalance; for example, a cold and moist imbalance may express itself through runny head colds, certain kinds of headache, asthma, chronic upset stomach, constipation with soft stools, impotence, skin problems, etc. Temperament is not a substitute for diagnosis, it's a tool to help with diagnosis and treatment.

There's another wrinkle that has to be kept in mind, though, because many common "illnesses" are actually the body's way of cleansing itself of imbalances and toxins. Any illness that consists primarily of one or more bodily discharges—most colds, "stomach flu," etc.—should be treated by bed rest, plenty of fluids, and gently warming herbs and foods, not by methods that try to stop the body's natural cleansing process. Don't stop the symptoms unless the illness goes on for more than a few days, or worsens as it proceeds. Never override your body's cleansing process just because its timing is inconvenient; the imbalances and toxins you keep in your body now may cause a serious disease later—which will be much more inconvenient.

And now we get to the practical core of the art of elemental healing. It's also the place where otherwise sensible people lose their marbles and start rolling around the floor speaking in tongues and foaming at the mouth. Yes, we're about to talk about diet.

Let's start with the unavoidable fact that nobody in America is sane about food. Nobody. I think it's a hangover from our Puritan past—and I mean "hangover" here in the head-pounding, gut-twisting, kneeling at the porcelain altar while repatriating all of last night's party snacks sense of the word. H. L. Mencken, I think it was, once defined Puritanism as the haunting, unshakable fear that somebody, somewhere is having a good time. The essence of the Puritan mindset is that whatever you enjoy is bad; you need to figure out what it is and get rid of it, and then you'll be good. We've gotten past that sort of delusional thinking in our spiritual lives—at least most of us have—but we still think that way about food. Ninety-nine times out of a hundred, when somebody comes up with a new diet, what they've done is identify some food as the latest version of Evil Incarnate, and the diet consists of getting rid of it. Cholesterol is bad for you; polyunsaturated fats are bad for you;

meat is bad for you; carbohydrates are bad for you; fat is bad for you; you name it, somebody says it's bad for you.

I sometimes suspect this is why the old elemental way of healing has been banished into the outer darkness with wailing and gnashing of teeth and all that because one of its basic rules is that there are no forbidden foods. None. Every food has its own temperament, which means that people who can handle that temperament easily can eat it freely, while those who might be unbalanced by that temperament need to balance it out with something else.

Let's take the most obvious example, the one that will have already come to the minds of a large proportion of the audience here: chocolate. Pure dark chocolate is cold and dry in the Second Degree; its appropriation is to the nerves, its property is calmative and its virtue is as a treatment for lovesickness. Which was a disease discussed in quite a bit of detail in the old texts, by the way; they didn't have chocolate available to treat it, but there were other medicines; there was also the preferred treatment which, if the cause of the illness was available and willing, was pretty much what you would expect.

If you're using chocolate as a treatment for lovesickness, that's one thing, and I trust you're under the care of a medieval doctor who is carefully monitoring the dose. If you're eating it as a food, though, you need to manage that yourself. Once again, temperament determines what you need to do. If you happen to be moderately melancholy by temperament, not only can you eat dark chocolate in moderation, it's good for you. If you're not melancholic, you need to figure out what to eat along with the chocolate to make it healthy. You're choleric? Add a heating spice, enough to cancel out the coldness; Mexican hot chocolate or those chocolate bars with hot peppers in them ought to be fine. You're phlegmatic? Butter, eggs, and wheat flour are all moistening; have a slice of chocolate cake with frosting. You're sanguine? Milk is warm and moist; milk chocolate's likely to be your best bet.

What if you don't like chocolate and don't want it? Don't eat it. Your body knows more about your real needs than anybody else; listen to it, notice what you like and what makes you feel good, and then eat that, balancing as necessary with other foods you like that keep you in balance. I know that trusting your body about anything is blasphemous heresy in a Puritan culture, but there it is; people in the Middle Ages were not Puritans; they had their own neuroses, to be sure, but those aren't the same as ours.

In the old way of healing, diet is the foundation of health and the first line of defense against illness. Eating a varied diet of wholesome foods suited to your temperament, taking the temperament of the season, weather, and other factors into account, will prevent most illnesses, and appropriate foods eaten during illness will cure mild ailments and assist in curing serious ones. Notice that what counts as a healthy diet varies from person to person; a diet that would suit one may be very unhealthy for another. No diet is suited to everyone, and as a rule, the more extreme the diet, the smaller the number of people who are actually going to find it healthy.

One of the interesting implications of the traditional lore is that your grandmother's recipes may be healthier than you think. Many traditional Western eating habits started out as medical advice; for example, serving mustard and horseradish (which are hot and dry) with beef (which is moist) brings the resulting dish closer to balance. In the same way, a lot of old-fashioned health advice comes out of the old system of healing. "feed a cold and starve a fever" works, because digestion heats the body; fasting in moderation helps cool off hot conditions, while big meals of warming foods are invaluable for cold conditions.

If you happen to have grown up in a Hispanic or Filipino community, you should pay particular attention to what Abuelita said about staying healthy. A few years ago an American anthropologist who knew a bit about the history of medicine finally got around to noticing that a very large part of the "folk medicine" practiced in Latin America and the Philippines is actually the old elemental medicine, straight out of Galen and Avicenna. Plenty of first-rate health advice can be taken from that source, and also some excellent rules for cooking and eating; it's not accidental that a very large percentage of recipes from the Latin American countries and the Philippines are very nicely balanced for midrange temperaments.

One other rule. Food should taste good! Food the patient doesn't enjoy does little good, no matter how nourishing it is in theory, while a tasty, well-prepared meal the patient likes will improve health no matter what it's made of. The old books strongly recommend giving a sick person "comfort foods" even when these aren't the healthiest thing to eat; the emotional benefits outweigh the temperature imbalance, and you can always take something else to balance it out. The time to make changes in lifestyle is after the acute illness is over, when the patient can handle the additional stress.

So, you've got your foundations: the theory of temperaments, the patient's own elemental balance, and the Six Externals that bring health and illness. How do you use this in practice? You start with diagnosis. With a little practice, it's not hard to figure out somebody's temperament, and the elemental nature of their illness, through simple observation and taking a case history. Somebody's normally sanguine but now they look pale and puffy, they feel chilled, their nose is running, and so on; the illness followed exposure to a spring rainstorm, they want to sleep all the time; it's a phlegmatic condition, and you treat accordingly. Observe yourself carefully, keep a health diary, and watch how what you eat affects how you feel, and you'll have this down in no time flat.

There are more advanced methods. The two most common, and most challenging, are pulse reading and urine observation. To learn to read pulses, you're probably going to have to apprentice yourself to somebody who knows how it's done. You can do this, too, if you're lucky or determined, because the system of medicine we're discussing is still practiced in India and some parts of the Muslim world; it's called Unani medicine—Unani is what happens when the word Ionian, that is, Greek, goes through Arabic and ends up in Sanskrit. A good Ayurvedic, Tibetan, or traditional Chinese doctor would probably be able to show you the basics, too, since they do a very similar kind of pulse diagnosis, and get equally good results from it. The pulse doesn't just tell you the state of the heart and the bloodstream; it gives you a glimpse into the functioning of the whole organism if you know how to do it.

Urine examination is another very important tool. Medieval doctors used to have little clear flasks in which they'd put the patient's urine, and then examine its color, layers, particulates, and so on, and use that to check the state of the kidneys, the bloodstream, the digestion, and much more. That also has to be learned from a qualified expert; I'm not one, so don't ask.

Fortunately, there's another set of advanced diagnostic tools you can learn on your own: divination. Every doctor in the old days used either astrology or geomancy as a diagnostic tool. The astrologically minded doctor would cast a chart—called a decumbiture—for the time when the patient first took sick, and then interpret it like a horary chart. The astrologers here will know that the sixth house governs illness; the element ruling the sign in the sixth house generally tells you which direction the patient's system is out of whack, and the location and condition of the planet that rules the sign in the sixth house tells you what other systems are involved. Some other houses play a role; the first house governs mental factors, the twelfth house governs chronic illnesses, and then there's the eighth house, which governs death; if the ruler of the sixth house is in the eighth, and you don't have some major positive aspects influencing the chart, your medieval doctor would be likely to suggest that you make out your will. Modern astrologers tend to be squeamish about making statements like that; but in the Middle Ages and Renaissance, people routinely asked an astrologer how long they would live and how they would die, and the astrologer told them.

Geomancy was the other common option. I don't know how many of you are familiar with it, but in the Renaissance it was nearly as common as astrology, and the standard method at the time used the same twelve houses as astrology. A physician who preferred geomancy would cast a chart for the patient and interpret it; he'd check the figure in the sixth house, see whether it had a mode of perfection connecting it to the first, eighth, or twelfth, and so on. Robert Fludd, the great Hermetic encyclopedist of the seventeenth century, wrote a treatise on medical geomancy, which I've translated and studied; it's interesting stuff, and just as useful in this context as medical astrology.

Treatment follows diagnosis. When somebody's healthy, you maintain their elemental balance, and when they're sick, you restore it by countering the imbalance. For a hot and dry illness, you use cold and moist medicines—mostly herbs, in the traditional practice, for acute illnesses; chronic illnesses usually require changes in diet and other lifestyle issues. You also choose the remedy with an eye to the intensity of the illness; you don't give strong medicine for a mild illness, or you may make the patient sick in the other direction! For home use, herbs in the 2° or 3° are good. The 4° is too strong to use unmixed, and for home use, again, you want to use simples—that is, single herbs taken by themselves—rather than mixtures. You can use more than one herb for a given illness, and very often that's the right thing to do, but you don't blend them into a single compound unless you know the right way to do it.

Compounding medicines was one of the great arts of the elemental healer, and it required a branch of knowledge that next to nobody knows today: proportional mathematics. You have one herb that's hot in the 3°, another that's hot in the 1°, and another that's cold in the 2°; you want to blend them together in such amounts that the end result will be exactly temperate; how much of each do you use? There are simple math methods for doing that. What makes this embarrassing is that most schoolchildren knew those methods in 1500; they were part of the ordinary school curriculum, along with logic, Latin grammar, and music theory, among other things. I considered walking the lot of you through the basics of proportional math, but you know, there comes a point at which people's neurons start dribbling out of their ears, and adding a whole new system of mathematics on top of the theory and philosophy of elemental healing would push that barrier a bit.

At this point, we can look at a relatively simple example: treating a chest cold. The patient (temperament moderately cold and dry) reported wheezing from mucus in the chest, productive cough on rising, feeling easily chilled, wanting to sleep all the time. His skin was damp, his tongue had a brownish coating on it showing poor digestion; his pulse was soft and sluggish. These are all signs of a phlegmatic condition, a good deal colder than the patient's temperament, so the treatment had to be drying and gently warming. The remedy prescribed was as much rest and warmth as possible, a warming diet involving foods the patient enjoyed, plenty of hot drinks, candied ginger (hot and dry, three degrees, stimulant) between meals, cayenne pepper (hot & dry, three degrees, general tonic) added to food according to taste, and elecampane (hot & dry, three degrees, pectoral, expectorant) tea 2–3 times per day or whenever chest congestion was apparent. After two days the congestion was gone, and he felt well again, but I had him keep the same regimen until it no longer appealed—that took most of the remainder of the week.

That probably just sounds like common sense. It is common sense. Most healing, when it's really healing and not simply an attempt to make another million in annual profits for the shareholders of pharmaceutical companies, is the application of common sense to matters of health. Of course the same thing can be said of most of the teachings of the Western world's occult traditions, or for that matter of any other kind of esoteric spirituality; they are common sense, and the only reason they look exotic in today's world is that our contemporary culture abandoned the last traces of common sense a long time ago. It's not the sleep of reason that produces monsters but the obsessive pursuit of reason divorced from reality; I challenge anyone to show me a medieval dragon or giant that devastated half so much as, say, the recent housing bubble.

As our world slowly shakes itself awake from the dreams and delusions that have entangled it for so long, some of the old habits of common sense—or, to return to the metaphor I used earlier in this talk, some of the pieces of the great machine we've been able to put back into working order—may be well worth getting back into use. I've come to think that the old art of healing through the elements is one of those. Those of us who practice herbal medicine can use it; those who practice spagyrics can do the same; all of the many occult traditions that make use of the four elements already know the basics of this system, and just need a little practice putting them to use.

There have been a few books in recent years that have touched on one dimension or another of the old art of elemental healing—I've listed them at the end of the handout—and there's also been a great deal of scholarship on the subject in academic circles; your local university library will probably be able to provide you with old herbals and medical texts that will give you more to work with than you can easily imagine. The material is out there. If this talk inspires any of you to look into the art of healing through the elements, and to apply even a bit of it in your own life, then I've done my job.

Healing through the elements

Four qualities

- Hot, Cold, Dry, Moist

Four elements

- Air—Hot and Moist
- Fire—Hot and Dry
- Water—Cold and Moist
- Earth—Cold and Dry

Elements and qualities

Four degrees

- Temperate—zero point
- First Degree—Mild
- Second Degree—Moderate
- Third Degree—Strong
- Fourth Degree—Damaging

Four characteristics of medicines

- Temperament—the balance of elements
- Appropriation—part of body influenced
- Property—general effect on body systems
- Virtue—specific effect on particular illnesses or conditions

Four factors in temperament

- Constitution—the health factors you inherit
- Habit—the cumulative impact of past choices
- Lifestyle—the way you are living right now
- Illness—any specific health condition affecting you

Six externals

- Air—purity, temperature, and humidity

- Food and Drink—type, purity, and elemental balance
- Sleep and Waking—length and timing in the daily cycle
- Exercise and Rest—intensity and type of exercise, amount of rest
- Fullness and Emptiness—quantity and quality of food, drink, and excreta
- Affections of the Mind—including memory, will, and emotions

Four temperaments

Hot and Moist: Sanguine
Hot and Dry: Choleric
Cold and Moist: Phlegmatic
Cold and Dry: Melancholy

Basic concepts of healing

- The basic cause of illness is an unbalanced temperament, caused by the Six Externals. Any of the elements can also become *adust*, that is, inflamed.
- Each elemental type, and each individual, has a different elemental balance and therefore different health care needs; one size emphatically does not fit all.
- An imbalance of temperament can cause various diseases, and the disease, as well as the imbalance, must be treated; temperament is not enough by itself.
- Many common "illnesses" are the body's way of cleansing itself of imbalances and toxins. Let them run their course to prevent worse illnesses later on.
- Diet is the foundation of health and the first line of defense against illness. This does not mean that some foods are "bad;" if a food is unbalanced, eat it with something that balances it.
- Do not make changes in diet and lifestyle when the patient is dealing with an acute illness—the additional stress will not help the healing process.
- The digestion process heats the body; thus, "feed a cold and starve a fever."
- Emotional factors are as relevant as strictly physical ones; thus, tasty food is medicinal! "Comfort foods" are valuable allies in healing.

Tools for diagnosis

- Observation and case history determines the elemental balance
- Examining pulse and urine are advanced methods requiring training and experience
- Astrological or geomantic divination—look to the sixth house of the chart

Principles of treatment

- Balance the illness, e.g., use hot and dry treatment for a cold and wet ailment
- Temper the treatment to the illness—do not use strong medicines for a mild ailment
- Acute conditions are best treated with herbs; chronic conditions require changes in diet
- Simples are best suited to home use; compounding requires proportional mathematics

Example: treating a chest cold

The patient (temperament cold and dry) reported wheezing in the chest, productive cough on rising, feeling easily chilled, wanting to sleep all the time. The skin was damp, the tongue had a coating, and pulse was sluggish. These are all signs of a cold and moist condition. The remedy was rest and warmth, a warming diet, plenty of hot drinks, candied ginger (hot & dry 3°, stimulant) between meals, cayenne pepper (hot & dry 3°, tonic) added to food according to taste, and elecampane (hot & dry 3°, pectoral, expectorant) tea 2–3x per day or whenever chest congestion became apparent. The patient was well after two days.

Sources

Chishti, Hakim G. M., *The Traditional Healer's Handbook* (Healing Arts Press, 1991).

Culpeper, Nicholas, *Culpeper's Complete Herbal and English Physician* (Meyerbooks, 1990).

Greer, John Michael, *The Encyclopedia of Natural Magic* (Llewellyn, 2000).

Tobyn, Graeme, *Culpeper's Medicine* (Element, 1997).

CHAPTER NINE

Paganism and the future

I'd like to thank you all for coming to this talk. As I think you all probably know by this point, I'm John Michael Greer; I write and blog about a variety of subjects, including Paganism and the future; and I've given plenty of talks at Pagan events over the years about Pagan and occult history, which have by and large gotten a very enthusiastic reception.

This talk is not going to get an enthusiastic reception. It's also about history, in several different senses. I'm guessing that some of you showed up this afternoon because you're interested in where the Pagan movement is going, what its own future is likely to be; and some of you showed up because you're interested in where the world is going, what its future is likely to be, and what Paganism might have to offer to the world ahead of us; and some of you may be curious about both. I do have something to say about both, and about what history has to say about both.

Some of you may be expecting the sort of rousing call to arms we've heard fairly often over the last thirty years; the world needs us, we've got to get out there and change history, and so on. There's going to be a bit of that but not necessarily where you expect it; and of course there's another side to the story, which is that the modern Pagan movement has its own trajectory, and there's reason to think we may be very busy dealing with that for a while, and not necessarily in any shape to get out there and save the world; and that, again, has a lot to do with history.

We have a complicated relationship with history in the Pagan movement. A lot of us like to think of ourselves as practicing the Old Ways, doing something that has roots in the distant past. That's an important source of inspiration, but it also tends to be a source of confusion, because paying attention only to the very distant past is sometimes a way to avoid paying attention to the more recent past, which often has a lot more to say about what's actually going on in a recently founded alternative spiritual movement like this one. And that complicated relationship is made even more complicated by the way history is understood, or misunderstood, and used, or misused, in modern industrial societies, and the way that these misunderstandings and misuses affect the way we think about the future. Talking about that is explosive stuff, and it's one of the reasons that some of you are probably going to storm out of this room in a state of blind fury well before I'm finished with today's talk.

That can't be helped. There are times when the things that nobody wants to talk about are the things that have to be faced; when chugging ahead under the influence of familiar assumptions and accepted taboos stops being a workable plan and turns into a fertile source of disasters. I'd like to suggest that now is one of those times. A lot of today's talk will be about the reasons why; and we can start exploring that by glancing back at those dim and distant days far in the past when the oldest of the Pagan traditions we practice first emerged from the primeval mists of the very dawn of Time.

Yes, I'm talking about the 1970s.

Now, of course, the dawn of Time is a highly mobile point for Pagans. For Wicca, the dawn of Time was around 1947, when Gerald Gardner cobbled it together out of a variety of older materials—we don't have to get into just what those were right now. In the case of Druidry, the dawn of Time was a little longer ago, back in the eighteenth century in fact; and so on down the list. But none of those had much of a presence in America until the 1970s. A scattering of pioneers brought a few of these things over from the far side of the Atlantic a little further back—in the case of Druidry, quite a bit further back, but what was practiced then had almost nothing in common with most of the Druidry we've got these days. For the most part, until the 1970s, Pagan spirituality was something you read about in books, and the alternative traditions you could actually expect to encounter here in America, again, had very little in common with the thriving scene today.

It was a very different world in the 1970s, and not merely because we had to suffer through bell bottom pants and the Bee Gees. It was also a world where magic was much less publicly available than it is today. When I first took up magical training, during that decade, there were all of five Tarot decks available for sale in well-stocked magical bookstores in America. That was a major step up; one of my teachers used to talk fondly about the days, only about a decade earlier, when you had your choice between the Marseilles deck and a cheaply printed knockoff of the Rider-Waite, take your pick, and you got them by mail order from Ty-Rad or Mar-Lar unless you lived in one of a few big cities. Books on magic and Pagan spirituality that actually told you how to do anything were rare as hen's teeth. I remember how excited I was in 1976 when Francis King and Stephen Skinner's little paperback *Techniques of High Magic* showed up in a Seattle department store book section, of all places, as part of the first big wave of mass-market occult paperbacks. It's not actually that good of a book by today's standards, but, by the standards of the time, I might as well have found the Holy Grail.

A few of the old occult orders were still around, teaching their stuff, but most of those went to ground or went to pieces in the 1960s, and if you could find one that was still active, you could count on spending a chunk of money and putting up with a lot of very old-fashioned formalities to get in. Other than that, what there was was pretty much the standard condition of occult studies since the end of the Renaissance, a very small subculture of occultists pursuing their own very diverse paths, piecing together rituals and practices out of odds and ends, and supporting the odd bookstore and a few small publishers, most of whom published in mimeograph with spiral or staple bindings.

You had a couple of other spiritual scenes at that time in very nearly the same condition. One of them was a very loose movement that drew on equal parts leftover Theosophy, Asian mysticism, and a bunch of avant-garde movements in the sciences ranging from parapsychology to systems theory. It didn't even have a name yet, but some of the people who were more or less in a leadership role had begun to talk now and then about the possibility that the world was going to enter a new age. The other scene was gradually emerging out of a fusion between the Jesus Freaks of the late counterculture and what was left of the old, weird, Bible-toting Protestantism that had its last big period of popularity in the 1910s and 1920s when a set of pamphlets titled *The Fundamentals* went viral in the American underclass. You still heard talk now and then about fundamentalists, usually uttered in tones of high disdain by the very liberal Christian clergy who still dominated the national religious scene at the time.

Exactly what happened next is an issue that deserves much more historical research than it's gotten. Over a fairly short time in the late 1970s and early 1980s, all three of these very marginal movements became popular in a big way. In each case, there was a catalyst, something that caught the public imagination and dragged the movement into the limelight. The resurgence of fundamentalism was set off by a clever ad campaign in 1976, focused on the phrase *I Found It!*—some of you will remember that. The rise of the New Age movement to mass popularity was kickstarted by the 1983 publication of Shirley MacLaine's visionary memoir *Out On A Limb*. For Paganism, it was Margot Adler's *Drawing Down the Moon* and Starhawk's *The Spiral Path*, both published in 1979. That's when Paganism went pop, and that's when we began the journey to a world where there are so many Tarot decks on sale that nobody on Earth can even find time to look at them all.

Now, I know it's not exactly popular in present company to suggest that contemporary Paganism, the New Age movement, and Christian fundamentalism have things in common. Still, there's more than a little family resemblance, and I've sometimes thought that the hostility among them is more or less sibling rivalry. The New Age movement is the insufferably smug older sister who insists that the other two will agree with her once they grow up; Fundamentalism is the angry, uptight brother who's into acting out and saying nasty things about his sisters; modern Paganism is the bratty kid sister who likes to shock people and thinks that her elder siblings are stuck up and no fun.

You can use other metaphors if you prefer. Still, the crucial point is that all three of these movements, formerly banished to the fringes of American society, became relatively large, and relatively popular, right around the same time. One measure of that is that it became possible for a writer like me to make a living from writing books for the occult market without having to have a day job, or write porn under a pseudonym or something. It became possible for a publisher like Llewellyn to move out of Carl Weschke's basement, hire some real live staff, and bring out some new books alongside the handful of occult and astrological classics that were its bread and butter for years. And eventually, it became possible for anything up to a couple of thousand Pagans and occultists to meet in a hotel in some perfectly respectable corner of America without having the local police show up to shut 'em down.

It's interesting to note, in terms of similarities, that all three movements very quickly embraced some very enthusiastic ideas about what the future would hold for them. The New Age movement, well, as the name suggests, its basic theory from the start was that a new age of the world was about to dawn, and one of the central features of that new age was that everybody was going to be a New Ager. The fundamentalists started out with pretty much the same notion, which gradually morphed into the traditional Protestant premillennialist claim that everybody who disagreed with them was nasty and evil and would get the ever-living crap kicked out of them for all eternity once Jesus showed up with his hobnailed boots on, which of course he was going to do sometime very, very soon.

I'm pleased to say that fantasies like this last were nothing like so popular in the Pagan scene. The late Isaac Bonewits did write a nasty little song, once fairly popular in some parts of the scene, about how we'd all be Pagan again once we hanged every preacher from a tree and burned out every church, and you had a certain number of visions of a future where everybody would be a happy Pagan forever, but it wasn't all that common. The way that the Pagan movement embraced the image of the witch, who is a marginal figure by definition, was, I suspect, a major barrier in the way of these Utopian fantasies. It's kind of hard to be a marginal figure unless you have a bunch of people who are willing to marginalize you, and that's hard to arrange if everybody in the world agrees with you.

What you did get, and do get, in the Pagan scene is a great deal of fascination with becoming a big respectable institutionalized presence, with paid clergy and large buildings and invitations to say the opening prayer when the city council or the state legislature starts a new session, and so on. This can be taken to absurd lengths on occasion. I recall a conversation I had once with an influential reconstructionist Druid who insisted that since the ancient Druids advised kings, we ought to advise presidents, and the presidents damn well ought to listen. It didn't do a bit of good to point out that the ancient Druids earned the respect of the Celtic kings by their wisdom and good advice, and to be quite frank, we haven't. It didn't do any more good to point out that the only thing we really have in common with the ancient Druids is that we chose to borrow the name, and by the same logic I could start calling myself God and expect people to fall down and worship me. That's one of the things about a movement that adopts an imagery of marginalization; the craving for unearned respect runs deep.

Now, of course, there are plenty of people who are pursuing respectability in less counterproductive ways. I'm thinking here of the people in many different Pagan traditions who have gone to work in the field of prison ministry, and have earned the respect of officials who tend to be fairly difficult to impress. There are Pagans volunteering in soup kitchens and hospices, and doing a lot of other things on the same scale. They're becoming respected, which of course is the one guaranteed way to become respectable.

And that's actually part of the problem because, on the whole, people who are attracted to contemporary Paganism aren't looking for something respectable. On the whole, they're looking for something edgy and transgressive and iconoclastic. If they wanted something respectable they'd become Methodists. Right there you're looking at a chasm that's opening up within the Pagan community, but more importantly, between the Pagan community and its own future.

To make sense of that we're going to have to take a step back and look at the Pagan community, and the popular Paganism of the last thirty years, in a much wider context. Pagans tend to see modern Paganism as something that stands apart from the rest of American culture's religious options and religious history; again, if they put it in any historical context at all, it's something from a couple of thousand years ago at least. From a wider perspective, though, contemporary Paganism is simply one more American popular alternative religious movement. I've compared it to the New Age movement and the current round of Christian fundamentalism, but other comparisons go much deeper.

There's a book that some of you may have read and most of you should know about: it's titled *Nature Religion in America* and it's by Catherine Albanese. Albanese is a historian of religions, and the topic of this book is a particular current in American religion that goes back to colonial times, a current that's produced a long string of popular alternative religious movements. Everybody in this room knows a fair amount about that current, even if you don't know a lick of the history Albanese explores, because contemporary American Neopaganism is very much a part of that current. We draw from the same stock of ideas, we share a common set of ideals and attitudes; we like to see our traditions in relation to archaic Pagan faiths from various exotic corners of the globe, but in fact, we're part and parcel of a movement within American culture that's been around since the end of the seventeenth century.

The current that Albanese calls "Nature religion" is only one of these continuing themes in American religious life. The New Age movement and Christian fundamentalism are the current representatives of two other currents with equally long pedigrees, and of course there are others still. The thing to keep in mind is that much of the time, any given current is simply part of the background noise of American popular spirituality, with a modest following here and there, a few small publishers and so on; and then every so often something pulls that current up into public favor, and it becomes a popular movement for a while, before fading out into the background again.

There have been a huge number of these popular movements; one way or another, they make up something like half of American cultural history. From the first flowering of American occultism in the 1680s and 1690s, when German Rosicrucians and English religious radicals arrived in Pennsylvania and Maryland and laid the foundations for a lot of what's now Pennsylvania Dutch braucherei; the Great Awakening of the 1720s—sinners in the hands of an angry God!—and the deist and freethinking countermovement a little later; the Quakers, the Shakers, the Mormons, the Millerites, the Transcendentalists, the Spiritualists, the Theosophists, New Thought, American Rosicrucianism, and the list goes on; at any given point in American history, there are two or three alternative spiritual movements that have caught the public imagination and attracted a following and a lot of attention; and then a few decades later, something else hogs the spotlight.

It's possible to be a bit more precise than that. The lifespan of any one of these popular movements, from the time when it bursts into public awareness to the time when it either crashes and burns or fades quietly into the spiritual background, averages thirty to forty years.

I think you see where I'm going with this.

The other two movements I mentioned a little while ago, Christian fundamentalism and the New Age movement, are already on the last part of their trajectories. With the fundamentalists, it's an easy call, because they're making the same mistakes and moving into the same death spiral that swallowed the first wave of fundamentalism, which ran from a little before 1900 to just after the 1929 stock market crash.

Now as then, they allied themselves with the far right—in the 1910s and 1920s, it was the Ku Klux Klan; you had a popular fundamentalist author, the Reverend E. F. Stanton, publish a book in 1924 titled *Christ and Other Klansmen, or Lives of Love*—and now as then, they found out the hard way that politicians were willing to say anything to get their votes and their volunteer hours come election time, but once the election was over it was, "Bye, see you in four years"; which is why, thirty years into the current wave, most of the items on the fundamentalist political action list are as far away as they were in 1980.

Now as then, they trusted in the Holy Spirit to guide them in their choice of leaders, which meant—and means—that the movement has been a happy hunting ground for scoundrels who can put on a show of godliness. I trust I don't have to remind anybody here of the number of fundamentalist ministers who have been caught with their pants around their ankles in one sense or another. If you think that's something new, I encourage you to read Sinclair Lewis' brilliant and scathing novel *Elmer Gantry*. It's the story of a corrupt revival minister of the 1920s, and every detail could come straight out of today's headlines.

The results? A lot of people on the Left like to portray Christian fundamentalism as Godzilla bearing down on Bambi, but if you read fundamentalist publications, and I recommend the exercise, you get a very different story. A study run and funded from within the fundamentalist community a few years back found that only around eight percent of their own children keep their faith after they turn twenty-one. The average time that a convert under age thirty stays with fundamentalism is about two and a half years; then they're gone. The latest source of panic is what's called the Home Church movement; many thousands of devout evangelical Christians—nobody seems to know how many, or if they know, they're not admitting it—are getting sick of the begging for money and the politics disguised as religion and the unending drumbeat of scandals; they're dropping out of their churches, they're not paying tithes anymore, they're meeting with a handful of Christian friends in somebody's living room every Sunday to pray and study the Bible. As that catches on, and it's catching on in a big way as we speak, the fundamentalist movement as we've known it is deflating like a punctured whoopee cushion.

As for the New Age, its doom is near at hand; the Grim Reaper is breathing down its neck as we speak, ticking off the days until it's time to swing that sickle. I can tell you right down to the day when the New Age movement is going to roll over and die; but to explain how I know that, I'm going to have to tell you a story from American religious history.

Right after the War of 1812, the United States went through its first great wave of social reform, equivalent to the Progressive Era or the 1960s. You had a lot of serious political reformers, and you also had a lot of idealists pursuing the progressive causes of the day: pacifism, the very first stirrings of American feminism, opposition to slavery, opposition to alcohol—Prohibition was a liberal cause in those days; it's one of the ironies of history that the nineteenth-century Left was opposed to mind-altering substances just as passionately as the late twentieth-century Left was in favor of them. But, the even richer irony is that a great many of these idealists were evangelical Protestant Christians. What we would now call fundamentalism, back then, was the religion of the far Left, while those people who were dabbling in magic and Paganism were mostly on the Right. Times change.

Plenty of important reforms got put in place in those years, but the big name causes—the abolition of slavery; the abolition of war; the abolition of alcohol; and so on—those turned out to be mostly out of reach; and worse, as the nineteenth century drew on, it started to become clear to a lot of people that they could abolish slavery or they could abolish war, take your pick, because if you wanted to get rid of slavery, it was going to take one helluva war to do it; and so, just as a lot of radicals in the 1960s ended up getting involved in religious mysticism in the hope of finding the freedom the political system wasn't going to give them, a lot of radicals in the 1820s and 1830s ended up getting involved in their own kind of religious mysticism, which again, was some form of radical Christianity. And that's where the situation was when William Miller came along.

Miller was a New England hardscrabble farmer who became convinced that he'd decoded the Bible and figured out the approximate date when the world was going to come to an end: sometime in 1843 or maybe 1844. In the late 1830s, he started going from meeting hall to meeting hall in New England and upstate New York, in his very sober New England way, letting people know that the Second Coming was about to happen and maybe they might want to get ready to say hi to Jesus. Now, of course, there are people like that all the time; but Miller found very much to his surprise that a lot of highly educated liberal Christian reformers wanted to hear what he had to say. They wanted it bad.

And the reason they wanted it, and wanted it bad, was that the apocalypse was basically the only way they could think of that they could get the world they wanted. Once Jesus showed up and pounded the stuffing out of Satan and his legions, they figured, he'd abolish slavery and war and alcohol, and give women equal rights, and do all the other things that ten and twenty years before, they'd hoped they could do themselves. So, the Millerite movement, as it came to be known, became a mass movement drawing on a huge number of disappointed liberals. Miller and the coterie of ministers around him finally settled on a date: October 22, 1844. Thousands upon thousands of people—I don't think anybody knows exactly how many, but there were a lot of them—went up onto hilltops on the sunset of the day before and spent the next twenty-four hours waiting, expecting literally moment by moment to see the skies open and light stream through the clouds as Jesus showed up right there in front of them.

And it didn't happen; the Sun came up on October 23 on the same old world; and shortly afterward, the entire movement imploded. Not just the Millerite movement, the whole complex of progressive social movements and liberal religion that fed into it. It's one thing to face persecution, and a lot of these people had done that already; it's quite another to face humiliation—to have everybody in America laughing themselves sick at everything you believe in, and at you, personally. And they were. A few Millerites kept the faith, and a generation or so later they became what's now the Seventh Day Adventists; others went and joined other radical sects of the time, notably the Shakers, and when Spiritualism got going a lot of former Millerites ended up there; and a lot of others simply headed west to the frontier, where nobody knew that they'd made fools of themselves—Joshua Himes, a Boston clergyman who more or less ran the movement during its last years, ended his days as a missionary on an Indian reservation in North Dakota. But the first American progressive counterculture was dead as a doornail, and it wasn't until the 1890s that something like it got going again.

The New Age movement has a very similar pedigree. A lot of people who became part of it came out of the social and political movements of the 1960s and turned to mysticism when the Age of Aquarius failed to show up on schedule. Now they've committed themselves to a date for the end of the world: December 21, 2012. This time around, William Miller's name is Jose Arguelles; he's the guy who invented the 2012 Mayan prophecy business out of whole cloth back in the 1980s, with a little help from Terence McKenna. The whole New Age movement, and a lot of people who don't call themselves New Age and who you'd think have more common sense than to fall for yet another round of warmed-over millennarian fantasy, are getting sucked into the 2012 prophecy. For the New Agers, there's good reason for that; for years now, they've been insisting that they could create their own reality, but reality hasn't shown any particular willingness to cooperate; so 2012 becomes the date when the reality they've been trying to create shows up all nice and gift-wrapped, and all the skeptics get to eat crow.

And when December 22, 2012 dawns like any other day without benefit of Quetzalcoatl or mass enlightenment or the space brothers, the New Age movement is going to become a worldwide laughing stock, and it will implode.* Some New Agers will keep going; a hundred years from now there's doubtless going to be some small sect somewhere in Montana that treats the writings of Shirley MacLaine and Jose Arguelles as sacred scripture, and if you sit down with them they'll explain to you very earnestly that 2012 was a *spiritual* apocalypse, and that everything really has been different since then, and so on; but the movement as a significant social force will be dust in the wind.

That's one of the ways that popular alternative spiritual movements can die: not the most popular but common enough. What happens to a movement that dodges that kind of self-inflicted bullet? Most of the time, it imitates the old soldier in the proverb and just fades away. It rarely fades away completely; there's always that background noise of American popular spirituality, where you can count on finding just about anything chugging away on a small scale; and it happens fairly often that organizations that come out of popular spiritual movements undergo a metamorphosis. You're probably thinking about the caterpillar and the butterfly, but it's the other way around; what used to be a flighty, short-lived butterfly turns into a patient, long-lived caterpillar; a popular movement turns into a denomination. That's where most of the current religious denominations in American life come from; those stolid, respectable, unexciting religious bodies that a certain subset of Pagans regard with ill-concealed envy—most of them used to be fly-by-night radical movements every bit as far from the status quo of their time as modern popular Neopaganism is from the status quo of ours.

---

*As it has been doing, on schedule, since that date.

Now, of course, there's a significant fraction of Pagans who would like to see our movement turn into a denomination, and have the respectability, the real estate, and the salaries for clergy that denominations in America generally have. They may get their way, but it'll be a while. To begin with, the only people I've ever heard insist that Pagans ought to have paid clergy are people who want to be the paid clergy. I have yet to meet anybody who's eager to sit in the congregation and hand over the cash, which means that there's a supply and demand problem: the supply of paid Pagan clergy far exceeds the demand. Part of that is that too many people have taken notions of clergy straight from liberal Protestantism—you know, weekly services, rites of passage, a little amateur counseling, a bit of political activism, that's what clergy do. The problem is that the denominations where this is what clergy do are losing members so fast that some of them—some of the big names among them—are going to be extinct in fifty years if nothing changes. Again, supply and demand: if the things you want to offer are things that other people are going broke offering right now, there's a flaw in your business plan.

There's also that metamorphosis that has to happen first, and—to extend the metaphor a bit—before the butterfly can turn into a caterpillar, it's going to have to crawl into a chrysalis and spend a good long while there. I don't know of any spiritual movement in American history that made the transition straight from being a popular mass movement to being a respectable denomination; what comes between those two is the period when your movement isn't fashionable anymore, but it isn't respectable yet, and what that means is that during that time, your movement tends to be very small.

Is today's Paganism moving toward that awkward and intermediate state? There's good reason to think so. Over the last few years, you may have noticed that a fair number of people who used to be in the Pagan community have been leaving it. Some of them are going back to the faith they were raised in, some of them are going on to other religions such as Buddhism, and still others are chucking religion altogether and taking up the atheist materialism that's the established faith of modern industrial society. At the same time, and even more telling, you'll have heard from a lot of people who are still more or less in the community but no longer share its ideas, values, and beliefs. There's a lot of talk these days about "cultural Pagans" and "secular Pagans," basically people who like the trappings of the movement and enjoy the parties, but who aren't willing to accept the idea, or even explore the possibility, that magic works and the gods are real. If you've kept an eye on the Pagan blogosphere recently you'll have seen a number of people coming out and saying, "You know, I just don't believe in that stuff anymore."

If our movement follows the usual trajectory, there's going to be a lot more of that in the years just ahead of us. One of the reasons why that happens is exactly the clash between the craving for respectability I've mentioned and the driving force that's basically built the Pagan movement since 1980, which is—well, without too much distortion—we could call it the desire to shock your mom. To do something edgy and iconoclastic and transgressive. Now, of course, there are other reasons; there are always other reasons, since you decided to become a Pagan when you could have taken up any number of mom-shocking options; you could have grown dreadlocks or joined the Hare Krishnas or become a Young Republican, but you became a Pagan instead; and of course as we get older and creeping respectability sets in, a lot of us insist even to ourselves that the desire to shock our moms was never really a factor in taking up Paganism, no, at age fourteen we were profoundly intrigued by the philosophical implications of a polytheistic thaumaturgical orthopraxy. Sure we were.

But, the problem slips in as the leaders and the members of a movement age, because the older your leaders and members become, the less interested they are in providing new recruits with opportunities for being edgy and transgressive, and the more interested they get in looking respectable and claiming the perks of respectability. That's fine for those who are already in, but it means that the next generation of kids interested in shocking their moms goes somewhere else, and so do the people who are along for the ride because it's fashionable, and—well, basically, anybody who doesn't have a strong commitment to the ideas, beliefs, and values of the movement, because once an alternative spiritual movement stops being popular, it isn't as much fun. The music starts to sound like the stuff from last year, and the parties turn into gatherings of middle-aged folks who sit around and sip drinks and talk about how cool it was back in the 1990s, and the crowds get thin and the excitement trickles away.

And then you're in the in-between place, the chrysalis time, where a Pagan conference in 2020 might have a total attendance of forty people, and the book table is selling used books because the publishers who used to churn out Pagan books by the truckload have all moved on to something else.

Now there's life after the chrysalis, or there can be. There's the example of Christian fundamentalism, which came barrelling back up out of the fringes fifty years after it finished its first period as a popular movement and went through the whole cycle again. Plenty of other movements have done the same thing. On a more enduring scale, there have also been any number of movements that have morphed into denominations, become respectable, and are still chugging merrily away a couple of centuries after their initial rise and fall. The question is getting from here to there—getting through a couple of decades or so, during which you're not fashionable anymore but you're not respectable yet either.

And getting through the next few decades is going to be more of a challenge than usual, for reasons that are going to need another step back, from the history of religious movements to the history of empires.

Empires aren't fashionable these days, which is why so many people insist that America doesn't have one. Of course it does; we have troops garrisoned in a hundred and forty countries around the world, and they're not there for their health; we're also the beneficiaries of global economic relationships that see to it that the five percent of humanity that lives within US borders gets to use a quarter of the world's energy resources and a third of its raw materials and industrial products. That doesn't happen because the rest of the world doesn't want those things, and it doesn't happen because we produce something so cool that everyone else is willing to go hungry in order to buy it. We don't produce much of anything, in fact, and yet we're the world's top consumers; but it's considered very impolite to suggest that all those garrisons, and an annual military budget that's roughly equal to all the other military budgets in the world put together, have anything to do with the matter.

This is one of the places where history is helpful. Look at the last few centuries, and it's not too hard to recognize that we've got the same imperial role now that Britain had a century ago, when it was the British who got the lion's share of the world's resources and industrial production, and not incidentally owned a quarter of the Earth's land surface outright and had naval bases pretty much everywhere that there was salt water. A century before then, Britain was going at it mano a mano with France for who was going to be the big imperial power; those two spent the entire eighteenth century duking it out. Before then it was Spain, though Holland made a stab at it, and before Spain, Portugal tried but didn't quite make it; before then the technology for a global empire didn't exist, and the big imperial states were regional land-based states like the Ottoman Empire and the Chinese Empire.

So empires are nothing new. They rise, they plateau, they decline and then somebody else shoves them aside and grabs the goodies. The rise of America's empire was nothing unusual, starting in the 1820s, when we started exerting economic control over Latin America in the name of the Monroe Doctrine. About the only wrinkle is that when push finally came to shove, we didn't have to invade and conquer the previous empire; instead, we saved their bacon twice in thirty years when they were at war with the other main contender for Next Big Empire. You know the story from there; Germany lost, we won, and Britain handed over her empire to us but got the consolation prize of a spot in our inner circle of allies.

Now, you're probably wondering what this has to do with the future of the modern Pagan movement. The critical point is that empires don't keep, they have a very limited shelf life; and ours is in decline. It's the usual problem, the one Paul Kennedy documented so well a while back in *The Rise and Fall of Great Powers*; maintaining an empire isn't cheap, and the costs tend to rise over time while the income shrinks. So, you end up with a bloated military budget and an economy that's more and more geared to a permanent state of conflict, and less and less able to compete with the rest of the world in any other field; your infrastructure starts to suffer from malign neglect; your domestic industries ditto; you end up with a hollow shell of a society propped up by increasingly desperate and increasingly ineffective short-term measures. If none of this sounds familiar, you probably need to get out more.

A lot of people in this room are probably planning on cheering when the US empire goes down, and that's understandable. But there's a downside, or more precisely, two downsides. The first is that the end of our empire isn't the end of empire; as ours goes down, it's pretty clear who's itching for the spot, and the results of the changeover may not be an improvement for the world as a whole. The second is a bit more direct. Remember that point I made earlier, that twenty-five percent of all the world's energy resources, and thirty-three percent of its raw materials and industrial product, goes to the five percent of us who live in the United States? As our empire goes away, so does all that lagniappe; in fact, it's already going away, which is why our economy is contracting while China's is growing at ten percent a year. And that means that over the next few decades, pretty much all of us are going to experience something like an eighty percent decline in our standard of living—which among other things cuts into the resources that make it possible for all of us to come here.

That's one of the big problems with empires. People in an imperial society get used to taking absurd amounts of wealth for granted and then find themselves discomfited when the empire goes away, and they have to make do with a lot less. Now of course they can make do with a lot less; nobody actually needs the wealth of the late American middle class in order to survive fairly comfortably; the average European gets by on a third of the energy per capita we're used to squandering, and they're not living in caves; but it's going to take getting used to. And during that time of getting used to the end of extravagance, the odds are pretty good that people who don't have a fairly strong commitment to the ideals and values of modern Paganism are going to find something else to do with their very limited resources.

The economic contraction we're facing—which is not just an ordinary, common or garden-variety great depression, but a long wave phenomenon that's going to be shaping the rest of our lives—has another wrinkle, because it happens to come right after the world's petroleum production has peaked. Some of you have probably heard a bit about peak oil, as it's called: the point at which conventional petroleum production worldwide runs into hard geological limits and starts to decline; also known as the end of the age of cheap abundant oil. It's not the end of oil; we're nowhere near running out, but we are past the point at which we can count on the steady year over year increases in petroleum production that have driven the last century or so of economic growth in the US and the rest of the industrial world.

It's a source of great amusement to those of us in the peak oil scene to listen to one end of the mainstream media warn that we could hit peak oil in ten or twenty or thirty years, and the other end insist the market will take care of it—you know, prices will go up and then new supplies will become available in a puff of twinkle dust. Ahem. The worldwide peak of conventional petroleum production was in 2005; since then the price of oil has nearly tripled, and that's not even counting the 2008 spike to $143 a barrel; and the new sources of supply that have come on line since then—yes, that includes the shale oil that's getting so much hype—haven't even made up for the oilfields that are being pumped dry. The only reason production hasn't dropped since 2005 is that people are throwing tar sands, natural gas liquids, ethanol, biodiesel, anything that will burn into the mix, and even so they're falling behind. The lesson is simple: when the laws of physics and geology go head to head with the laws of economics, the laws of economics lose.

Now you'll find plenty of people who insist that some new and even more lavish energy resource has to be out there, just because we happen to want one. Belief in progress is the real religious faith of our time, and trying to suggest that we might not be able to power all the toys we want in some kind of Jetsons future is like trying to tell a medieval peasant that heaven with God and all the saints isn't there anymore. You'll also find plenty of people who insist that we're going to suddenly run out of oil and then it's mass dieoff time, with people being devoured by zombies. You won't find many people looking at history. If you look at history, you'll find that it's par for the course for civilizations to outrun their resource base. They do it all the time, and when they do it, they decline.

You can't even talk about decline these days. It's a concept most people don't even have in their heads. We're so addicted to the fantasy of infinite technological progress that most of us think that the only alternative to some Star Trek fantasy of humanity metastasizing across the galaxy is some sort of Hollywood apocalypse where everybody dies next Wednesday, with or without the benefit of zombies. But, in fact, just as popular religious movements rise and fall, and empires rise and fall, civilizations rise and fall. Slowly. Rome wasn't sacked in a day.

We could get into a long digression about the reasons why I think Western industrial civilization is in decline, why it's headed for the same compost heap of history as so many past civilizations, and why it'll take a couple of hundred years to get there—mind you, it'll be a rough couple of centuries, with catastrophes that will be world-class whoppers, but that's business as usual for the decline of a big civilization. Still, people either get that or they don't. If you think I'm crazy, if you're convinced that somebody or other has promised humanity a grand destiny out there among the stars, fine; it doesn't actually matter that much in terms of the specific points I want to make today. Still, there's a reason I bring it up, and that's one of the points that Arnold Toynbee made repeatedly in the twelve volumes of *A Study of History*: when civilizations tip into decline, there's usually a new religious movement that emerges to pick

188 A MAGICAL EDUCATION

up the pieces, and that new religious movement becomes the chrysalis from which, centuries later, a new civilization is born. It's not guaranteed, but it happens pretty often; and it's a helluva long shot, but that new religious movement might be us.

The thing that sets one of these new religious movements apart from the competition, you see, is that its basic assumptions are straight out of left field, in terms of the fundamental beliefs of the society in which it emerges. To the educated classes of ancient Rome, this bizarre cult called Christianity wasn't just one more mystery religion; it was sick and wrong, which is why you got some very tolerant and learned people back then calling Christians "enemies of the human race" and things like that. Buddhism was the same way in the context of late Han dynasty China, and so on down the list. One of the things that sets contemporary Neopaganism apart from most of the competition, in turn, is precisely that its core assumptions break with two thousand years of Western religious history.

Paganism isn't talking about salvation. It's not offering people an escape hatch by which to bail out of the world of Nature and natural limits, which is what you get from Christianity, from the New Age movement, from most of the popular spiritualities and mysticisms of today. The heart of the Christian faith is the image of the resurrection and ascension—the godman dying and then coming back to life, not just spiritually, but right there in the body; and then rising up to heaven to sit in a bucket seat next to God, again, not just spiritually, physically. That was the promise—that the right religion could tear open the sky, break the laws of life and death, and chuck us out of the grubby realities of existence into eternity. Thus, it's rather telling that these days, the core Christian image of the resurrection mostly appears in the form of vampire and zombie flicks. Jesus is back, but now he wants to eat your brain.

But, since the first image of the whole Earth from space got spread around the globe, a lot of people have started to think of Nature, and Time, and the Earth not as a prison we ought to escape from, but as a home we probably ought to take better care of, even as a mother whose patience is running very thin and who may just bend the lot of us over her knee to administer an old-fashioned spanking. That's the core of the modern Pagan idiom: the sense of Nature as divine, and as a divine context in which humanity exists and from which humanity gets not only what it needs for physical survival but what it needs for its inner life, its resources of meaning and value and purpose. Catherine Albanese, who I mentioned earlier, talks about that in her book, as the thing that sets Nature religion apart from most other spiritual movements nowadays. That might just turn out to be the core theme of the civilization that will rise from the rubble of the one we live in, hundreds of years from now.

But again, all that's speculative at this point. Trying to time the decline and fall of a civilization is no easy task, and beyond suggesting that the first wave of decline set in around 1914, and the second one may be setting in right about now, I'm not prepared to guess. What we do know is that if we're going to have any chance of fulfilling that role, we've got to get through the decades ahead of us, and the history of other popular alternative spiritual movements suggests that that may not be as easy as it seems. We have to face that chrysalis time when Paganism isn't fashionable anymore and isn't respectable yet. Christianity went through the same thing back in the day; first it was a fad, and then it stopped being popular as fashions changed, but enough people stuck with it to give it institutional stability; it cycled up and down, going in and out of fashion, as the late Roman world came gradually unglued, until it was basically the only social institution left standing; and you know the rest of the story.

So, do I have any recommendations for today's Pagans? As it happens, I do.

First, and hardest, to everyone here who's been edging toward the exit doors of the Pagan community, if that's what your heart says is right, do it. Don't try to pretend. If you don't believe that magic works and the gods are real, then you don't, and that's simply the way it is. But, if you could do the rest of us a favor, don't insist that the rest of us ought to drop our belief in these things so you'll be less uncomfortable in your unbelief. You're going to go your own way, and that's cool, but your way isn't everyone's way.

A lot of you are going to move out of Paganism into other religious movements. Some of you are going to become Methodists or atheists or Buddhists or members of some other established denomination. Some of you are going to move into one of whatever the next waves of popular alternative spirituality turn out to be. If I had to bet, I'd guess that one of those waves will be the African diaspora religions—Vodoun, Santeria, and the like. Those have plenty of spiritual and philosophical depth, and they've also got what it takes to be edgy, transgressive, and iconoclastic, at least for the white middle-class kids who make up the bulk of new recruits to an alternative religion. Possession trance, animal sacrifice, and the still very strong racism of white American culture make for a very high mom-shocking potential. Incidentally, the clergy of African diaspora religions do a lot more than liberal Protestant clergy; they offer services for which there is a much greater demand, and there again, they could do very well.

And of course, there are also options that don't look religious. In times of serious economic trouble—like, oh, right now—political ideologies that make quasi-religious claims of salvation can substitute for alternative religious movements, the way Marxism did for many people in the 1930s. Or the Methodists could have the last laugh after all, and turn into a mass movement again for the first time since the 1850s. Or it could be something out of left field—or right field. It's anybody's guess.

But there will be those who remain Pagan after the parties are over and the cheering stops. There may be a fair number of them if today's Pagan leaders can avoid the temptation to predict the end of the world the way William Miller did, or do any of the other dumb stunts that popular alternative religious movements do in their last days when they suffer from a poorly concealed death wish. We'll assume that our current Pagan community is sensible enough to steer clear of that sort of attention-getting disaster. Given that, we need to talk about what Pagans and occultists can do to up the chances of making it through the chrysalis period, and keeping a much smaller scene going during the years when everyone else is going, "Oh, yeah, that stuff—I used to be into it back in the day."

There are things that reliably work. The most important is to remain open to new members, but don't lower your standards in a misguided attempt to keep membership up. The people who come to you won't be showing up on the doorstep because they're interested in coasting through with the least possible amount of work; there are a lot of people like that in the Pagan scene right now, but then lots of people like that are one of the typical signs of a movement near its end. The ones you get in the chrysalis years are going to want the real deal, the full experience, and if you've lowered your expectations they're going to be disappointed. Now, of course, they're going to have to be able to find you, which means that a public presence is essential; whatever media and networking options exist, you need to use them. Between the 1930s and the 1970s, when the occult scene was in its last chrysalis period, those magical orders that survived kept quiet little ads in the classified pages of astrology magazines and other periodicals that appealed to their potential audience. The technology will doubtless be different this time, but the principle is the same.

I'd like to suggest also that those of us who are clergy, or otherwise in leadership roles in Pagan traditions, might want to take a good hard look at how clergy in different cultures support themselves and what services they provide to their clients. The hunger for respectability that's convinced too many senior Pagans that the only way to be clergy is to imitate the Methodists is a problem now; it's likely to become a fatal problem at a time when our traditions aren't fashionable anymore. If you want to support yourself as a Pagan priest or priestess, you need to be able to offer people things that they can't get from the Methodists, and this means you need to recognize that you're not the one who will decide what people want to pay you to do; they make that decision. In the past, a lot of occultists supported themselves as astrologers or teachers of various useful things; there are broader possibilities this time around, but when you're neither fashionable nor respectable, trying to get people to pay you for something they can get from somebody fashionable or respectable isn't going to get you far.

We—and here I mean all of those people who stick with Pagan and occult traditions when the music stops, and the crowds go somewhere else—also need to take a hard look at what the last thirty years of popularity have done to our teachings. The habit of lowering standards to attract members is part of that, but there's more to it. One of the things you get is a massive pressure to conform to certain stereotypes. In the days of Theosophy, every occult tradition had to say something about Atlantis. No matter how irrelevant lost continents were to your teachings, you had to have a rap about Atlantis or nobody would take you seriously. Nowadays—well, there are a couple of factors; one is gendered duotheism—you know, all the gods are one god and all the goddesses are one goddess, thank you, Dion Fortune. Another is the eightfold year-wheel. Neither one of those were part of Paganism until fairly recently in historical terms, but those of you who teach traditions that don't have them, as I do, know how much pressure gets put on you to force your tradition into that pair of Procrustean beds.

The time for that is over. More generally, the time for what I suppose you'd have to call generic pop Paganism is over. Just as the occult traditions after the age of Theosophy gradually got rid of Atlantis, and the rings and rounds and root races that everybody demanded back then, and got back to teaching what they actually had to teach, our traditions will need to reclaim their original diversity: their own calendars, their own deities and theologies, and so on. With all due respect to the man, do what Scott Cunningham teacheth shall no longer be the whole of the Law.

More generally, the thirty-year trajectory of popular Paganism has had a remarkable flattening out effect on the once very diverse magical traditions of this country. To a very real extent, a lot of people in today's Pagan and magical scene act as though all of magic was invented in England between 1887 and the very early 1950s. We borrow symbolism from all over the place, granted, but our techniques are drawn from a very narrow field; if the Golden Dawn or Aleister Crowley or Dion Fortune or somebody in the first generation or so of public Wiccans didn't do it, many people don't even know it can be done. There are whole worlds of magic we've forgotten about, and a loss of magical diversity is as bad for an occult community as a loss of ecological diversity is for an ecosystem. It's past time to recover as much as possible of that diversity; to remember, just to pull a few examples out of thin air, that there used to be American magical traditions involving hardcore physical exercise; that alchemy isn't just a metaphor for psychological symbolism; that there used to be a whole world of magical lodge technique that even most of today's magical lodges have forgotten; and so on.

And if you end up as the last custodian of the rituals and teachings of some Pagan tradition or other, for the gods' sakes do something to make sure it's not just hauled out with the trash when you die. Even in recent times, there have been scores of traditions that are now not even a memory because nobody made sure the teachings would survive. Now it happens that I've been part of the rescue team for a couple of traditions now; the Druid order I now head is one of those, but it's not the only one; I've helped to piece things together again from some very fragmentary materials, which I happened to be in the right place to rescue before their last custodians died of old age; and so I can all too easily imagine a future where people are saying, "Well, we know there used to be this thing called Wicca, but nobody knows what it was about—none of the teachings or rituals survived." That happened to some very major nineteenth- and early twentieth-century traditions. As Israel Regardie showed, it's better to publish a secret tradition, and have future generations be in a position to learn about it from a book, than have it go extinct and have nobody able to learn about it ever again.

We've got a lot of material to preserve. More so than in the past. In fact, I'm not sure how many people realize just how remarkable the last thirty years have been. Back in 1969, a man named Edward T. Whitney wrote a book titled *The Coming Great Golden Age of Esotericism*. It's been a very long time since I read it, but if I remember it correctly, the guy deserves top ranking among prophets, because he was right. He was about a decade ahead of one of the most spectacular golden ages of occultism the Western world has had in a very long time: a period when occult teachings were right out there in public to a degree that's basically never happened before, when a lot of creative work got done, when—well, as I commented earlier, just the number of Tarot decks in existence boggles the imagination.

This is not the way things usually are, and I think a lot of us have gotten a bit spoiled by the abundance. I know I have! But if I'm right, and over the next decade or so the crowds go elsewhere and most of those Tarot decks go permanently out of print, and the publishing companies that keep us supplied with books end up publishing mystery novels or Methodist devotional literature because the market for books on magic and Paganism just isn't there anymore—well, at that point there's a new imperative.

Everybody likes to think of themselves and their generation as being the ones that matter, the ones poised on the hinge of history. That's what drives things like the Millerite movement and its current New Age equivalent, and it's also one of the things that make it difficult to keep one's own spiritual beliefs in historical context; what we're doing has to be the most important thing ever, it can't be just another link in the chain of American Nature religion, and just maybe a first faint foreshadowing of the religious movement that's going to pick up the pieces as industrial civilization slides down the arc of its decline and fall over the next two hundred years or so. But the irony here is that in a certain sense, we are poised at a time that does really matter.

We've lived through an extraordinary period—those of us who have been around a while have lived through it; those of you who are a little more recent on the scene have come in partway through, and had the chance to enjoy it while it lasted; for a couple of centuries to come, quite possibly, people are going to be riffing off the things that were created or made public during the last thirty years, the way that the great occult revival in Britain in the mid-1600s basically defined Anglo-American occultism until the coming of Theosophy at the end of the nineteenth century. The task ahead of us now is getting as much as possible through the transition, through the chrysalis time, and into the hands of the Pagans and occultists of the future. And the most important tool in doing that, I suggest, is to pay attention to how well we're walking our talk.

What that means in practice works out at least a little differently for each of us. As I suggested earlier, if you really don't believe in the core ideas and values of Paganism anymore, if magic and the gods simply aren't real to you, this is probably a good time to 'fess up to that, at least to yourself, and consider what you need to do if you're going to live in accordance with what you actually believe. If when it comes right down to it, you belong with the Methodists, or the Buddhists, or at a hounfor somewhere taking part in a Vodoun ceremony, then that's where you belong. If, may the gods help you, your heart tells you that the place you need to be is waiting for the space brothers to arrive on December 21, 2012, then get out there and watch the skies; maybe having an entire planet full of people laughing at you from December 22 onwards for years to come is a karmic experience you need to have.

But, if when push comes to shove, you stand with one of the modern Pagan traditions, or one of the occult traditions that have ended up associated with them, or maybe more than one, you have your work cut out for you. Exactly what that work will be is going to be different for every one of us, so I won't try to suggest a laundry list; what it's going to take in the case of any given tradition to deal with a decline in membership, a decline in popularity, and a decline in readily available resources, without suffering a decline in enthusiasm or in the willingness to do the work yourself and teach the students you do have—it's going to vary quite a bit. And of course the thirty-year lifespan is an average; it's not something you can set your watch by; we may have a few more good years ahead of us, or the backlash from the approaching 2012 fiasco could land on the whole range of current alternative spiritualities like Godzilla diving into a Tokyo-sized mosh pit.

It's hard to say. What's clear is that history doesn't justify the notion that things are just going to keep on going onward and upward from here—for modern Paganism; for the United States; for modern industrial civilization—and as things head south, those who have at least considered the possibility of decline and contraction, and maybe even taken some steps to prepare for it, are likely to land easily while those who are blindsided by it all land hard. If I'm right—and of course any statement about the future has to be prefaced by those words—we all have a lot of work ahead of us; and I hope that some of the points I've made are of some help in getting that work done. Thank you.

INDEX